On Perpetual Peace

ON PERPETUAL PEACE

A TIMELY ASSESSMENT

Dieter Senghaas

Translated by Ewald Osers

Berghahn Books
New York • Oxford

Published in 2007 by

Berghahn Books

www.berghahnbooks.com

First published in Germany as
Zum irdischen Frieden. Erkenntnisse und Vermutungen, Frankfurt/M.
© 2004 Edition Suhrkamp

English language translation © Ewald Osers 2006

Library of Congress Cataloging-in-Publication Data

Senghaas, Dieter, 1940-
  [Zum irdischen Frieden. English]
  On perpetual peace : a timely assessment / Dieter Senghaas ; translated by Ewald Osers.
    p. cm. -- (Methodology and history in anthropology)
  "First published in Germany as Zum irdischen Frieden. Erkenntnisse und Vermutungen,
Frankfurt/M."
  Includes bibliographical references and index.
  ISBN 978-1-84545-324-4 (hardback : alk. paper)
  1. Peace. I. Title.

  JZ5595.S4813 2007
  303.6'6--dc22

                                    2007034700

British Library Cataloguing in Publication Data

A catalogue record for this book is available from
the British Library.

ISBN 978-1-84545-324-4 (hbk.) 978-1-84545-325-1 (pbk.)

CONTENTS

ACKNOWLEDGEMENTS

This book is the fruit of my decades-long interest in research on peace, conflict and development issues. The thematic foci shifted again and again during this time, for example from research on deterrence, arms control and disarmament to the analysis of dependency structures in the world economy, the structural analysis of the international system and of the world society including cultural dimensions, and, generally, from non-war peace structures to political configurations of stable peace. My greatest intellectual debts all the way along are to my former teachers, namely Ralph Dahrendorf and Iring Fetscher, and to sources of intellectual inspiration such as Max Horkheimer, Theodor W. Adorno, Jürgen Habermas, Anatol Rapoport and Ernst-Otto Czempiel. I am, however, particularly indebted to Karl W. Deutsch, eminent scholar, teacher and close friend with whom I was once lucky enough to work intensively, as particularly documented in chapter 3 of this book: an earlier version of which we co-authored. Having had Michael Zürn as a young, inspiring close colleague for the last decade was also a highly stimulating and rewarding experience.

The translation of the original German version of this book (published in 2004) was made possible by a grant from the Berghof Stiftung für Konfliktforschung (Munich) to which I am most indebted. Ewald Osers receives my grateful thanks for having produced a meticulous translation most faithful to the original.

Bremen, Germany
D.S.
May 2007

INTRODUCTION

This book is about perpetual peace, but its subject matter is, in its tendency, comparable to those earlier essays that reflected on durable, everlasting or indeed eternal peace. In all these instances the issue was, and still is, reflections on the conditions in which peace is possible and also on the probability of these peace programmes being realised at any given time.

If explicit reference is made in the subsequent text to peace on earth, or perpetual peace, then this is not because the concept of eternal peace has been repeatedly and prominently addressed in the discussion in the eighteenth and nineteenth centuries, notably of course in Immanuel Kant's essay, the philosophical peak of this discussion, and which indicated a downright endless history of successor discussions. Besides, the change in conceptual content is not based on the fact that talk about eternal peace might again give rise to the obvious and still frequently encountered misunderstanding that the relevant essays necessarily refer to utopian ideas, or to the creation of chimeras, or that they treat of a totally different, i.e. a transcendent, world.[1] These misunderstandings are already refuted by the early peace drafts, which endeavoured to present a contemporary peace concept, realisable in the given circumstances, in a realistic manner.[2] However, it is quite possible that the fixation of theoretical and practical discussion upon Kant's essay and its discourse supported such an erroneous perception. The specific concepts of the original German title of the present book, *Zum irdischen Frieden*, therefore signal nothing other than that its subject is peace under the conditions of the twenty-first century.

In consequence, this book contains no discussion of the early debate mentioned,[3] and no further contribution to Kant studies, which, seeing that Kant has by now been reinterpreted infinitely often and certainly with new insights, are of gradually diminishing marginal utility today.[4] Nor will there be a recapitulation of the history of peace ideas inside and outside Europe,[5] let alone, as one would have to formulate today within the scientific community, a 'reconstruction' with a view to specific topical requirements. All such enterprises with regard to the history of ideas have been made repeatedly and in many places, and there is therefore no urgent need to continue them now.

Why then yet another discussion about peace, whose problems and dimensions must surely have been discussed in a vast amount of literature?[6] My motivation for publishing this book was as follows. In many more recent essays on peace this is treated either in abstract general terms and more or less non-empirically, as it were in terms of a category (thus mainly in many contributions to political philosophy); or else it is (mostly without methodical reflection) presented as a sector, in regional terms (thus mainly in social science contributions) with the result, in the latter case, that the non-thematical partial worlds and the world as a whole rarely find themselves at the focus of analysis. However, the problems of peace present themselves not on an abstract general plane, but in specific concrete contexts; with the world as a whole, that favourite (abstract) point of reference of philosophical reflection, being just one of these. The peace-philosophy discussion in most cases lacks not only concreteness but also the mediation of the overall perspective, in each specific instance, of the partial worlds actually present in the world.[7] On the other hand, sector-type analyses of partial worlds, however persuasively presented by social science (e.g. on the security dilemma inherent in Indian–Pakistani relations, on integration efforts in South America and elsewhere, etc.) are incapable of offering a realistic overall picture.[8]

What, strangely enough, remains disregarded is the fact, elementary for an analysis of present-day peace problems, that today's world is, in its dimensions, an extremely stratified structure abounding in rifts, gradients and the asymmetries resulting from these: in an economic, social, cultural and political respect the really existing world is a downright quintessence of structural heterogeneity.[9] Concepts that, because of their abstract nature or as a result of their insensitivity towards structurally different action contexts, simply, blind to experience, presuppose worldwide parallels, in other words a kind of homogeneity of the world, and therefore evade a fact-based contextualisation of arguments, cannot claim to be truly contemporary. Yet the simultaneity of unequal development in a persistently disjointed world renders factual categorical differentiation inevitable, even though it is lacking in most peace discourses or else smoothed out on a kind of Platonic model.[10]

Hence a contemporary essay on perpetual peace cannot in its analysis concentrate only on the security dilemma resulting from the so-called 'anarchy of the world of states'. Instead, this dilemma should itself be thematised in connection with a structural development dilemma that has meanwhile become a worldwide problem, since the concrete manifestation of the security dilemma depends largely on the development-conditioned situation of individual states within a markedly hierarchical world society. The constant talk, within the peace discourse, of the growing interdependence in the present world similarly lacks analytical persuasiveness, unless the widely differing interdependences existing in reality, along with their peace-policy implications, are analysed with regard to their specific profiles. Besides, it is only on this basis that the question of the 'interdependence of interdependences' (Willy Brandt) arises. And a category with worldwide reference, such as 'globalisation', can be used meaningfully and make sense only if very disparate but simultaneously observable experiences are considered in the conceptualisation of globalisation: for example a relatively unproblematic globalisation that is enriching in economic, social and cultural respects (World I: 'Globalisation de luxe'); differently, a globalisation that, in a few parts of the world, actually opens up an upward movement or upgrading within the hierarchy of an international division of labour (World II); next, a globalisation that, in major parts of the world, clearly accentuates an anyway existing, mostly politically virulent, developmental crisis and moreover provokes system-motivated and power-politically motivated struggles (World III); and finally: a globalisation that, in the world's chronic problem zones, definable by failing or even failed states and violence markets, lets a political, socio-economic and cultural regression turn virulent over a wide area (World IV). Any contemporary peace discourse has to address such realities, quoted here by way of examples, and thus reveal the complexity of the really existing world and its partial worlds even in statements intended to generalise.[11]

On Perpetual Peace is designed to offer those realisations, insights and assumptions, and especially knowable worldly-wise knowledge, that are important for a contemporary differentiated understanding of the present and near-future worldwide peace problems. The informative intention of the present book – if not in its title or contents, then certainly in its motivation and presentation – follows the classic Kantian model: In the preliminary reflections (Chapter 1) a non-peace-conducive action slogan ('si vis pacem, para bellum') is very briefly criticised and the 'para pacem' slogan is presented in outline. In the subsequent voluminous second section (Chapter 2) the strategic defining conditions for peace – the so-called 'civilisatory hexagon' – are briefly developed. The question is: Through what and how does peace constitute itself under the complex conditions of our present? This is followed by a third section (Chapter 3) with the paradigm-like pointed discussion of the no less important, though strangely enough scarcely ever asked, question: Through what and how does peace-policy reason, i.e. a reason promoting peace, constitute itself? A fourth section (Chapter 4) discusses critiques of previously published expositions on the civilisatory hexagon. These four sections (Part I of the book) gather together the core statements on perpetual peace.

In a second part of the book the Supplements further develop specific aspects of the definitions and corresponding experiences. The First Supplement (Chapter 5) presents four sets of peace programmes arrived at on an empirical basis: i.e. complex peace-policy programmes proving that peace-theory and peace-policy discussion requires not a reduction of analytical complexity but its increase. The *Second Supplement* (Chapter 6) thoroughly analyses historical experience of the creation of a zone of stable peace and the opportunity of extending it.

The contributions in the Appendices of the book (Part III) elucidate fundamental structural states of affairs whose knowledge is indispensable for an understanding of the peace-policy problems in today's world and for an appropriate set of peace programmes. Here conceptual differentiations are developed, such as are not only suggested but positively demanded by a complex analysis of reality, i.e. the present-day situation of the world. These differentiations concern the dilemmas (Chapter 7) built into the structure of the present-day world, the diverse experiences with interdependence (Chapter 8), especially, with a view to development problems, those that, contrary to common assumption, are worldwide (Chapter 9). The differentiations moreover concern the globalisation discourse, which, in its customary form, is today especially characterised by a lacking sense of structurally disparate action contexts. This discourse is elucidated by examples taking particular account of the problems of cultural globalisation (Chapter 10).

These four chapters of Part III will also render plausible the methodological premise of this book, which is the result of factual insight and not simply of some arbitrary approach – more precisely the result of a way of arguing in which disparately located action contexts are seen in a differentiated, i.e. a context-sensitive, way. The consequence of this is that, on such a basis of reality-saturated experience, the politically motivated peace discourse is similarly exposed to an appropriate cue to move towards argumentative differentiation, without such analytical or practice-oriented argumentation losing the synoptic view of the complex, yet structured set of peace-policy problems in which the world finds itself. As the modern, and more especially today's, world is increasingly a unit of structural weight of its own, albeit a staggered unit of non-homogeneous, though interrelated, parts, an appropriate assessment of the situation can anyway only be achieved in so far as a synoptic analysis of the world's overall structure and its structurally diverse 'partial worlds' is accomplished.[12]

One final observation at the beginning: the title of this book is no swindle with labels. The book deals with *peace*, hence not with violence or war. Research into the courses of violence and war is important and its essential findings do, of course, whenever necessary, flow into this book.[13] Such research, however, remains inadequate while the core question of causes-of-peace research calls for an answer – i.e. what are the restrictive and promoting conditions and premises necessary for the 'architecture' of a durable and stable peace, one that is a peace that is marked by sustainability. The fact that bridges are generally possible between one and another focus of research, and hence also intellectual attention, is documented in this book, as well as the fact (notably in Chapter 3) that in the peace discourse there are meaningful conceptual bridges between diverse levels of the peace problem – the macro, meso and micro levels.

Notes

1. See Wolfgang Burgdorf, *'Chimäre Europa'. Antieuropäische Diskurse in Deutschland (1648–1999)*, Bochum 1999.
2. See the list of peace plans since the Renaissance in Kurt von Raumer (ed.), *Ewiger Friede*, Munich 1953; Hans-Jürgen Schlochauer (ed.), *Die Idee des ewigen Friedens*, Bonn 1953; John Sylvester Hemleben, *Plans for World Peace through Six Centuries*, Chicago 1953; Jacob ter Meulen, *Der Gedanke der Internationalen Organisation in seiner Entwicklung*, vols. 1–3, The Hague 1917–40. Evidence that the peace drafts did not emerge aloof from political reality is provided by Thomas Fröschl (ed.), *Föderationsmodelle und Unionsstrukturen. Über Staatenverbindungen der frühen Neuzeit vom 15. bis zum 18. Jahrhundert*, Munich 1995. Without trying to be really topical, this volume exhibits an almost day-to-day topicality if one compares the early discourses with those that took place in the so-called constitutional convention of the European Union (2002/3).
3. See a detailed documentation, along with evaluation, in Anita and Walter Dietze (eds), *Ewiger Friede? Dokumente einer deutschen Diskussion um 1800*, Munich 1989.
4. On the more recent reception of Kant's essay *On Eternal Peace*, mostly in connection with the bicentenary of that publication and a consequential discussion, see Otfried Höffe (ed.), *Immanuel Kant. Zum Ewigen Frieden*, Berlin 1995 (with an extensive bibliography also of the earlier literature on Kant's essay); Matthias Lutz-Bachmann and James Bohman (eds.): *Frieden durch Recht. Kants Friedensidee und das Problem einer neuen Weltordnung*, Frankfurt/M. 1996; Reinhard Merkel and Roland Wittmann (eds), *'Zum Ewigen Frieden'. Grundlagen, Aktualität und Aussichten einer Idee von Immanuel Kant*, Frankfurt/M. 1996; Matthias Lutz-Bachmann and James Bohman (eds),*Weltstaat oder Staatenwelt? Für und wider die Idee einer Weltrepublik*, Frankfurt/M. 2002; Comprehensive interpretations of Kant's essay in the context of his philosophy were offered by Wolfgang Kersting, *Wohlgeordnete Freiheit. Immanuel Kants Rechts- und Staatsphilosophie*, Frankfurt/M. 1993, 2nd edn.; Volker Gerhardt, *Immanuel Kants Entwurf 'Zum Ewigen Frieden'. Eine Theorie der Politik*, Darmstadt 1995; Otfried Höffe, *Königliche Völker. Zu Kants kosmopolitischer Rechts- und Friedenstheorie*, Frankfurt/M. 2001.
5. See the brilliant survey by Wilhelm Janssen, 'Friede. Zur Geschichte einer Idee in Europa' in: Dieter Senghaas (ed.), *Den Frieden denken*, Frankfurt/M. 1995, pp. 227–275, as well as Michael W. Doyle, *Ways of War and Peace*, New York 1997.
6. An extensive selected bibliography on the basic literature alone will be found in Senghaas, *Den Frieden denken*, pp. 490–503.
7. This does not have to be the case, as superbly proved by the volume of Christine Chwaszcza and Wolfgang Kersting (eds), *Politische Philosophie der internationalen Beziehungen*, Frankfurt/M. 1998.
8. The state of affairs is banal and is being continually confirmed by a multitude of new publications.
9. The concept originates, as would not be suspected differently, in development research. There it means a stratified socio-economic, sociocultural and political reality, whereby the stratifications stem from symbiotically interlinked but hierarchically related modes of production. See Dieter Senghaas, *Weltwirtschaftsordnung und Entwicklungspolitik. Plädoyer*

für Dissoziation, Frankfurt/M. 1977, pp. 21ff. The concept originated in the Latin-American *dependencia* discussion ('heterogeneidad estructural').

10. An analytical differentiation, not from a scholar but from a practitioner, is found in Robert Cooper, 'Gibt es eine neue Weltordnung?' in Dieter Senghaas (ed.), *Frieden machen*, Frankfurt/M. 1997, pp. 102–118; more extensively: Cooper, *The Post-modern State and the World Order* (n.d., accessible via the internet). Idem, *The Breaking of Nations. Order and Chaos in the Twenty-First Century*, London 2003.

11. This four-part world analysis is found in Dieter Senghaas, 'Die Konstitution der Welt – eine Analyse in friendenspolitischer Absicht', in *Leviathan*, vol. 34, issue 1, 2003, pp. 117–152.

12. Such analytical mediation, finally concluded with the presentation of a state of affairs, presupposes in the cognition process the so-called progressive–regressive method proposed paradigmatically by Jean-Paul Sartre – i.e. a continuous switching, in the cognition process, between empirical analysis of detail and the analysis of overall connections, continuing along those lines at least until one believes one is able to present a cognitionally defendable finding. Finding then means: the exploration of a state of affairs emerging and consolidating in the cognition process, hence its analytical elaboration as a subject-related theory-constituting process. See Jean-Paul Sartre, *Critique of Dialectical Reason*, vol. 1, London 1991, Chapter 1.

13. On causes-of-violence research see now Wilhelm Heitmeyer and John Hagan (eds), *Internationales Handbuch der Gewaltforschung*, Wiesbaden 2002; on causes-of-war research see Manus Midlarsky (ed.), *Handbook of War Studies*, Ann Arbor 2000, 2nd edn.

Part I

Instituting Peace

On the Constituent Conditions of
Reasonable Peace and Peace-policy Reasoning

Chapter 1

FIRST SECTION

Containing Preliminary Reflections
on Perpetual Peace
('para bellum')

'Si vis pacem, para bellum' runs the conventional maxim for ensuring peace, a maxim still received and accepted with understanding in many parts of the world: skilful war preparation ('para bellum') is to prevent war and thus also to enhance the probability of peace (minimalistically defined as non-war). The circumstances that make violence potentials ripen, and potentially make violence virulent, do not stand at the centre of attention in this popular maxim. Instead it reacts to merely suspected, to actually threatening, or to already realised, violence, no matter of what origin; against this a militarily backed power management that serves diplomacy as reinsurance in general and, in particular, with reference to the worst case is postulated. In this sense this maxim and any policy in line with it are not cause-oriented but symptom-oriented.[1]

Because of its premise, its orientation towards confrontational security, the para bellum maxim is inevitably non-sensitive to the question of whether the instruments envisaged by it – an instrumentally conceived policy of threat, usually becoming chronic, as well as military armament of any kind – do not in fact exacerbate the escalation potential of violent situations instead of counteracting and restraining potential escalation. The point is that a militarily backed power management can be pursued with different accents – as a mere deterrence strategy (for instance in the sense of non-provocative defence), as a strategy of deterrence and restraint with significant defensive and/or offensive components, and as an offensively planned strategy of potential forward defence, of pre-emption and pro-active prevention that scarcely differs from a purely offensive strategy.[2] Under the last-named premises in particular it is impossible to arrive at a functioning, or indeed even cooperative, security community in which the security dilemma chronically existing between sovereign, even more so between hostile, states might at least be cushioned and rendered unproblematical.[3]

Moreover, any militarily oriented peace insurance is, and remains, by definition focused on the separation of the opponents. It is therefore lastingly dissociative, which means that there is always a danger of its ending in a continuous, politically barren, arms race.[4] Hence the frequently observed proneness of confrontational armament to evolve a growth dynamic of its own, especially if armament reaches a substantial scale, and to produce a well-differentiated apparatus with a multiplicity of competing interests.[5] And the reason why this security measure is barren is that, given military primacy, other instruments of securing peace are relegated to secondary importance, as for instance the instruments of peaceful dispute settlement and even relatively near-military instruments such as provisions for cooperative collective security, as in the meaning of the United Nations Charter (there Chapter VII) – not to mention peace insurance through a broad-spectrum activisation of political arrangements or in-depth institutionally backed economic, social and cultural relations.[6]

Viewed historically and sociologically such a para bellum maxim reflects the search for a stable 'state peace order' on the premise of territorially conceived states, or national states, such as have developed mainly in Europe but also in recent decades elsewhere (since the beginning of the modern age).[7] The maxim presupposes a stable monopoly of force within such territorial-state societies, i.e. the overcoming of the danger of a civil war: the 'situation hobbésienne' (R. Aron). Upon this basis problem situations between states are addressed by a combination of diplomacy and military measures, including, if necessary, in a borderline situation, warlike actions. Diplomacy, as a rule, is directed towards one or other variant of an always threatened balance of power order and, in the borderline case, of a no less fragile hegemony order that, mostly, can only be maintained temporarily.[8] The above maxim has a parallel in classic international law as an at least marginally effective social agency on the international plane, based on the sovereign individual state; until the first half of the twentieth century it regarded wars (and hence also the armament preceding them) as legitimate and is to this day, albeit with some qualifications, oriented along the principle of non-intervention in internal affairs.[9] In both cases, the maxim being underpinned by armament measures and by classic international law, the point at issue was the coexistence of sovereign state agents, once the coexistence of conflict-generating social groups within the states was checked by the creation of an appropriate authority of the state.[10] Authority of the state means here the existence of an, initially crude, power monopoly, in no way constitutionally or democratically constrained, a monopoly that has, as a rule, come into being through a warlike state-formation process and that has, for a long time, been backed only by force and in no way legitimately.[11]

The concept of peace as non-war, that underlies such a contemporary para bellum maxim, is therefore narrow and undifferentiated. Likewise, from the perspective of a historically earlier, relatively broad and conceptually rich, idea of peace of the European Middle Ages the contemporary concept is focused solely on *'securitas'* (security) or perhaps *'tranquillitas'* (ceasefire). The earlier more comprehensive perspective of international peace as the result of a superior legal order (*'iustitia'*) is no longer contained in one and the same peace concept, nor is *'caritas'*, always included in the medieval peace concept in the sense of a benevolent attitude to the needs of one's neighbour. Reflections on such orientations are omitted from later, e.g. post-medieval, peace-theory discussion.[12]

Thus the para bellum maxim is based on a conceptually narrow idea of peace within the state (*pax civilis*), moreover in the double direction of effective compelling force (*pax effectiva*) backed internally by administrative and police measures (with a presumed chance of relatively durable success) and a militarily based compelling force outwardly with an expected high probability of recurring warlike conflicts resulting from the 'anarchy' of the world of states.[13]

However, such a conceptual and practical orientation does not lack an alternative. Thus the contrasting maxim 'si vis pacem, para pacem' reflects those violence-breeding sets of problems that lead, time and again, to an upsetting of internal and international peace: the quest for imperialist hegemony, the undermining of a potentially existing balance of power among the great powers, or the obsession with power and expansionism, an arms race (preparatory and catch-up armament), political discrimination, contempt of human rights, economic exploitation, or disparities with related inequality of opportunity, power-politically anchored autistic orientations and enemy-image projection. Unlike the para bellum maxim, the para pacem maxim is conceived broadly and in a differentiated manner since it sees the starting point of threats to peace in such and similar problems. It is cause-oriented and focused on the elimination of such nuclei of non-peace. With it, too, prevention of violence and war is the supreme aim: efforts for associative peace-promoting intra-societal and international structures are designed to prevent any violence potentials from evolving. At the same time it is realised that in a world in continual transformation this aim will not always be optimally attainable – wherefore appropriate provisions must be made for the borderline case, a potentially necessary, legally circumscribed, forcible containment of violence.[14]

Unlike the para bellum maxim, the sociological background of the para pacem maxim is to be seen in the social mobilisation of once relatively stationary and traditional societies into modernising and modern societies, because in such socially mobile societies (and only in them) internal and external peace policy can no longer be managed as in the days of traditional despotism and autocracy, i.e. absolutist rule. Peace can no longer be reliably secured upon a crude monopoly of force or power – an elimination struggle with subsequent assertion of power, pure and simple. In consequence, peace today can no longer simply be understood as protection from violence (non-war), but, as will be shown in later sections of this book, also as protection of liberty, protection from hardship and protection from chauvinism and comparable mental and emotional attitudes.[15]

Such extended orientations reflect the demands for a contemporary peace concept and hence for a peace policy for socially mobile societies, from which stems irrefutable pressure for peace-policy action, seeing that a socially mobile society needs broad chances of participation and a variety of conflict-regulating mechanisms. The economically conditioned production of social inequality in modern, i.e. market-economy and capitalist, societies, giving rise as a rule to a considerable politicisation potential, requires long-term equalising social-policy and educational-policy measures. Upward and downward mobility, the result of continual social change, produce – especially if relevant social strata collide – problematic psychological orientations that can only be deproblematised if they are embedded in a relatively vibrant political culture of constructive conflict management. Moreover, the legitimation of social relations under the conditions of the rule of law is accepted only if the law is felt to be democratically legitimated and fair. Regardless of any still existing differences, which will be expounded in subsequent chapters, we see the emergence of basically comparable requirements of a viable peace order also at the international level – and hence also comparable peace-policy imperatives. The fact is that socially mobile societies are not like monads. The political dynamics resulting from their profiles transfer to multiple, albeit variously located, worldwide effective interdependence structures in which they are embedded.

Between the individual components of a peace concept for our time (here mentioned only by way of illustration but systematically discussed in the second section of this book) and hence an intra-societal and international peace structure – there exist feedbacks with reciprocal intensification effects. We can then proceed from the fact that such a structure, if fully developed and therefore relatively stable, is characterised by a multiple (redundant) causation: individual components can then be variously strongly marked without the relatively stable overall structure being affected. This is the factual background of why under present-day conditions – socially mobile societies politicising themselves, as well as worldwide international interdependences likewise politicising in the dimensions mentioned – peace has to be seen conceptually on the analytical level as a configuration, and why in reality a peace structure has to be shaped in a correspondingly configurative manner. For only a redundant causation in a configurative structure provides the basis for 'overdetermination', i.e. for a relatively upheaval-resistant stability of such a peace, though, if only for reasons of caution and political wisdom, it should be seen, in peace concepts and in reality, as always under threat.[16]

This elementary state of affairs – configuratively redundant causation – can also be presented in a negative respect: fairness of distribution can become accentuated on the inter-societal and the international planes, group-psychological or mass-psychological problems can become militant, conflict regulation based on legitimation can collapse for lack of legitimacy or fairness. If this, or something similar, occurs in exacerbated form and moreover together, there is a danger – and, in the event of an exacerbation of the problems, a high degree of probability – of these conditions condensing into a configurative negative scenario with built-in reciprocal intensification mechanisms, thus bringing about a redundantly caused civilisatory regression.

The peace concept extensively and systematically expounded in Chapter 2 is designed effectively to counteract such a situation. In it the strategic definitive provisions for peace on earth are comprehensively developed. The question asked is: Through what and how does peace constitute itself under the complex conditions of the present? The answer is found, in concentrated form, in the expositions of the so-called '*civilisatory hexagon*'. In this historically inspired paradigm, which systematises empirical findings resulting from comparative analysis, peace is presented as a project of the civilisation of modern conflict within and between societies. Where this is successfully realised, the para bellum maxim is forced back, marginalised in its traditionally dominant political importance or, as in the case of emerging 'peace zones' (see Chapter 6), either entirely suspended and thus replaced by a structure that corresponds, in intention or altogether, to the alternative para pacem maxim. The preconditions of this (rarely systematically elucidated) process and its result will be explained in the next three sections (Chapters 2–4). Their length contrasts deliberately with the brevity of this Section: after all, what matters here is the constructive presentation of a historically inspired and systematically elaborated peace concept and not the critique of a maxim (para bellum) that has today, if not before, become dysfunctional with regard to peace, along with its consequences in thought and practice. The reader is presumed to be familiar with this frequently presented critique.

Notes

1. Oddly enough, such an orientation is labelled by its champions as 'realistic' in conceptual as well as in practical respects, which means that reality is so structured that such an orientation is synchronised with reality. The significance of such a situation assessment, as well as necessary critique of it, is discussed, most recently, by Gert Krell, *Weltbilder und*

Weltordnung. Einführung in die Theorie der internationalen Beziehungen, Baden-Baden 2000, Chapter 6, and by Ulrich Menzel, *Zwischen Idealismus und Realismus. Die Lehre von den Internationalen Beziehungen*, Frankfurt/M. 2001, Chapters 2 and 8.

2. On the last variant of a strategy of pre-emption and prevention see, as a recent example, the security-policy strategy of the U.S.A., published in September 2002, *The National Security Strategy of the United States of America*, ed. by the White House, Washington (17 September) 2002.

3. See Harald Müller, 'Erfordernisse einer "friedlichen Militärordnung"', in Dieter Senghaas (ed.), *Frieden machen*, Frankfurt/M. 1997, pp. 362–375.

4. The distinction between a dissociative and an associative peace strategy (the latter will be mentioned below) is elucidated in Johan Galtung, 'Theorien des Friedens', in Dieter Senghaas (ed.), *Kritische Friedensforschung*, Frankfurt/M. 1971, pp. 235–246.

5. On the connection between scale and internal dynamics of military and armament apparatuses see Dieter Senghaas, *Rüstung und Militarismus*, Frankfurt/M. 1972, Parts II and III, as well as idem, *Aufrüstung durch Rüstungskontrolle. Über den symbolischen Gebrauch von Politik*, Stuttgart 1962, pp. 81ff.

6. On this now, superbly, Ernst-Otto Czempiel, *Kluge Macht. Außenpolitik für das 21. Jahrhundert*, Munich 1999.

7. An instructive essay on this subject, in the series Kontroversen um die Geschichte, is now Edgar Wolfrum, *Krieg und Frieden in der Neuzeit. Vom Westfälischen Frieden bis zum Zweiten Weltkrieg*, Darmstadt 2003.

8. See Werner Link, *Die Neuordnung der Weltpolitik. Grundprobleme globaler Politik an der Schwelle zum 21. Jahrhundert*, Munich 1998.

9. Still particularly instructive on this matter is Wilhelm Grewe, *Epochen der Völkerrechtsgeschichte*, Baden-Baden 1988, 2nd edn.

10. On the different legal character of intra-societal and international law see Otto Kimminich, 'Das Völkerrecht und die friedliche Streitschlichtung', in Dieter Senghaas (ed.), *Den Frieden denken*, Frankfurt/M. 1995, pp. 142–161.

11. On the process of transition from forcible to legitimate backing see Chapter 2 of the present book.

12. An impressive account of the development of the peace concept in the European history of ideas can be found in Wilhelm Janssen, 'Friede. Zur Geschichte einer Idee in Europa', in Senghaas (ed.), *Den Frieden denken*, pp. 227–275.

13. Police backing of effective compelling force internally used to be understood and practised in a much broader sense than in the modern meaning of the term police. Thus Ernst-Wolfgang Böckenförde, *Vom Wandel des Menschenbildes im Recht* (Gerda Henkel lecture), Münster 2001: 'Police power thus seen is comprehensive. It includes the professional police as much as the morality and public finance police, the household and economic police, etc. Its measures and regulations combine care for a well-ordered society with the pursuit of mercantile utility' (p. 10). From this 'police science' (*Polizeywissenschaft*), which had been elaborated particularly on Germany in the eighteenth century and which positively reflected this state of affairs, modern political science gradually developed.

14. See the contributions in Senghaas (ed.), *Den Frieden denken*, as well as the monograph treatise by Ernst-Otto Czempiel, *Friedensstrategien*, Opladen 1998.

15. The systematic location of these orientations or imperatives will be found in Chapter 2.

16. For an earlier justification of the importance of a configurative analysis taking account of redundant causality, see publications listed in note 5. Without the use of the term configuratively planned conceptualisations of peace are found in the contributions by Heinrich Schneider, Georg Picht, Johan Galtung and Karl W. Deutsch in Senghaas (ed.), *Frieden machen*.

Chapter 2

SECOND SECTION

Developing the Definitions of Perpetual
Peace ('para pacem'): Through What
and How is Peace Constituted Today?

1. The Doctrine of 'Causative Pacifism'

Through what and how is peace constituted today? This elementary question
was put at the centre of pacifist programme study by Alfred H. Fried, one of
Germany's leading pacifists during the first two decades of the twentieth
century. The slogan was 'causative pacifism': 'He who wishes to eliminate an
effect must first eliminate its cause. And he who wishes to see a new desired
effect instead of another must replace that cause by one that can produce the
desired effect.'[1] This sounds methodologically abstract, but was meant quite
literally. If war is the consequence of an 'international anarchy' still prevailing
in relations between states, then this anarchy has to be eliminated in order to
eliminate its consequence, war. Anarchy must therefore be replaced by a
'social order', as a result of which conflicts can be reliably managed without
force, so that, in the political meaning of the concept, peace is established.

The doctrine of so-called 'causative pacifism' is therefore based on the
attempt to reflect systematically on premises and conditions that render
peace possible and probable. In an analytical respect the doctrine of
'causative pacifism' was therefore comparable to today's efforts towards a
contemporary peace theory.[2]

'Causative pacifism', whether or not this specific term was used by
individual authors, was therefore both a fundamental scholarly and a
practical issue in the classic discussion of pacifism. It is part of the tragedy

of the past century that this perspective lost attention in the pacifist trends and eventually became a non-theme. In that twentieth century of tyranny, wars, genocide and the mutual threat of annihilation within the framework of the deterrence system anti-militarism – quite understandably and comprehensibly – became a predominant orientation of pacifism, governing thinking and action. However, a gap was left behind, an 'empty hole' (Vlasta Jalusic). Antimilitarism aims at liquidating structures and mentalities causing aggression, violence and war. In contrast, 'causative pacifism' aims at erecting durable peace-promoting structures and mentalities. For this reason 'causative pacifism' and comparable orientations can be described as pacifism aiming at the construction and architecture of peace, i.e. a 'constructive pacifism'.

The classic doctrine of 'causative pacifism' – thus explicitly formulated by Alfred Fried in 1918 – aimed at the establishment of a 'new world order'.[3] This intention was not based on any eschatological idea, but on a peace-technical, manageable one, 'imbued with a purposeful spirit of peace'. This new world order was seen as the result of an ongoing process of 'state socialisation' leading to a 'social contract between states'. This would, formulated in present-day terminology, lead not to the liquidation of conflicts, but to conflict transformation, 'to the transformation of an inter-state relationship that would lend to conflicts a character ensuring that it becomes removed from violent resolution and becomes entirely suitable for judicial treatment.'[4] Such conflict transformation, 'the transformation of the character of the conflict', therefore means precisely what is described in the present-day peace-theory discussion as 'civilisation of the conflict'.

However, whereas in the classic doctrine of 'causative pacifism' a civilised management of conflicts on the internal scene was regarded as more or less successfully accomplished – here, with regard to Europe, a successful 'socialisation' had taken place according to the assessment of the situation at the time – today this premise can no longer be assumed as a matter of course. A glance at the world shows that, at least at this moment, scarcely any wars between states are being fought (even though the world of states has by no means been 'socialised' yet); on the other hand we observe a break-up of states and a multitude of militant internal conflicts within states, above all civil wars of the most diverse character.[5] In consequence, the rendering possible of internal peace – and not just the 'new world order' – once more becomes an important analytical and practical orientation of constructive reflection on peace. A contemporary theory of peace must therefore relate to both planes, the internal and the international.

2. Pluralisation and Politicisation
of Traditional Societies

The need for a cause-of-peace research to re-examine also the conditions of internal peace arises from the far-reaching transformations that affected the Western world at an earlier date and the extra-Western world mainly in the twentieth century. When the idea of 'causative pacifism' was formulated at the end of the nineteenth and the beginning of the twentieth century, the world, including the major part of today's industrialised countries, was largely organised on a peasant basis. The past 100 hundred years (1900–2000) – a matter rarely considered – will go down in history as the century of the deruralisation of the world and its consequences. Today, unlike at the beginning of the twentieth century, most people no longer live under subsistence conditions and its typical mutual dependence of people within a small-scale radius. Instead they live in territory-wide economies with increasingly broad-spectrum economic relations. Developing countries are no exception, even though marked gradations continue to exist in this respect, for instance between East Asia and black Africa.

In contrast to peasant communities in the traditional village frame, this new socio-economic milieu has brought to people an enormous broadening of horizons and range of activity. The urbanisation that goes hand in hand with the structural change moreover intensifies communication and for the first time in world history makes the mass of the population capable of political organisation. A simultaneous literacy drive on a mass basis produces a large-scale mobilisation of intelligence, i.e. intellectual emancipation and a revolution in skills: the human competence level rises dramatically. A conversion is taking place: 'from ignorance to awareness, to connection with the world', as a nun working in India's under-stratum once accurately put it (*Frankfurter Allgemeine Zeitung*, 6 January 1999). It is here that, unlike in traditional society, the opportunity for social upward mobility is based. Worldwide media, moreover, make life expectations and lifestyles comparable. It is possible that the globalisation of such demonstration effects is today more effective than a mere globalisation of economies.

In this way traditional societies become politicisable and in fact politicised societies. In them traditional identities become questionable. 'Truths' can no longer be simply defined. ideas of justice are multiplied, as also are interests. What makes a 'good society' becomes a problem in the face of the plurality of offers of system-political projects and definitions. The *'tranquillitas ordinis'*, the 'tranquillity of order', once written about, in the milieu of traditional societies, by Augustine and many other European and, chiefly also, extra-European authors, is no longer to be apprehended. There arise, viewed in terms of their structure, social constructs prone to producing conflicts or even violence, constructs that can no longer be reduced to a common denominator, except forcibly by dictatorship or despotism. These, however, are doomed to failure sooner or later under the socio-economic and sociocultural conditions shown: the fact is that sociocultural, socio-economic and hence also political plurality are insuperable, just as the politicisation of identities, truths, ideas of justice and interests is irreversible. The consequence of all this is the demand for political participation, audible from every corner of the world.[6]

The 'modern social conflict' resulting from politicised difference thus becomes a problem of the whole society with considerable external consequences: if social, socio-economic and cultural conflicts present themselves as political, and if political conflicts present themselves as social, economic and cultural, we are faced with fundamental politicisation. As a result, many societies today are acutely confronted with the question of coexistence in spite of fundamental politicisation. The questionable alternative to coexistence, in the extreme case, is civil war – something we are taught anew by what we see around us every day.

3. The Civilisatory Hexagon or the Need to Civilise the Modern Social Conflict

But how, in such a situation, does one avoid civil war? The above-outlined reconstruction of the world occurred first as a consequence of agrarian and industrial revolution about the middle of the eighteenth century and, above all, in the nineteenth century in the Western part of Europe. Not surprisingly the just outlined set of problems – coexistence in spite of fundamental politicisation – first became acute here and that is why some results of the tackling of that set of problems can best be observed here.[7]

Above all, six conditions of a civilised, i.e. durably non-violent, management of indispensable conflicts need emphasising ('civilisatory hexagon').

First: To start with, there is the *legitimate state monopoly of power*, i.e. the *safeguarding of the rule-of-law community* – this is of fundamental importance for any modern peace system. Only a 'disarming of citizens', the deprivatisation of force, compels them to settle their identity and interest conflicts by argument and not by force. Only thus are the parties to potential conflict compelled to resort to argument and hence to a policy of deliberation in the public space. The significance of this state of affairs becomes dramatically obvious wherever the power monopoly collapses and a rearming of citizens takes place, i.e. when feuds and warlords rise again in new garb, as may be observed at many militant war centres in the world today.

Second, the power monopoly requires control by the rule of law unless it is to become simply an expression of arbitrariness. Without such control, which is at the core of the modern constitutional state, the monopoly of power would remain legally uncircumscribed, in fact nothing other than dictatorship, the rule of the stronger, the rule of force. Rule of law lays down the rules of the process of political opinion formation and will formation, as well as of decision making and of the legal enforcement of legal requirements as defined. Alongside general principles, such as those laid down in catalogues of fundamental rights, these constitutionally fixed rules of the game are of basic importance just because in politicised societies there is usually no agreement on substantive issues.

Political systems based on the rule of law ensure that the monopoly of power is fenced in; only thus does it become legitimate. With this first step it loses its original character of being simply an instance of predominance achieved by force, ultimately by military or warlike means.

These ring-fenced, controlling, legitimated principles transforming the monopoly of power include, among other things, the protection of fundamental freedoms, the guarantee of human rights by law, the equality of citizens before the law. As one of the principal points they guarantee the separation of powers, free elections and the right to political participation, the constitutionally delimited action of governments, the subjection of government and administration to the law, the principle of transparency, administrative justice, especially the instruction on legal means in the findings of judges, the independence of the judiciary and the public prosecutor's office, the unambiguity of the rules laid down for criminal proceedings, the right to legal assistance in the event of criminal prosecution, the right to public and fair legal proceedings, the right to defence, criminal prosecution only on the basis of legally defined circumstances, the presumption of innocence until judicial proof of guilt.[8]

Orders based on the rule of law are also distinguished in the social sphere by a multitude of institutionalised forms of conflict articulation, conflict management, conflict regulation and conflict resolution. Conflicts of any kind, whether conflicts of interest or of identity, are regarded from the outset as 'normal' and legitimate; in intact rule-of-law conditions conflicts of interest are more frequent than conflicts of identity and, as a rule, are more easily manageable than the latter.[9]

Political systems thus conceived allow for the emergence of soft and incomplete problem solutions for a time; they are subject to a trial-and-error process. A rule-of-law system could therefore be interpreted, with regard to conflict management, as an institutionalised permanent learning process about the handling of conflicts that are of significance to the public. Its product is lawfully arrived-at (legal) authoritative decisions, valid for a time, which fail to become the starting points of serious conflicts, in the extreme case of civil wars, if they are accepted as legitimate from procedural and substantive points of view and are perceived as, in principle, capable of revision.

Concerning the relation between monopoly of force and rule of law the following should, in terms of logic, be stated: Without the previous constitution of the monopoly of force, a democratic rule of law is not even conceivable. The state based on the rule of law, where fully developed, itself becomes the quintessence of control of the monopoly of power. The monopoly of power is legitimised. Although therefore only a rule-of-law circumscribed, moreover democratically based (see below), monopoly of power is conducive to a civilising of the modern social conflict, the separation performed in the civilisatory hexagon between monopoly of power and its control is conceptually meaningful, if not downright obligatory, because in the historical process, as a rule, power conditions initially produce only a crude monopolisation of power before, in usually prolonged disputes, i.e. in the conflict history of societies, control bodies and control modalities are established and eventually acknowledged as legitimate (constitutionalisation process).

Third, another essential condition of internal peace consists in affect control, which stems from multiple interdependences. Deprivatisation of force ('the disarming of the citizens') and its socialisation into a multitude of institutionalised conflict regulations imply a control of affects. Such self-control is significantly supported by the development of large-scale networks (in Elias's sense of 'long chains of acting') because these, as can be observed mainly in division-of-labour economies, require a considerable measure of calculability and, in consequence, bring with them reliability of expectation.[10]

Modern societies are differentiated in many directions: people in them are multiple 'role players' with a range of loyalties. The demand for multiple roles, as taught by conflict theory and by everyday experience, leads to conflict fractionalisation and to a moderation in conflict attitudes, to a taming of affects, because without these coexistence would not be thinkable in complex milieux such as presented by modernising or modern societies.

Affect control – the result of sublimation of affects – means self-control or self-restraint resulting in differentiated societies from diverse sets of action. It is the basis not only of the inhibition of aggression and renunciation of force, but, developing from these, of tolerance and readiness for compromise. Neither is conceivable without preceding self-discipline. With it the autonomy striving of individuals and groups, which characterises all modern societies, finds an indispensable corrective.

Fourth, there is a need, on the other hand, for democratic participation. Because where people cannot involve themselves in public affairs, whether due to legal or other discrimination, 'judicial unrest' (S. Freud) arises, in the worst case a build-up of conflicts, which in politicisable societies can become a focus of violence. Democracy as the basis of institutionally regulated development of the law is therefore not a luxury but a necessary condition of peaceful conflict management.[11]

Societies in which large-scale interdependence textures develop become socially mobile societies. In them, as pointed out above, a fundamental transformation process takes place that can be outlined by the following keywords: deruralisation or proletarianisation, devillagisation or urbanisation, as well as, for mobile societies fundamentally, a literacy drive. Such a transformation process leads to the emergence of entirely new social strata that, according to their place in society and depending on their potential upward or threatening downward mobility, articulate and defend specific interests and develop their own identity profiles. For the past few decades, as a result of progressive democratisation, gender-specific role assignations, as well as the patriarchal relations underlying them, are being questioned.

In politicisable communities interests must be capable of articulation on a broad front and capable of integration in the ongoing political process. The more open and flexible the democratic rule-of-law institutional structure, the more resilient to stress it will be in the event of persistent or possibly increasing political demands.

Generally speaking, subordination relations on the basis of gender, race, class or other characteristics are no longer tolerated by those concerned in advanced, socially mobile societies. In democratic rule-of-law states with a high politicisation potential such discrimination undermines political stability.

Fifth, such conflict management in politicised societies, however, is durable only if there are continuous efforts for social justice. Socially mobilised societies with a widening participation are societies characterised by a high degree of lobbyist organisation by many (albeit not always all) interests and hence by a large measure of potential or actual politicisation. In them, social justice, in the double meaning of the concept – i.e. justice of opportunity and justice of distribution – inevitably becomes a persistent virulent problem.

In societies with a considerable politicisation potential an active policy of *justice of opportunity and distribution*, supplemented by *justice of basic needs* (safeguarding of basic requirements) is indispensable because only then does the mass of the population feel *protected with fairness*. The material enrichment or buttressing of the rule of law, especially in the sense of fair participation in welfare, is therefore not a political orientation that can, but need not, be pursued by such societies according to their inclination; instead it is a constituent condition of the viability of rule-of-law systems and hence of the internal peace of societies.

Societies based on the rule of law are therefore well advised never to let the issue of justice come to rest, especially when the economies on which they are based – as a rule capitalist market economies – in their systemic nature tend to produce inequality rather than equality. Unless this dynamic towards inequality is continually counteracted, explosive social rifts develop in such societies. Unless continuous efforts are made to achieve fairness of distribution, the disadvantaged will question the credibility of the rule of law because the rules of its game are no longer perceived to be fair. In contrast, serious efforts for social justice and fairness are conducive to a constructive conflict management; they lend legitimacy to public institutions, a legitimacy feeding on direct everyday experience.

Sixth, if in the public space there are fair opportunities for the articulation of identities and for the reconciliation of diverse interests it can be assumed that such an arrangement of conflict management is reliably internalised and that compromise-oriented conflict situations, including the toleration necessary for them, become a self-evident orientation of political action. The monopoly of power and the rule of law and democracy – in short, the democratic state based on the rule of law – become anchored in the political culture. Moreover, the culture of constructive conflict management becomes the emotional basis of the community. Material performances ('social justice') prove to be an important bridge between the structure of institutions and their positive emotional safeguards ('public attitude'). To use a concept of Ralf Dahrendorf, appropriate 'ligatures' come into being, i.e. political and cultural ties or socio-cultural in-depth ties, definable as the 'subjective inside of the norms that guarantee social structures'.[12]

The development of geographically bounded dense interdependence textures is, as a rule, translated not only into a unified juridical area, into a unified economic area (characterised by a common currency), but also – mostly overlooked – into a corresponding 'emotional area'. This is a late product of prolonged modernisation processes and is reflected in 'national identity' or also 'regional identity'.[13] On its basis develops the ability to think and act empathetically with regard to a far greater number of people than those close to one.

The political culture of constructive conflict management does not stand at the beginning of the evolution of modern coexistence. Instead it is a late product in the historical process. And, like the other five components, it is not foreshadowed in European (read: Western European) culture. On the contrary, the evolution of every single component is more of a reluctant process. Viewed historically, disarmament as a rule was the outcome of victory and defeat in elimination struggles: the stronger was victorious over the weaker, a superior instance above subordinate rule of law had its origin in historically contested compromise arrangements wrested from the conflicting parties, arrangements that, naturally enough, were not loved and initially understood as concessions in fragile power situations. As for affect control, self-determined existence in concretely overseeable small-scale connections was invariably preferred to integration in self-dynamic (as we say nowadays, self-referential) functional systems. Since Sigmund Freud, if not longer, we have known that affect control is determined by the imperatives of the reality principle and not the pleasure principle, with both principles being inexorably in conflict with one another.

Moreover, the struggle for the extension of participation always encountered hard defensive fronts, as, in a world of system-conditioned inequality, did the dispute about justice and fairness in distribution. Political participation and just distribution had to be wrested from the status-quo powers. Eventually a culture of constructive conflict management only came about under the fortunate conditions that the above-listed building blocks of civility, each in turn, became historical reality, moreover reinforcing one another and ultimately anchoring themselves emotionally. Only under such extreme preconditions did a civilisation of conflict and hence the basically non-violent settlement of conflicts become probable in a milieu of fundamental politicisation.

The process itself can therefore be understood only as the historical result of numerous conflicts that took place in the European context in line with the above-mentioned sequence of six stages. Besides, this historical state of affairs is reflected also in the history of modern political thought. Synoptically reconstructed it presents itself as follows. In the modern peace discussion Hobbes emphasised the pacifying effect of the state's crude power monopoly in view of acute and threatening civil wars. Kant's contribution was focused on the rule-of-law circumscription of that power monopoly ('republican order'), as well as on the confederative networking of states in a 'peace league'. Liberal thought in numerous variations supplemented the civilising effect of division of labour, of free exchange of goods, and (albeit over a long period and with considerable limitation) of democratisation. Socialist tradition laid great emphasis on fair distribution and social equity. Later the psychological (especially the psychoanalytical) argument was focused on self-awareness, strength of ego, affect control and empathy. Feminist thinking, wherever it was capable of a positive turn, accentuated many of these aspects. In retrospect these diverse thinking traditions, one building upon another, reveal the configurative complexity of the civilisation project – its constitutional, institutional, material and emotional dimensions.

What has arisen is a construct of conflict management – here called the 'civilisatory hexagon' – which has constitutional, institutional and material dimensions, but is also marked by specific mentalities and generally – this has to be emphatically stated – represents a civilisatory artefact (see Figure 2.1 on page 24).

It can be plausibly argued that circumstances that, in emancipated mass societies, characterise fundamental politicisation, such as the demand for absoluteness, fixation on a particular interest, emphasis on a special identity, possessive individualism, lobbyist inclinations, etc., are immediate, in a sense 'natural', whereas tolerance, sensitivity to rules, moderation,

Power monopoly

Rule of law

Interdependences
and affect control

Political participation

Social justice/equity

Culture of constructive
conflict management

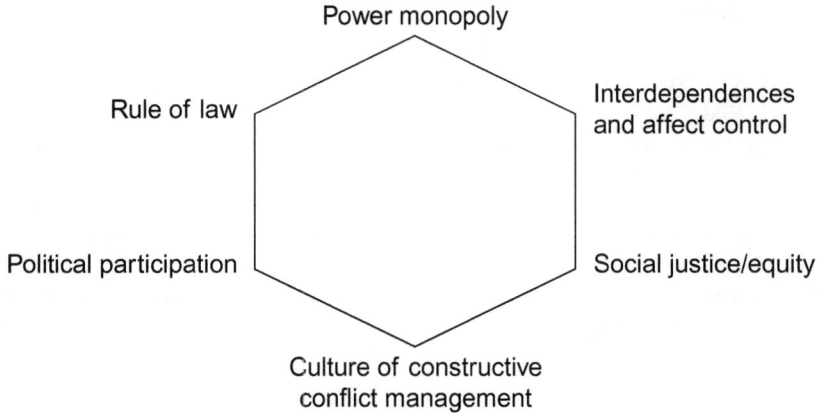

Figure 2.1: The 'civilisatory hexagon'

separation of powers, readiness for compromise, the sense for more than one's own interest (empathy) are, in a sense, 'artificial', i.e. the result of laborious collective learning processes. All these extensive civilisatory achievements were attained, especially in Europe, against its own old-European class-society tradition, in struggle and in conflict with that past. Thus the democratic rule-of-law state is not the result of culture-genetic premoulding. Instead it is the expression of an innovation, or of a sum of innovations, moreover, in the framework of two and a half millennia of European history, a very recent development.[14]

The above-mentioned six components of the civilisatory hexagon should be seen configuratively, not monothematically or in terms of a one-dimensional and narrow-minded theory, but as the premises and conditions for lastingly civilised conflict management. Monothematic thinking concentrates on one of the six named points of the hexagon, in order to illuminate it positively or critically (including fundamental critique). The complexity of the configuration is lost in this process. All six components are important, as also their feedbacks, because these provide support for the individual components and reciprocal reassurance, causing relative stability configuratively or through redundancy.

If this configuration is inadequate, stability cannot be expected either. Without a secure power monopoly there is no rule of law or violence-free democratic participation; without fair distribution there is no guarantee of endurance for a rule of law that is perceived to be fair and legitimate and, in consequence, no reliably ring-fenced power monopoly and no conflict culture. Without democratic participation and fairness of distribution there is no civic mentality, there are no 'ligatures'.

If one views the civilisatory hexagon from its components and their feedbacks, it presents itself as a fragile construct that, as it is built up from its corner points, is also always threatened with collapse from their direction. The force monopoly can flip over into a police state; rule of law and democratic processes can turn out to be just a façade and thus lose legitimacy; overwhelming, no longer transparent, interdependences can lead to identity loss and, in consequence, to a renewed liberation of affects; unfair distribution is one of the politically most sensitive dangers. When such and other negative conditions bundle together, even constructive conflict culture stands no chance. The sequence of steps of

'Lebanonisation' – exemplified by Lebanon, once the often-quoted 'Switzerland of the Middle East', and its collapse in a fifteen-year-long civil war – offers a representative scenario: perceived and politically increasingly virulent inequality of opportunity and of distribution as a starting point, delegitimation of constitutional formulas of coexistence, collapse of conflict culture, reprivatisation of force, as well as disrespect for and collapse of the rule of law, arming of the conflicting parties, breakdown of traditional interdependent action patterns, including the economy, release of parochially determined ethnopolitically motivated affects, civil war and unleashing of affects – until the eventual exhaustion of those involved and the intervention of an external hegemony (Syria).[15]

The civilisatory hexagon, in view of its collapse-threatened points, is therefore an enterprise that has to be secured time and time again. Successful opposition to the threats therefore requires persistent efforts in all the areas designated by the six corner points. Configurative thinking is necessary not only in the analytical but also in the practical respect.

4. Historical and Topical Experience ('Hexagon variations')

In the civilisatory hexagon historical experience from modern history of certain parts of Europe – the region of democratic constitutional states – is conspicuously bundled together. Viewed historically, the monopoly of power was the first to take shape since the end of the Middle Ages in Europe – the result of prolonged elimination struggles (as a rule of feuds and wars) for hegemony. Along with the emergence of the power monopoly the conflicts for the control of this power monopoly began immediately. In the long run these resulted in the institutionalisation of the rule of law. Differentiation and interlinking of modern societies with an increasingly large-scale territorial economy and increasingly dense and close communication structures took place with a time lag. The struggle for democratic participation, imaginable only on the basis of societies that have become socially mobile, went hand in hand with arguments about social justice, especially fairness of distribution. Parallel to this a political conflict culture of liberal character developed step by step.[16]

The variations in the developmental process within this basic pattern were certainly remarkable. Thus England had a long struggle for the rule of law behind it at a time when the power monopoly in the large-area countries of the European continent still maintained its absolutist and autocratic position. Generally the struggle for democratic participation depended on the scale and the speed of the transformation of traditional societies into modern ones. Where the labour force potential was, or became, small the political struggle for social justice was facilitated. This was the case, for instance, in the European settler colonies (especially in New Zealand, Australia and Canada); moreover they were not burdened with the heritage of European feudalism, which is why the development of the civilisatory hexagon, albeit starting late, proceeded especially fast and with regard to all six components. Experience on similar lines was also shared by the Scandinavian countries, where, long before the rest of the European continent, a completion and rounding off of the civilisatory hexagon took place. A certain 'maturity' of the civilisatory hexagon is observed only in the democratically and market-economy oriented constitutional states of the West (OECD states) after 1950, without however the above-mentioned break-up danger being eliminated in principle.

Although Eurocentrally rooted, the civilisatory hexagon is not anchored in any original 'cultural genes' of Europe. Its first outlines appeared 500 years ago; 100 years ago it began to differentiate in a few individual instances; as recently as in the twentieth century there were dramatic regressions and it remains to be seen whether the relatively positive experiences in the OECD sphere during the past 50 years can be seamlessly extended into the future. Just as no certain origin can be established in Europe, so there is no guarantee of endurance for the civilisatory hexagon in Europe or in the Western world generally. And since this construct represents a sum of politically institutional innovations, it would be a mistake to assume that innovations beyond the forms of the hexagon known today would be improbable over future centuries, let alone millennia.

Maybe such innovations will come about in other regions and cultural spheres of the globe, such as, during the next few decades, in the East Asian or South-East Asian area. Here one could speak of an emerging hexagonal development process, especially in Korea and Taiwan, but as a trend in all reasonably successful developing countries of East and South-East Asia. The sequence observed in these cases may be described as follows. The starting points were dictatorial development regimes in the form of military dictatorships, which, in the time after 1950 enjoyed a generally uncircumscribed power monopoly. By the customary economic criteria the development policy pursued by them was exceedingly successful – especially in comparison with the results of development policy in other Third World continents. The consequence of successful development policy manifests itself in a dramatically swift transformation of traditional into modern societies, which, viewed in terms of social statistics, increasingly approach the OECD average.[17] This transformation, as always in history, led to struggles for political recognition, i.e. efforts by new social strata for political participation. As a result, democratisation appeared on the agenda of those societies. One of its aims was the enforcement of rule-of-law principles, in particular a constitutional control of the power monopoly. Since a dramatic growth of the economy has meanwhile exhausted the manpower potential and since the conflicting groups of modernising society are organising (creation of 'strategic groups'), the dispute about social justice will become further exacerbated.[18] An interesting question will be whether, in a cultural sphere previously disinclined to conflict (such as the Confucian-Buddhist), a political culture can establish itself that will gradually develop a positive attitude to conflicts and conflict management.

What we observe in the Far East is the scenario of a hexagon unfolding in specific sequence ('emergent hexagon'): crude power monopoly, efficient economy, democratic participation, rule of law, fair distribution, conflict culture. As always in history, this is ultimately a wrestling for new forms of coexistence, basically therefore for constitutional issues, the answers to all of which may be historically inspired, but are by no means predetermined. There is therefore always scope for politically institutional innovation.

The East Asian experience of an emerging civilisatory hexagon stands in clear contrast to the failure of the real-socialist experiment. In the political, social, economic and cultural respect real socialism was based on power monopoly – the monopoly claim of the Communist Party. Although real socialism vigorously promoted the transformation of traditional into modern societies, especially industrialisation, urbanisation and literacy, it was unable to meet the growing complexity of society, economy and culture through correspondingly increasingly complex political control instruments and, eventually, step by step, to abolish the monopoly claim of the single party and to open up to democratisation based on pluralism. Instead of acceptance of a scenario of an emergent hexagon there was enforcement of a crude power monopoly with more or less undisguised repression. Thus real-socialism manoeuvred itself into a civilisatory blind alley. The planned economy typical of it, despite considerable and increasing capital expenditure, performed less and less efficiently, which meant that for the mass of the population the ideologically promised fairness of distribution was replaced by increasingly widespread shortages. Rule of law remained unknown; self-organisation of social conflict parties ('civil society') was frowned upon. When social movements eventually forced a change, the initial result of democratisation was not infrequently chaos – a process entirely comprehensible in the light of the civilisatory hexagon. Ethnicisation – the lowest common denominator of politics – often became the pseudo-biological vanishing point of political movements. In the light of the civilisatory hexagon the reconstruction programme following the political turn (1989–92) had dramatic dimensions. The power monopoly was often contested by civil war; the rule of law, until then unknown, had to be gradually established, democratic pluralist politics had to be rehearsed. This actually required a political conflict culture, which had a poor chance unless the reconstruction of efficient economies helped to defuse the social problem. Tasks of this kind and this scope arose therefore abruptly ('dilemma of simultaneity') and continue to present themselves in all six dimensions of the hexagon at the same time. This has no parallel in history. It is not therefore surprising if all societies affected are struggling with these facts and that many of them cannot as yet see the light at the end of the tunnel (although the image of 'the tunnel at the end of the light' may be exaggerated[19]).

The emerging hexagon in the Far East points to growing – albeit not yet secured – opportunities for civilised conflict management in the political sphere; the real-socialist 'anti-hexagon' focused only on the power monopoly points to the violence-proneness of such a construct, given a socially mobile politicisable society. Other experience shows that in the large Latin American societies, which, in their history, have already known limited periods with democratic experience (Argentina, Brazil, Mexico) the opportunities still exist for an emerging civilisatory hexagon, for instance in the less populated countries (such as Chile and Uruguay). At least it is worth noting that Latin America at present does not belong to the worrying conflict sources in the world – quite unlike large parts of black Africa, where political institutions, economic potentials and infrastructures are, in many places, falling apart or are being wrecked, even though, on the other hand, certain individual democratisation processes can be observed, albeit with an as yet entirely open result. With regard to civilised conflict management Latin America (though perhaps only on the surface) may give rise to optimism, whereas black Africa gives rise to profound pessimism. In other parts of the world, especially in the Arabic-Islamic sphere, existing institutions of conflict settlement, such as the post-colonial secular state (where existing), find themselves, in the face of an expanding and deepening developmental crisis, under the political fire of fundamentalist Islamic forces. Unfortunately trends in that direction can be observed also in an ethnopolitically divided India ('Hindustan'), where more than a billion people will have no choice but to preserve the secular state as an institutional platform for more or less civilised conflict management or, replacing it, find (or invent) a new platform that would fence in ethnic conflicts – but what platform could that be other than the secular state?

Whether China, the world's existing more than one-billion society, will grow into an area-wide emerging civilisatory hexagon is a particularly suspenseful question. The scale of the task is unprecedented: efforts to fit into the civilisatory hexagon in the sense of conflict-prone collective learning processes have so far taken place successfully in small countries, such as Scandinavia, or in settler colonies, and most recently in Taiwan. But how can one visualise such a process in a vast country with, at present, more than 1.3 billion inhabitants? Can such a process, given our experience, even be expected? The answer is open, but there is one noteworthy state of affairs: as in the rest of East Asia, the forces in China that have an interest in the development of one or another variant of the democratic rule-of-law state are being strengthened by a dynamically unfolding economic basis, whereas the material power base of the status-quo forces, trapped in an ageing centralised planned economy, tend to shrink. Unlike the reformist forces in the eastern half of Europe, which at zero hour (1989–92) had no new economic basis at their disposal, the reformers in China will be able, in the impending inevitable political conflict about the direction of future development, to throw their own economically founded political weights on to the scales. Here is a clear difference from the development in the eastern half of Europe, especially Russia, following the world-political about-turn.

5. The Worldwide Civilisation Problems from a General Perspective

What Europe had to learn laboriously and painfully, by trial and error, by direct and roundabout roads and sometimes wrong roads – tolerance as a solution of a pluralisation initially perceived as a threat to the status quo – is a process that will have to be repeated in other parts of the world, if not in detail then certainly in principle: the non-postponable mastering of coexistence problems in the face of a spreading fundamental politicisation, as the consequence of the above-mentioned transformation of traditional into socially mobile societies, is increasingly on the agenda there. However, just as once in Europe, no provision is made in any of the various extra-European regions for these modern problems in their traditional political culture. Their self-comprehension, too, was largely 'cosmocentrally' oriented. In it – especially in the manifestation of high mythology – the cosmos, society and people were understood as a unit from an integral perspective. This was envisaged as a well-ordered and well-constructed hierarchy. Its architecture was viewed statically. Besides, the roles and role play of the actors were prescribed. Cyclicity determined historical self-comprehension, which in reality was not historical in the modern sense, because the cycle – in analogy to the processes in the annual cycle of nature or to events in the political sphere (rise, flowering and decay of imperial structures or empires) – kept returning to the same starting point. The idea of a plurality of truths was, on the whole, unimaginable.

If on such premises especially the institutions of community and governance appear as an organic entity, the conflicts are, as a rule, regarded as dysfunctional. They are, as in ancient China, understood as the 'great unrest under the sky', that is as the starting point of the danger of chaos or as an expression of an already existing chaos. Counteracting thinking is then seen as a contribution to the overcoming of just that chaos, as a chaos control strategy designed to restore the 'cosmic order'.[20] However, for the requirements of mastering the modern coexistence problems, such orientations are no longer helpful. That is why, also in the rest of the world, new perspectives of conflict management suited to our time, and hence new formulas and forms of internal peace will have to emerge under the compulsion of circumstances.

Unlike the endogenous Western development, the collective learning processes in the extra-European world are massively co-determined by earlier developments within the West: these, being earlier, define the history-making international context that shares in shaping local events. In this process, just as once in Europe in its relations with hexagonal pioneering societies (like Britain, France and Scandinavia) or with latecomers (e.g. Germany), four prototype forms of reaction can generally be observed in the extra-European world today:

Modernistic-imitative is a reaction that accepts the challenge of the West as well as its experiences and 'solutions offered', viewing the West therefore as a model and fighting against the weight of its own tradition, including its own traditional political culture. In the first half of the past century such orientations were found in many places, above all in China; they remained unsuccessful at their time. Today, however, they are strikingly successful, e.g. in two of the four threshold countries in East Asia – Korea and Taiwan. There, as demonstrated above, newly industrialising countries (NICs) become 'newly democratising countries', whose political culture, despite all local colour, will in the foreseeable future be barely distinguishable from that of western countries.

Where modernisation upheavals occur and coexistence problems become acute, the preservers also appear: *traditionalists*, also reactionaries, generally conservatives. They endeavour to turn back the wheel of history or at least to halt modernisation. This type of reaction can be observed wherever in the world Western modern ideas clash with traditional ones. Gandhi could be quoted here as a soft-minded example, because his tradition-based philosophy of life was village-oriented, anti-commercial and egalitarian. It envisaged small units and therefore favoured a direct democracy based on consensus in an area of manageable size, i.e. not representative democracy to which, in populous societies, there is no alternative anyway. Today comparable ideas, albeit controversially discussed, are still found, mainly in black Africa.

Where upheavals occur *half-modernists* also appear on the scene. They pounce on western know-how, but try to keep all other ideological influences away. Japan has successfully pursued such a project since the middle of the nineteenth century, whereas the real socialism of the twentieth century remained unsuccessful. The so-called 'Singapore school' became prominent during the last three decades of the past century for such an orientation of half-modernism, and Islamic fundamentalism is pursuing it to this day. Yet the political problems of an increasingly complex pluralising society, be it in Singapore, in China, in the vast sphere of Islamic societies or elsewhere, are not resolved by such a system-political programme or even brought nearer to a solution – least of all where attempts are made to proceed with theocratic recipes of Islamic provenance. These reveal astonishing parallels with historical antecedents, but also prove the hopelessness of a 'theocratic counter-revolution' against modernism, such as was observed, for instance, in Europe in the first half of the nineteenth century as a reaction to the French Revolution. Pluralism was, and is, considered in this anti-modernist programme as an amoral community-disturbing idea, as an expression of the decay of values and culture, as the quintessence of moral blindness ('jahiliyya'); unrestricted religiously motivated rule was, and is, considered right for our time.[21]

However: even in the extra-European world *innovations* will ultimately be necessary where modern and traditional ideas clash and irreversible upheavals follow. Just as they were unpredictable in the European zone, so they cannot be predicted in the extra-European world. Internal European experience will be repeated: As soon as traditional political order and culture are confronted with modernisation thrusts, when societies undergo a structural and hence mental upheaval, these systems and cultures get into conflict with themselves with merciless inevitability, experiencing a 'clash *within* civilisation'. From this stem the necessary collective learning processes – and also problematical wrong developments.

That the innovations of modernism in the European western sphere have totally exhausted themselves with regard to the mastering of coexistence problems – this is the assumption underlying Francis Fukuyama's thesis of the *'end of history'* – does not seem likely. On the contrary, four fifths of humanity will, over the next few decades and as a rule reluctantly, have to experiment with the discovery of new appropriate answers to the problems of social mobilisation and fundamental politicisation. It is unlikely that these answers, which will ultimately have to prove effective, will be invented in abstract form at the drawing board.

More likely, also in this respect, is a repetition of European experience: that which eventually proves its worth as a viable arrangement of coexistence, i.e. of internal peace, will have come about as an unintended consequence of profound political conflicts.

Extra-European society will not therefore be spared Europe's difficult, painful and conflict-abundant experiences on the road to the democratic rule-of-law state, its institutions and its ethos. The process is comparable to that in Europe, even though its final outcome could be different, especially if genuine innovations are actually implemented. In this case, however, the result would reflect not the deep dimension of traditional political culture, but something new – against one's own tradition.

Pluralisation as a perceived threat, institutionally protected and emotionally anchored tolerance as a solution: this, viewed worldwide, is one of mankind's great challenges for the twenty-first century, no less weighty than the intensifying worldwide environmental problems. A glance back at the twentieth century reveals the explosive nature of these problems. In that century the 'alternatives' to tolerance were rehearsed in many areas: marginalisation, ghettoisation, apartheid, expulsion, 'ethnic cleansing', genocide and, above all, civil wars in many variants.[22] Unlike the 'causative pacifism' at the beginning of the twentieth century, the search for system-political normative, institutional, material and mental conditions of coexistence *within* societies, therefore, in view of the irreversibility of pluralisation, remains high on the agenda. Internal peace is not therefore a marginal problem, but has become an acute existential core problem – more than ever before, seen worldwide. For even in the last corner of the earth the matter-of-course nature of traditional orders is crumbling away, which is why indispensable orientation conflicts are inevitable in a mixture of power disputes and system-politically motivated culture conflicts. The exacerbated conflicts in Iran since the 1980s are a good example.

6. Shaping of a World Order Policy

Constructive Conflict Management on the International Plane

The civilisatory hexagon was initially explained with an eye only to the civilisatory requirements of politics within societies. In such individual hexagonally organised societies an increasingly coherent sequence of actions arises in consequence. Can these reflections be transferred to the plane beyond individual societies? What would civilisation of politics mean on the international plane?

A transfer of the civilisatory hexagon from the intra-state intra-society plane to the international plane would have to understand the world either as a sum of hexagonal societies or even as a single hexagonally structured civilian world society. Its emerging development, viewed in the abstract, might be imagined as follows: first, the emergence of increasingly dense transnational inter-societal interconnections within the traditional world of states, from which, initially in regional link-ups and later beyond these, a transnational 'societal world' and 'economic world' would develop; gradual relativisation of the world of states and step-by-step development of a world society, principally through globalising system relations in the dimensions of worldwide economy, transport, information and communication; next, the development of corresponding, in the final effect common, normative and judicial horizons, as well as of corresponding overarching institutions, of accepted rules and political control mechanisms that would contribute to a civilised management of conflicts and to the cultural development and stabilisation of a civilian world society. If such a world society were also to tend to become a homogeneous community of values, then today's world of states would eventually be transformed into a world community with the individual states playing an important, albeit ultimately subsidiary, role and function in such a worldwide network of actions. Within such an overall construct – the civilian world society – the realisation of a large-area civilisatory hexagon would now become imaginable on the highest possible, i.e. worldwide, plane: the development of a power monopoly, acknowledged as legitimate (however institutionally shaped in detail), control of this power monopoly in a manner analogous to the rule of law on the state plane, worldwide interdependence links and resulting disciplinary constraints with the result of affect control; democratisation at least in the sense of appropriate possibilities of representation of essential collectives and groupings; economic equalisation to achieve social justice on a worldwide plane; as well as internationalised conflict culture, mainly in the sense of tolerance as the fundamental contents of a world ethos.

There is nothing to prevent us from indulging in an abstract mental experiment (like the one just rehearsed) and imposing the civilisatory hexagon in its separate components and as an entity upon such a future world, regardless of whether we regard such development as desirable or reprehensible. As for desirability, we might, in this context, recall Kant's scepticism as articulated in *Zum ewigen Frieden* (1795). He championed the thesis that mutually independent neighbouring states may justify a state of war (unless a federative unification of them prevents the outbreak of hostilities), but that, according to reason, a federative unification of such independent states is preferable to an amalgamation into a power overarching all individual states and transforming itself into a world state. His reasoning was: 'because the laws, with the enlarged size of the government, lose more and more of their weight and a soulless despotism, having exterminated the germs of good, ultimately descends into anarchy'.

And, although the dissimilarity of languages and religions bears within itself the tendency towards mutual hatred and towards a pretext for war, this very dissimilarity was being utilised 'by nature' to prevent nations from intermingling and to keep them apart. Growing culture and the gradual rapprochement of people to common principles and to consensus with regard to peace would engender rivalry and eventually an equilibrium that would be more peace-promoting than 'despotism'.

In the language of the newer theory: the abstract extrapolation of the civilisatory hexagon from the individual civilian society to the world as a whole would aim at the creation of an 'amalgamated security community', i.e. a new federal state on a supranational plane. Kant's critique of this is oriented positively towards this or that variant of a 'pluralist security community' (K.W. Deutsch), i.e. towards imaginable variants of a confederation.[23] Also imaginable are models of political constitutional shape between federal state and state federation, such as the 'league of states', which was the label given to the European Union in a judgment of the German Constitutional Court. A 'league of states', accordingly, would be less integrated than a federal state, but far more integrated than a mere state federation, a 'confederation'.

What is possible, what is probable and what, moreover, is sensible does not, of course, primarily depend on such abstract extrapolations, but on the reality of the world and foreseeable trends of development. To start with, this reality does not present itself as a single homogeneous and coherent pattern of actions, but as a fissured and hence heterogeneous system of relations.[24] And the likelihood of the world as a whole gradually, and in the foreseeable future, becoming homogeneous over large areas and achieving worldwide effective systemic, moreover institutional and mental, coherence continues to be slight.

If this is difficult to accomplish within societies, and if even there it should, under optimal conditions, be seen only as a fragile construct without any guarantee of endurance (which is why, as demonstrated, continuous efforts for internal peace remain necessary even with a fairly stable starting situation), then this is, *not extrapolated in the abstract, but concretely analysed relating to the existing reality*, a much more difficult task on the international plane: namely. to achieve and safeguard international coexistence with world order politics.

Hence first the question: what systematic reflections result, with regard to the existing reality, from the preceding reflections on the civilisatory hexagon concerning the transformation of the character of international conflicts? What would have to be done in the real existing world in order to 'formally institute peace' (Kant) also on this plane and hence to establish a 'social order' beyond individual states in the sense of the above-quoted causative or constructive pacifism?

First, the equivalent of the disarming of the citizens within the state would be a 'disarmament of states'. Potentially or actually armed states – as defined by the 'anarchy of the world of states' situation – live under the conditions of the so-called security dilemma which, in the event of appropriate conflicts of interests, goes along with the threat, or the use, of force. 'Peace' under the premises of the security dilemma, as Alfred Fried has pointed out, initially means only armistice. However,

> such peace would ... only be a latent war, its time limit given by a mutual outbidding of means of force, by the fear of one state of a sudden attack by the other, a peace that could be maintained only by the sacrifice of all the productive forces of the states, forces that should serve the enhancement of a happy life of the nations, for the longest possible extension of a period between a recently finished and the next war, a period misnamed peace. Just as a person cannot be regarded as in good health if, for a predetermined time, he is free from an acute attack, so the world of states is not pacified by a transformation of an acute state of war into a latent one that one knows is bound to retransform itself into acute war.[25]

If, however, the security dilemma were to be replaced by reliable expectation, predictability and hence assured behaviour, what institutional provisions would be necessary for achieving such a state of affairs? What would be the functional equivalent of the intra-state rule of law and its power of enforcement, i.e. to the intra-state monopoly of legitimate power? A negative answer is easy: a stable monopoly of legitimate power on the international plane could not be simply the result of victory and defeat in an international elimination struggle, or the result of a hegemony order based solely on power. Least of all is such a monopoly imaginable in a deterrence or equilibrium system of the powers – or in an arrangement between military alliances (whether oriented regionally or worldwide). The justification of the last-named systems, which have characterised the history of international relations to date, explicitly contradicts the idea of a legitimate monopoly of power. Moreover, none of these arrangements are durable. A hegemony-based order is always prone to erosion: systems of equilibrium or deterrence usually find that the ground on which they believe they rest securely is pulled from under their feet by uncontrolled and uncontrollable processes. On an international plane and in a persistent heterogeneous environment a monopoly of legitimate power, given the continued existence of separate states, is imaginable only within a system of collective security as conceived, albeit only in embryonic shape, in the Charter of the United Nations since 1945. This system is based in principle on a prohibition of power – not to be confused with the monopoly of force – which is why international law can only claim to be an international law *of peace* since 1945. The only exception from the prohibition of force is time-limited individual or collective self-defence until the instruments of the collective security system are set in motion, i.e. effective help is provided for the victim of force, i.e. the attacked state, with its defence against the aggressor. This state of affairs was conceived in analogy to one that exists also within rule-of-law political systems: in acute emergencies individuals are entitled to self-defence until the lawfully competent state bodies come to their aid.

In theory the system of collective security as enshrined in the UN Charter is conceived entirely logically. That its instruments have not been fully implemented is not the fault of the concept (of collective security), but of the states that continue to refuse to fully implement such a system – with the result that it is not properly effective. What does its logic consist of? For the event of conflicts of interests that are apt to lead to force or have indeed led to force, it has provisions for peaceful conflict settlement, negotiation, investigation, mediation, arrangement, adjudication, judicial decision and other peaceful means of its own choice. In the event of a failure of such efforts, and if aggression has taken place, there is a gradation of measures: assessment of aggression having taken place, peaceful sanctions in the sense of an economic embargo, evaluation of the efficacy or inefficacy of such peaceful sanctions, possibility of military sanctions for which a whole range of provisions exists (so far unrealised special agreements between the Security Council and the UN members obliged to assist; holding of air forces in readiness; drawing up of plans for the application of force of arms by the Security Council with the support of the general staff committee; execution of the resolution of the Security Council according to its judgment by all or some members of the UN; possibility of authorisation of one or more members, i.e. authorisation of appropriate actions).

Whatever differences there are in detail, the ban on the use of force, laid down in international law since 1945 on the international plane is based, just as in the intra-state sphere, on two elementary premises: the individual (here the state, there the individual or group of individuals) is prohibited in principle from resorting to force except in the event of self-defence. There is no kind of exception. Besides, since even a ban on the use of force in principle is no guarantee that force will not be resorted to, the second premise really consists in the duty, under the law, to come to the assistance of the victim of aggression – the conceptually logical counterpart to the prohibition of force. If such assistance, though urgently required, does not take place on the international plane, or only rarely, or only for opportunist reasons, this means that the community of nations in reality lags behind what it has itself explicitly and without any reservation undertaken to do. Today's international world is therefore, in respect of a security guarantee, a rule-of-law community in the formal sense, whereas in political reality it usually acts as if judicial anarchy prevailed. This means that relevant decisions (e.g. in the Security Council) are taken arbitrarily as a contingent result of political bargaining processes and not always or cogently in the light of the situations viewed and assessed from judicial points of view. As a rule, therefore, we still see à la carte decisions motivated by power politics or interest politics instead of decisions resulting from the assessment of a situation in the light of judicial demands.

The fundamental problem of the collective security system as it exists today in international law in accordance with the UN Charter is that it is practised as a power figure that is manipulated by opportunist considerations in all possible directions instead of a mandatory instance of law. If political actions were at the level of an international law with its own value, the weighting would have to be exactly the other way about. The legal character of the decisions to be taken in the UN, especially in the Security Council, would have to be the primary consideration, with aspects of political opportunism holding second place. The fact that this is not so indicates that the much-invoked 'community of nations' at top level still sees itself as a power-politically defined 'world of states' and not, especially with regard to very elementary police-type international order-restoring functions, as a legal federation. However, there will be no world peace order until this emphasis is changed in line with the fundamental demands of the existing international law of peace.

Secondly, the question about a rule-of-law-analogous control of enforcement measures arises also outside the individual state. This is the problem of the rule of law on the international plane. Who is it, on this level, that actually controls the executor of sanctions against a threat to peace or a breach of peace: who today controls the Security Council?

This problem is of fundamental significance for the development of a world peace system. If we look at the present system of collective security, as laid down in the UN Charter, the question immediately arises of what controlling body those affected by the resolutions of the Security Council can turn to in the event of feeling violated in their own rights. In the intra-societal sphere there are a multitude of legal procedures and judicial levels serving the protection of the individual. Only in combination with such protective and control measures does the intra-state monopoly of power become one of the pillars of the state based on the rule of law and thus the backbone of a genuine rule-of-law community. Hardly any comparable development is to be observed on the international plane and hardly anything has so far been institutionalised in an analogous manner if we disregard a few regulatory fundamental principles, such as the principle of proportionality of means. However, an international legal system that is to attain legitimacy is not thinkable without control by a decision-making sanctions-imposing authority. While the role of the 'world public' should not be underestimated, what would be truly relevant is appropriate institutionalised legal authorities,[26] i.e. independent fact finding in order to establish whether or to what degree a threat to peace or an actual breach of peace exists, furthermore an independent body that examines the facts found, assesses them in the light of international law and arrives at a legally justified judgment; next an authority that puts into effect appropriate sanctions in the light of that judgment; and finally an authority to which the sanction-imposed state, if it feels wronged, can complain against the procedure of the community of nations. The more intra-state outbreaks of violence, i.e. civil wars, are interpreted by the world security council as 'threats to peace' and hence as a legitimate field of activity of UN agencies,[27] the more an interpretation of legitimate intervention that is more than casuistic becomes necessary.[28] There is an urgent need, also in this respect, of differentiated judicial institutions that would actually establish the rule of law and hence a legitimacy of peace enforcement or law enforcement measures appropriate to our time; as a result they would overcome the quasi-absolutist character of the present state of the Security Council. Only then would it be possible to speak correctly of the existence of a monopoly of legitimate force also at the international level within the framework of a differentiated peace-constitutional law.

On the international plane no institutionally differentiated power monopoly, one to be qualified as legitimate, analogous to the rule of law, as yet exists. What does exist is a general prohibition of force – no less (what a progress in international law!) but also no more. On the basis of the UN Charter the Security Council is authorised by international law to take decisions regarded as mandatory. There is an 'authorisation monopoly for the use of force' (L. Brock). Admittedly these decisions are à la carte: they can, but do not have to, orient themselves along existing international law. Orientation points can also be single-state or coalition-determined interests, power-opportunist situation assessments, decisionist manifestations of will, etc. The dictum of Louis XIV 'L'état [le droit] c'est moi' might be legitimately varied by the members of the Security Council on the basis of the UN Charter to 'Le droit international c'est nous' – in point of fact a scandalous state of affairs that should be overcome, as a matter of urgency, by means of rule-of-law-analogous international provisions.[29] The urgency of reforms was emphatically revealed by the Iraq crisis in the winter of 2002/03.

Third, let us examine the other components of the hexagon, the interdependences and their consequences. As long as eight decades ago the above-quoted Alfred Fried (and many others similarly) formulated this observation:

> As a result of the revolution in transport and production technology a powerful tendency is observed towards a division of labour and systematic collaboration of nations, even in the remotest countries. This created reciprocal dependence between different states, both in material and moral respects. Nearly all activities today transgress the frame of the individual state. A community of civilised humanity has begun to develop before our eyes. That community strives for an

organisation in which people's actions would be adapted to the trend and the purpose of the new technology-influenced living conditions.[30]

Fried's observation is not incorrect, but it requires considerable differentiation; this is of major importance for the problems here discussed.[31] The point is that the interdependences in the world are very disparately located: symmetrically, asymmetrically or confrontationally. Symmetrical interdependences, as found, for instance, in the West European region, are based upon system-politically relatively homogeneous states (here, hexagonal rule-of-law states of the Western type). These structures are in turn characterised by comparable highly productive and efficient economic profiles, resulting in dense material networking of the type of substitutive division of labour, which in turn is embedded in correspondingly dense institutional networks at government level, at social level and at non-governmental level. The measure of self-regulation is relatively high. Explicit conflict-settlement mechanisms exist in the event of conflicts. This structure of relationships moreover gives rise to a constraint towards durable coordination at government level and increasingly also between social groups, as well as between governments and transnationally operating non-governmental organisations.

Needless to say, nothing similar is observed with regard to asymmetrical interdependences, as those existing between developed regions and little developed, misdeveloped or underdeveloped regions. Inequality, possibly (though not inevitably) with a growing tendency, is built into asymmetrical interdependence. The contents aspect of the exchange structure resembles, in the worst case, colonial relations: technology, machines and finished products are exchanged for raw materials. In the event of such an exchange the result is the structural enrichment of one side and a relative, often even absolute, structural impoverishment of the other. Such a competence gradient is usually safeguarded by dominance. Moreover, it is inherently unstable, erosion-prone and, for obvious reasons, prone not only to conflict but to violence.

In the event of confrontational interdependence (such as existed in the East–West conflict and can today be observed in many regional conflict situations, for instance between India and Pakistan or in the Middle East) there is always a danger of a clash of the agents, just because they are, through specific incompatibilities of interests, fixed directly upon each other, giving rise therefore to an interdependence *ex negativo*. This interdependence expresses itself in rearmament and counter-rearmament, i.e. in a rearmament dynamism or progressive military phases. If the conflict management concerned collapses, this means the threat of war or actual war.

The above-mentioned three-way differentiation is, in view of the very disparate action patterns observed in the world, not only of heuristic value, but is also important for political practice. Symmetrical interdependence is the only one with built-in self-stabilisation and self-enlargement mechanisms. Confrontational interdependence, on the other hand, tends to give rise to vicious circles. Asymmetrical interdependence in most cases runs counter to elementary demands of fair distribution and fairness and cannot therefore be stabilised. Wherever one of these three starting situations is given, practical action and policies are quite differently focused: symmetrical interdependence invites deepening; confrontational interdependence, on the other hand, given its inherent vicious circle, calls for considerable efforts to deconstruct it; asymmetrical interdependence requires, at least, restructuring. The action perspectives present in the two last-mentioned instances ultimately aim at symmetrisation. Symmetrical interdependence thus becomes a normative yardstick in analysis and practice. This justifies itself by the fact that the prospect of civilisation of international politics is enhanced by it. To achieve worldwide symmetry is probably an unrealistic goal. But it can sometimes be realised in a regional or sub-regional context. That is why as many world-order-building bricks as possible should be brought together at these levels.

With regard to affect control the implications of the above-listed differentiations are more or less clear. Confrontational interdependence allows affects to become exacerbated; special efforts are therefore needed to moderate them ('détente policy'). With asymmetrical interdependence a time-limited moderation of affects for overcoming power and welfare gradients gives the disadvantaged side a chance of avoiding discrimination ('empowerment'). Symmetrical interdependence sets restrictive conditions to affects. Affects are fenced round and cushioned; if they were mobilised this would have counterproductive and damaging consequences all round. Functional differentiation here – and only here – at the interstate and international level results in the same consequences as in the above-discussed intra-societal sphere.

The outstanding characteristic of the world is therefore a totally diverse position of the forms of interdependences, which defines the situation of the world in the overall view and in detail. Its characteristic is not homogeneity, but heterogeneity. This creates, looking at the world as a whole, a tendency towards major analytical and also considerable peace-policy problems.

Fourth, what might democratic participation on the international plane mean? Who – other than the states that are doing so already anyway – would have to organise on the international plane, and how, in order to avoid a violence-engendering accumulation of conflicts? Alongside the states, how about interest groups (such as multinational firms, employees' organisations, professional associations, etc.) or cultural and religious communities of every kind and size – or the much-quoted and rarely concretely defined 'civilian society' – along with Greenpeace, Amnesty International and Transparency International, who else? And what would a representative democratic constitution at a world level look like? What would 'citizens' participation' mean here?

Meanwhile on the international plane a consensus is developing (albeit still largely theoretical) that the authorities and institutions maintained and staffed by individual states are in urgent need, beyond the state level, of an institutionally buttressed feedback with the institutions of the individual civic societies in order to make participation possible, create transparency, enhance the effectiveness of decisions and their implementation and, beyond that, mobilise legitimacy. The problems concern the EU and, more especially, the international organisations all the way to the United Nations.

Ideas on this are of the most diverse nature.[32] Thus, for example, there is some discussion, at UN level, of establishing, as a supplement to the Security Council and the General Assembly (the representative body of the states), an 'Assembly of Nations' as a deliberate opposition and counterpoise to the étatiste ponderousness of the United Nations. Capable of development are also arrangements such as have meanwhile arisen at the great world conferences of the United Nations: non-governmental organisations are there given their own platform parallel to the official event or even, most recently, closely linked with it. Also imaginable is a more far-reaching involvement of all relevant forces in the consultation on specific problem areas, analogously to the 'committology' of the EU and the practice existing since the 1920s in the International Labour Organisation (ILO) and institutionally anchored, whereby representatives of the state, capital and labour (most recently also non-governmental organisations) cooperate with one another within the same international organisation.

Fifth, if the thesis that the so-called social and economic worlds each have a weight of their own and, as a rule, do not follow the action logic of the state, then their agents will, over time, demand participation in consultations and decisions concerning matters affecting them beyond the individual state. The corresponding procedures in the EU sphere are important here as examples. There is sufficient cause for such considerations in the dramatic extent of inequality and unfairness of distribution on the international plane and in the conflict matter latent in it or often already manifest. Only in some parts of the world is inequality diminishing, for instance between the old industrial centres and the 'new industrial countries' mainly of East Asia and South-East Asia. Elsewhere we observe a deepening of inequalities and hence an accumulation of conflict matter. Even though a worldwide and simultaneous eruption of this conflict build-up is not to be expected, such conflicts might nevertheless become virulent in local or regional contexts, resulting in worldwide consequences. At any rate, historical and topical experience points in precisely that direction

That much may be assumed. If the problems of fair distribution remain unmanaged, political stability cannot be expected on the international plane, any more than within societies and states. Chances of civilising the conflict remain slight. Formulated positively: on the international plane, too, serious efforts for fair distribution are needed, or at least efforts to mitigate gross neediness. Only thus can the accumulation of no longer controllable political explosive matter, resulting from privilege and discrimination, be avoided.[33]

Sixth, power to impose sanctions against a threat to peace or a breach of peace, existing formally but used à la carte, or even abused, lacking or inadequate rule-of-law-analogous institutions and control mechanisms, structural heterogeneity concerning interdependences, inadequate or only embryonic forms of participation, gross inequality – can a culture of constructive conflict management even exist at a world level in view of all these circumstances? The obvious answer is no. The surprising thing is that in spite of all controversial debates, now also about supposedly worldwide 'cultural conflicts', the point of reference for such disputes is, as a matter of course, universal values (human rights of the first or second generation) which act as a yardstick even where they are rejected. Perhaps the experience from the internal areas of hexagonal societies will repeat itself also on the international plane. There, too, constructive conflict culture was not the result of appropriate programmes, but the unintentional consequence of power-political situations, from which mutual tolerance of the contenders inevitably became a reluctant orientation, and only in the course of time became a kind of society-absorbed routine behaviour.[34]

Hence peace, also at the international level, is to be thought of no differently from peace within societies – only with a multidimensional configurative structure with constitutional, institutional, material and emotional components. To quote Fried's fundamental reflections once more: whoever wishes to see one consequence (peace) rather than another (war), must replace the one cause (anarchy) by another ('new world order') that can produce the desired result. Peace, i.e. the enduring civilisation of the conflict, cannot be instituted in a simpler way, not even conceptually. In consequence, peace has to be understood as a non-violent process, aimed at the prevention of the use of violence. By means of agreements and compromises such conditions for the coexistence of societal groups, or of states and nations, should be created as would, firstly, not endanger their existence and, secondly, not gravely violate the sense of justice or the vital interests of individuals or groups that, having exhausted all peaceful arbitration procedures, they believe they have to resort to force.[35]

Such a successful undertaking requires an astonishing amount of preconditions even on a minor scale, i.e. within societies and states; unfavourable circumstances often enough result, in the worst case, in civil wars replacing internal peace. Is therefore, viewed practically, a world peace order realisable at all on the international plane?

6.2 Global Governance as a Model of a World Order Policy

Indications that there is a chance of realising a world peace order are found not necessarily on the world plane itself, but in relevant subsystems of the world, such as, at present, exist mainly in the European zone. The Western half of Europe, today's EU Europe, has, since the end of the Second World War, been spared, if not civil-war-like disputes (as in Northern Ireland, the Basque country and Corsica), then at least major wars. More importantly, no one here expects the threat, let alone the use, of military force in spite of continuing conflicts of interests. However, the absence of such expectation in daily life – no one nowadays regards war as an instrument of policy – is, according to a classic definition, an expression (if not the actual constituent condition) of 'stable peace'.[36]

If one asks how this situation has arisen in the western half of Europe, the following explanation offers itself. All Western European states, viewed from a civilisation-theory viewpoint, became 'hexagonal societies' after 1950. In terms of constitutional politics they are democratic rule-of-law states, in terms of economics they are market-economy units with a comparable profile, closely intertwined with one another by symmetrical interdependence. Admittedly, equalising justice between them is only in its beginnings (e.g. the EU Regional Fund). Moreover, the institutional interlinking is so marked that the principal agents are under continuous coordination constraint and must willy-nilly orient their various selfish interests towards common positions. Since there are no reciprocal military dangers, it has become unnecessary to create a regional system of collective security. For defence against external dangers there is a defensive alliance going beyond its own region, NATO, as well as an (albeit only symbolical) regional security system in the shape of a Western European Union (WEU) having transformed itself into the EU. At an all-European level there exists, in embryonic shape, a security arrangement containing several (further developable) instruments for peaceful conflict settlement, the Organisation of Security and Cooperation in Europe (OSCE).

Thus the outlines emerge in western Europe of a geographically enlargeable regional peace order. This is the result of a protracted process of political community-formation, the finality of which, as proved by the continuing public discussion, is still undecided. A whole series of circumstances has contributed to this community emergence: the agreement of all major players on basic political values, the expectation of positive benefit and the intensification of frontier-crossing communication and economic-exchange processes, readiness to deal with the needs of the weaker ('responsiveness'), accentuated growth and the expectation of mutual advantage, increased ability to solve problems, the existence of core areas functioning as political 'draught horses', variable or flexible roles adopted in the course of time by individual countries, the enlargement of elites as a result of the opportunity for social upward mobility, the evolution of new lifestyles, above all the increasing predictability of motivations and behaviour (expectation stability), etc.[37]

These factors have contributed to institutionally safeguarded collective learning processes; these have progressed to a point where a drifting apart of this part of Europe has become improbable and almost unimaginable. What is often diagnosed as a shortcoming, namely, that Western Europe has not yet become a true community of memories, communication and experience, is not a serious shortcoming so long as there are no indications that, as used to be the custom in European history, these clashing interests will once more be settled by military means. Anyway, EU Europe is slowly moving towards becoming just such a community.

A comparable situation cannot as yet be observed in other parts of the world – in that respect not even in East Asia, where, especially in the case of Korea and Taiwan, new hexagonal societies are developing, although their reciprocal frontier-transcending networking, especially with Japan (and China) still exhibits considerable shortcomings, mainly a lack of substitutive division of labour – not to mention joint overarching institutions of cooperation and policy coordination.

What lesson can be learnt for a world peace order from the exceptional western European experience? The most promising road towards a world peace order will consist in regional systems evolving in many regions of the world, within which there is no threat or use of military force; this expectation would then have to be economically, socially and emotionally rooted and institutionally safeguarded. Such a peace order on a regional basis is durable only if the above-mentioned components work together as infrastructure and superstructure and if that 'social order' comes about which Alfred Fried has quite rightly described as the cause of the effect aimed at in causative pacifism, i.e. the cause of enduring peace beyond the individual state. This guiding perspective applies to Europe as a whole,[38] and also to other regions of the world.

Proceeding from such regional systems of lasting peace a world peace order would not be difficult to envisage: simply as the sum total of such regional arrangements – not as a world state (in the usual sense of the concept), perhaps as a federalist construct, certainly as a quasi-confederative arrangement of regions, which would all be anxious jointly to tackle the region-transcending, i.e. superior, world problems that even in peace-policy-protected regional relationships cannot be adequately managed. Global governance would probably be the appropriate concept, i.e. a world order policy based upon multiple solid individual-state and regional foundations.[39]

6.3. EU Europe as an Exceptional Case of an Emerging Multi-level Hexagon

EU Europe represents an outstanding case of an advanced political community formation with interesting practical and hence also conceptual implications for hexagonal-peace-theory reflections that, at some future time, might be relevant elsewhere in the world. As has been shown, the civilisatory hexagon evolved in a historical process in a single-state or national constellation. Building upon this and politically deliberately, the integration process in EU Europe has meanwhile developed to a point that has to be described as a post-national constellation.[40] This is the gradual result of political decisions that have led – and in a further integration process will continue to lead – to a derestriction of until now territorially restricted national states, hexagonally constituted in their internal structure. This process may also be described as 'denationalisation'.[41] The new frontier-transcending action patterns and transaction intensifications, especially with regard to an economy in course of transnationalisation (domestic market) and to increased mobility of all possible factors across hitherto fixed and guarded single-state frontiers (people, capital, harmful chemicals, drugs, criminality, etc.) give rise to incongruence between until now national-state-limited, mostly specific political, administrative and juridical regulation mechanisms on the one side and the new denationalised spheres of activity on the other.

It is improbable that, relating to the new spheres of activity, a new, spatially extended but structurally totally identical 'postnational hexagon' will simply replace the many former national hexagons. It is more probable that a 'multi-level hexagon' will develop, a graduated structure with a tendency to react to the denationalisation process and hence innovatively processing the new post-national constellation.[42] Such a development suggests that the attainments until now gathered in the civilisatory hexagon of the national constellation are newly reproducing themselves, or will have to be produced, across several levels in a postnational constellation, which is why the multi-level hexagon will be characterised by a number of remarkable specific features.

The following can be observed in detail: the monopoly of power does not, in line with traditional logic of verticality and hierarchy, have to be at the top of the new construct: it can remain, as now, anchored in the national framework. This is possible and probable because European integration is the outcome of far-reaching consensually negotiated political endeavours, because a great measure of voluntary rule observance can be presumed to exist, and in fact exists, without a supernational sanctioning body, so that the EU itself does not have to figure as the quintessence of a classic étatist power monopoly. Moreover, in spite of an evolving governance beyond the nation state, rule-of-law control remains unchanged at the level of the individual states. This, however, is complemented at the EU level by an institution like the European Court of Justice, whose increasing (largely self-created) weight is not to be missed. Admittedly, the democratic legitimation of will formation and decisions on regulations at the transnational level is generally still regarded as having shortcomings. However, this state of affairs is corrigible by the development of transnational parliamentary authorities, the well advanced evolution of associations at EU level and by a political public that is transnationally articulating itself beyond narrow party-political and lobbyist interests. With regard to public control the critical role of civic groupings operating in frontier-transcending networks, both nationally and transnationally, is of major and growing importance. In view of a politically driven frontier-disregarding economy, amounting to an interdependence step, and in view of inadequately developed social-political regulation authorities at the transnational level there is a danger of that much-quoted downward spiral (race to the bottom) of social standards becoming a threat to the transnational European multi-level system and hence also to national political systems. But it is unlikely that, in a denationalised sphere like the EU, the social question that used to be answered by national welfare-state measures would simply evaporate and become a non-problem. On the contrary: in the new context these problems will acquire a political virulence that will eventually make their management, also at supra-state level, inevitable. This point in particular makes it necessary to think configuratively. The problems give rise to action imperatives that cannot fail to have consequences for political awareness and for an appropriate political strategy. Thus a redistributive policy, albeit as a rule not yet imaginable today, will become reality also on the transnational-regional plane, even though it may be assumed that central endeavours towards social justice will continue to have their centres of gravity in the various national frameworks.

This means that in a graduated regional multi-level hexagon à la EU there will be stratifications between the separate levels, which, as a rule, will give rise to hexagonal building blocks of varying complexity, different from those familiar from national constellations. The process would be repeated elsewhere in the world, provided preconditions comparable to those in the EU were to develop there.

6.4 *Players in a New World Order*

These efforts for a world peace policy are therefore concerned, as viewed prophetically by 'causative pacifism', with the architecture and internal life of a world peace order: from the lower level of the pacified individual state (what a premise!) via its integration in loosely or variegated integrated regional associations or, as the case may be, emerging multi-level hexagons (again what a premise!) all the way to the top level, where international organisations and international regulations (international regimes) create durable institutional, also juridically conceived, framework conditions for a civilised handling of the conflicts that are inevitable in diverse conflict areas.[43] To counteract violent conflict settlement at all levels, indeed to overcome it in principle – that used to be the idea of visionaries; today these efforts must become the task of pragmatic Realpolitik.

But from whom can we expect such a world-order-oriented Realpolitik – i.e. a policy giving rise to a 'new world order' (a hexagonally inspired 'global governance')? Pacifists with a constructive programme used to believe that a new world order would result from the circumspect behaviour of crucial statesmen, i.e. from wise diplomacy guided by internationalist cosmopolitan norms and backed by international organisations. They had no problems with the state per se since they knew about the qualitative differences between states and were familiar with the concept of the 'rowdy state'[44] – which in the international community meant those players that chronically rejected international order (today they are called 'rogue states'). Thus their thinking, in line with conditions at the time, was state-centred, even though they regarded the civilisation of the international world and societal movements, such as bourgeois, feminist or socialist-motivated pacifism and their transnational or international links, as useful. Anarchist thinking was entirely alien to them. Admittedly, there are still states of diverse character; it would be irresponsible to underestimate this fact because from it can be derived indications for civilisation chances. Meanwhile, however, deepened and widened interdependences in the world, at least in the OECD sphere, are relativising the importance of state and statehood; they allow not only the players of the economic and cultural world, but also those of the social world, to become co-agents in international politics. Along with the long observed economisation of current foreign policy we can today observe an emergent socialisation of foreign relations with already marked repercussions on foreign policy. The media, interest groups, political parties, foundations, professional associations, non-governmental organisations (NGOs) and other societal groupings are increasingly interlinking across national frontiers; some of these already have considerable weight. The old question, 'Is foreign policy foreign policy?', thus extended and reformulated, acquires new topicality.[45] The answer can only be in the negative: in advanced societies of the type of the OECD world, foreign policy is a continuation of a self-internationalising domestic policy.

Moreover, in dealing with disasters and emergencies, more especially in the management of ethnopolitical conflicts, non-governmental organisations are downright indispensable in today's world. Here a new field of varied autonomous activities, or activities conducted in cooperation with state authorities, is opening for socially engaged citizens; all of these make diverse demands on personal presence and competence.[46] What we have in mind is activating assistance to politically and socially disadvantaged groups ('empowerment'), escort services for endangered persons, support for refugees and appropriate help and after-care ('post-conflict peace building'), reporting in the event of threatening conflicts and emerging escalations ('early warning'), observation of demonstrations, organisation of dialogues between hostile groups, assistance with mediation efforts, law-court observation, physical presence in areas of potential or actual tension, observation of elections, advice to official missions such as the UN or OSCE or EU. Such activities cannot, in the long run, be staged off the cuff; along with the necessary commitment they require situation-pertinent training, i.e. problem-specific and action-area-specific civilian peace service, indeed a specialised peace service, in which civic commitment can competently fulfil itself. Here a vast field of activity opens for societal agents and hence for constructive pacifism.[47]

The necessary conceptualisation of such services grows with demand, which reflects an objective need, and especially with first experiences. These experiences, especially if made in crisis situations and aggravated conflicts, show the extent to which societal and state activities are often dependent on each other, even though they operate at different levels and have different addressees. Even police and military security measures may, in certain circumstances, prove indispensable in order to make civic-society activities possible in an environment of conflicts that have become warlike. Dogmatically motivated fears of contact have proved counterproductive, while common learning processes ('multi-track activities' in the framework of 'security-governance' structures) have proved promising.[48]

Specialised peace services are helpful in the building of peace structures, as is peace-oriented diplomacy. Durable peace, however, will ultimately be found only where the local conflict parties eventually agree on universally accepted constitutional patterns and organise their activities accordingly.[49] This applies to separate societies as much as it does on the international plane. The difficulty of achieving such agreement on new rules of coexistence in the public sphere, even in the middle of Europe, is demonstrated over the past few decades by the sluggish process, driven by state and societal forces and marked by continuous relapses, of finding a constitution in Northern Ireland.[50]

7. Conclusion

The accents for 'thinking peace' and 'making peace' were at one time correctly set by 'causative pacifism'. Its constructive programme, so far largely disregarded, was to be an inspiration for congenial efforts suitable for our time. Its guiding idea in this can be that the yardstick of peace is peace itself. This is the legacy of an idea from the beginning of the past century – an idea whose time has now come, an idea that, after a terrible century and despite identifiable obstacles, needs to be revived.

Si vis pacem, para pacem: the para pacem maxim contained in this guiding perspective contains, at the individual state level, the regional level and the international level, several cognitive, constitution-political, institutional, material and emotional premises. It refers to the requirement of consensus-capable and legitimated coexistence formulas and appropriate institutions (constitution); it regards the material premises of constructive conflict management as a sensitive point of crucial importance for socially mobile and politicisable societies. Emotional reinsurance – 'ligatures' – is gained by such a maxim through the orientation of action along life preservation or life enhancement, with transparency and perceived fairness being important criteria of legitimacy. This clearly reflects the process character of peace as a civilisatory project: if, confronted with the requirements of mainly newly organised, newly of-age actors, the traditional internal or international political framework conditions prove incapable of adaptation, then – paradoxically (or perhaps not) – force, with inexorable logic, becomes a substitute for communication and, ultimately, a final resort perceived as having no alternative. Against this background we can understand why such starting situations will, more or less rapidly, slide into political upheaval situations, sometimes into civil wars or revolutions, and indeed into wars between states. Learning and adaptation capacity are therefore important categories for the civilisatory project 'peace'. And the demand for measures providing for 'peaceful change', though usually raised in the peace discussion by international lawyers, is of general and fundamental importance for a civilisatory or peace concept for our time.

Peaceful change in the conditions of a worldwide evident social mobilisation and politicisation, as well as a continually developing societal and economic world with inevitable conflicts about the direction of evolution of individual societies and the world as a whole, i.e. of system-politically relevant power-determined cultural conflicts, requires readiness to learn and adapt on the part of all actors at all levels. This, in particular, cannot be enforced by crude power potentials; it can come about only as a result of reciprocal persuasion efforts in the framework of materially and institutionally receptive transparent communication forums open to participation.[51] Since at the level beyond the individual state the actors cannot usually be compelled to base their actions on guidelines they do not themselves accept, there exists no alternative to persuasion endeavours through communication, i.e. through dialogues and discourses, through arguments and counter-arguments. Where suitable fora evolve in the shape of networks of private, public or mixed character, there politically relevant communication communities can develop, communities that learn to find common rules and consequently to accept the communicatively arisen power as binding. Such a result of collective learning, however, can be envisaged only if those concerned have a fair opportunity of participation, if the communication process itself is largely transparent and if fairness can be mutually expected.[52] As a result of discursive creation of plausible causes for a successful community creation we may then also expect those processes of rule-of-law creation, and ultimately of a reliable rule-of-law creation in international relations, in which the 'causative pacifism' referred to at the beginning of this second section has always been the quintessence of a 'new world order', i.e. of lasting peace.

As a final conclusion – though seemingly apodictically, but here and now well founded in these reflections on the defining conditions for peace – we are able to formulate this statement: the constituent conditions for a reasonable peace are known.

Notes

1. Alfred H. Fried, *Probleme der Friedenstechnik*, Leipzig 1918, p. 10.
2. Ernst-Otto Czempiel, *Friedensstrategien*, Opladen 1998; idem, *Kluge Macht. Außenpolitik für das 21. Jahrhundert*, Munich 1999; Dieter Senghaas (ed.), *Den Frieden denken*, Frankfurt/M. 1995 (with a comprehensive bibliography).
3. Fried, *Probleme der Friedenstechnik*, p. 42.
4. Ibid., p. 12.
5. Klaus-Jürgen Gantzel and Torsten Schwinghammer, *Die Kriege nach dem Zweiten Weltkrieg 1945–1992. Daten und Tendenzen*, Münster 1995; Mary Kaldor, *Neue und alte Kriege*, Frankfurt/M. 2000; Herfried Münkler, *Die neuen Kriege*, Reinbek b. Hamburg 2002. For an analysis of background conditions see the fundamental study by Günther Bächler, *Violence through Environmental Discrimination*, Dordrecht 1999.
6. See Karl W. Deutsch, *Tides Among Nations*, New York 1979; Ralf Dahrendorf, *Der moderne soziale Konflikt*, Stuttgart 1992.
7. The following reflections continue observations on the history of modern European development, as documented in Dieter Senghaas, *The European Experience. A Historical Critique of Development Theory*, Leamington Spa/Dover, NH 1985.
8. See *Dokumente des Treffens der Konferenz über die Menschliche Dimension der KSZE in Kopenhagen vom 29.06.1990*, which, after the world-political upheaval of 1989/90, summed up the fundamental principles of the rule of law as it was achieved or developed in European constitutional history; published in Dieter Senghaas, *Friedensprojekt Europa*, Frankfurt/M. 1992, pp. 191–210.
9. See John Burton, *Conflict. Resolution and Prevention*, London 1990.
10. See Norbert Elias, *Über den Prozeß der Zivilisation*, Frankfurt/M. 1976, vol. 2.

11. Sigmund Freud perceptively (in his famous answer to Albert Einstein's question) in Albert Einstein and Sigmund Freud, *Warum Krieg? Ein Briefwechsel*, Zurich 1996, pp. 43ff.; see also Dieter Senghaas, *Aggressivität und kollektive Gewalt*, Stuttgart 1972, 2nd edn., pp. 53ff.

12. Thus defined by Ralf Dahrendorf in *Auf der Suche nach einer neuen Ordnung*, Munich 2003, p. 45; see also Christian Graf von Krockow, 'Die Tugenden der Friedensfähigkeit', in Senghaas (ed.), *Den Frieden denken*, pp. 419–441.

13. See Deutsch, *Nationalism and Social Communication*, Cambridge 1966, 2nd edn., as well as idem, *Tides Among Nations*.

14. See Dieter Senghaas, *The Clash within Civilisations. Coming to Terms with Cultural Conflicts*, London/New York 2002.

15. As Rainer Tetzlaff has argued, especially with an eye to black Africa, there arises a 'Hexagon of Decivilisation as a result of state disintegration'. See his essay 'Staats- und Zivilisationsverfall. Wird Afrika anschlußfähig an die globalisierte Welt?' in Hans Küng and Dieter Senghaas (eds), *Friedenspolitik. Ethische Grundlagen internationaler Beziehungen*, Munich 2003, pp. 321–383. The hexagon of decivilisation has the following components: (1) fragmentation/privatisation of force; (2) rule of force, lawlessness; (3) overexploitation economy and self-help/affect explosion; (4) dictatorship, will imposition, enslavement; (5) self-granting of privileges/social polarisation; (6) war and terrorism/exclusion of enemy groups.

16. See Wolfgang Reinhard, *Geschichte der Staatsgewalt. Eine vergleichende Verfassungsgeschichte Europas von den Anfängen bis zur Gegenwart*, Munich 1999; Paolo Prodi, *Eine Geschichte der Gerechtigkeit. Vom Recht Gottes zum modernen Rechtsstaat*, Munich 2003.

17. This approach can be readily measured by indices. See Ulrich Menzel and Dieter Senghaas, *Europas Entwicklung und die Dritte Welt. Eine Bestandsaufnahme*, Frankfurt/M. 1986, Chapter 6.

18. See Hans-Dieter Evers and Tilman Schiel, *Strategische Gruppen. Vergleichende Studien zu Staat, Bürokratie und Klassenbildung in der Dritten Welt*, Berlin 1988; Günter Schubert et al. (eds), *Demokratie und konfliktfähige Gruppen in Entwicklungsländern*, Münster 1993.

19. A formulation by Claus Offe, *Der Tunnel am Ende des Lichts. Erkundungen der politischen Transformation im Neuen Osten*, Frankfurt/M. 1994. For an analysis of real socialism, largely in agreement with the one here presented, see Wolfgang Engler, *Die zivilisatorische Lücke. Versuch über den Staatssozialismus*, Frankfurt/M. 1992.

20. On the ideologies of high mythology see Ernst Topitsch, *Vom Ursprung und Ende der Metaphysik*, Vienna 1958.

21. See Ian Buruma and Avishai Margalit, *Occidentalism. The West in the Eyes of its Enemies*, New York 2004.

22. See Gunnar Heinsohn, *Lexikon der Völkermorde*, Reinbek b. Hamburg 1998; Mihran Dahag and Kristin Platt (eds), *Genozid und Moderne*, vol. 1, Opladen 1998.

23. See Chapter 5 of the present book.

24. See Dieter Senghaas, *Die Konstitution der Welt. Eine Analyse in friedenspolitischer Absicht*, Leviathan, vol. 31, no. 1, 2003, pp. 117–152.

25. Fried, *Probleme der Friedenstechnik* p. 29.

26. See Richard Falk et al. (eds), *The Constitutional Foundations of World Peace*, Albany 1993; and explicitly Michael Zürn and Bernhard Zangl, Weltpolizei oder Weltinterventionsgericht? Zur Zivilisierung der Konfliktbearbeitung, *Internationale Politik*, vol. 54, no. 8, pp. 17–24; Dieter Senghaas, Recht auf Nothilfe, in Reinhard Merkel (ed.), *Der Kosovo-Krieg und das Völkerrecht*, Frankfurt/M. 2000, pp. 99–114.

27. See Heike Gading, *Der Schutz grundlegender Menschenrechte durch militärische Maßnahmen des Sicherheitsrates – das Ende staatlicher Souveränität?* Berlin 1996; Martin Lailach, *Die Wahrung des Weltfriedens und der internationalen Sicherheit als Aufgabe des Sicherheitsrates der Vereinten Nationen*, Berlin 1998.

28. A suggestion for such casuistry is found in Dieter Senghaas, *Wohin driftet die Welt? Über die Zukunft friedlicher Koexistenz*, Frankfurt/M. 1994, Chapter 6.

29. International lawyers, usually focused on the political character of the Security Council, have mostly not been too inventive with regard to appropriate reform; mostly they put forward a critique of proposals viewed as utopian or illusionist. See, however, Mohammed Bedjaoui, *The New World Order and the Security Council. Testing the Legality of its Acts*, The Hague 1995; Bernd Martenczuk, *Rechtsbindung und Rechtskontrolle des Weltsicherheitsrates*, Berlin 1996.

30. Fried, *Probleme der Friedenstechnik*, pp. 46–47.

31. See Chapter 8 of the present book.

32. See Daniele Archibugi and David Held (eds), *Cosmopolitan Democracy. An Agenda for a New World Order*, Cambridge 1995; David Held, *Democracy and the Global Order. From the Modern State to Cosmopolitan Governance*, Cambridge 1995.

33. See Norbert Brieskorn (ed.), *Globale Solidarität*, Stuttgart 1997.

34. See Norberto Bobbio, *Das Zeitalter der Menschenrechte. Ist Toleranz durchsetzbar?* Berlin 1998; Michael Walzer, *Über Toleranz. Von der Zivilisierung der Differenz*, Hamburg 1998.

35. This definition of peace is elucidated and deduced in Dieter and Eva Senghaas, Si vis pacem, para pacem. Überlegungen zu einem zeitgemäßen Friedenskonzept, *Leviathan*, vol. 20, no. 2, 1992, pp. 230–251 (reprinted in Berthold Meyer (ed.), *Eine Welt oder Chaos?* Frankfurt/M. 1996, pp. 245–275.

36. Kenneth Boulding, *Stable Peace*, Austin 1978.

37. See Chapter 5 of the present book.

38. This guiding perspective for Europe as a whole is developed in a differentiated manner in Senghaas, *Friedensprojekt Europa*.

39. A complex conceptualisation is found in Otfried Höffe, *Demokratie im Zeitalter der Globalisierung*, Munich 2002, 2nd edn.; Dirk Messner and Franz Nuscheler, *Global Governance. Herausforderung an der Schwelle zum 21. Jahrhundert*, in: Dieter Senghaas (ed.), *Frieden machen*, Frankfurt/M. 1997, pp. 337–361; Paul Kennedy, Dirk Messner and Franz Nuscheler (eds.), *Global Trends and Global Governance*, London 2002; critically Ulrich Brand et al. *Global Governance. Alternative zur neoliberalen Globalisierung?* Münster 2000.

40. Thus explicitly Jürgen Habermas, *Die postnationale Konstellation*, Frankfurt/M. 1998, Chapter 4.

41. Michael Zürn, *Regieren jenseits des Nationalstaates. Globalisierung und Denationalisierung als Chance*, Frankfurt/M. 1998.

42. Michael Zürn, Vom Nationalstaat lernen. Das zivilisatorische Hexagon in der Weltinnenpolitik, in Ulrich Menzel (ed.), *Vom Ewigen Frieden und vom Wohlstand der Nationen*, Frankfurt/M. 2000, pp. 19–44. Also of interest in this context are the imperatives of a 'catch-up civilisation' of Europe, articulated by Emanuel Richter, who visualised a 'republican Europe'. See this author's *Das republikanische Europa. Aspekte einer nachholdenden Zivilisierung*, Opladen 1999. Christine Landfried's reflections on the utilisation of the rich experience of difference in Europe for a policy creation at European level can also be assigned to the concept of a multi-level hexagon. See that author's *Das politische Europa. Differenz als Potential der Europäischen Union*, Baden-Baden 2002.

43. The diverse planes are discussed in Senghaas (ed.), *Frieden machen*.

44. Thus Alfred H. Fried, explicitly, in *Friedenskatechismus*, published in 1894, reprinted in excerpt in Wolfgang Benz (ed.), *Pazifismus in Deutschland*, Frankfurt/M. 1988, p. 73.

45. See Ekkehart Krippendorf, Ist Außenpolitik Außenpolitik? *Politische Vierteljahresschrift*, vol. 3, 1963, pp. 243–266; Thomas Risse (ed.), *Bringing Transnational Relations Back In. Non-State Actors, Domestic Structures and International Institutions*, Cambridge 1995.

46. See Jörg Calließ (ed.), *Barfuß auf diplomatischem Parkett. Die Nichtregierungsorganisationen in der Weltpolitik*, Loccum 1998; Margaret E. Keck and Kathryn Sikkink, *Activists Beyond Borders. Advocacy Networks in International Politics*, Ithaca 1998; Norbert Ropers, Konfliktbearbeitung in der WeltbürgerInnengesellschaft. Friedensförderung durch Nichtregierungsorganisationen, in Ulrich Menzel (ed.), *Vom Ewigen Frieden*,

pp. 70–101; rather critically Elmar Altvater et al. (eds), *Vernetzt und verstrickt. Nichtregierungsorganisationen als gesellschaftliche Produktivkraft*, Münster 1999, 2nd edn..

47. See Christine Merkel (ed.), *Friedenspolitik der Zivilgesellschaft*, Münster 1998.

48. The 'security governance' concept is fundamentally argued in Elke Krahmann, *Multilevel Networks in European Foreign Policy*, Aldershot 2002. For experience reports on peace consolidation see Mir A. Ferdowsi and Volker Matthies (eds), *Den Frieden gewinnen. Zur Konsolidierung von Friedensprozessen in Nachkriegsgesellschaften*, Bonn 2003.

49. See John Paul Lederach, *Building Peace. Reconciliation in Divided Societies*, Tokyo 1994.

50. For a comprehensive presentation of the problem see Ulrich Schneckener, *Auswege aus dem Bürgerkrieg*, Frankfurt/M. 2002.

51. The state of affairs emerges from a fascinating observation by Karl W. Deutsch, one of the most important peace researchers of the second half of the twentieth century. He defined power 'as the ability to afford not to learn'; quoted from *The Nerves of Government. Models of Political Communication and Control*, New York 1966, 2nd ed., p. 111.

52. On this set of problems see the fundamental article by Rainer Schmalz-Bruns, Deliberativer Supranationalismus. Demokratisches Regieren jenseits des Nationalstaates, *Zeitschrift für internationale Beziehungen*, vol. 6, no. 2, 1999, pp. 185–244.

Chapter 3

THIRD SECTION

Elucidating Conditions for Reasonable Peace:
Through What and How does Reason Focused
on Peace Constitute Itself Today?

In a large part of political theory it has become traditional to describe the foreign-policy or international attitude of states as 'rational'. *Raison d'état* is indeed often presented as if it embodied a kind of logic that is more profound and more enduring than the reason of individuals or small groups.[1] Along with its towering importance, *raison d'état* is sometimes also characterised as inherently realistic. The political realist, as described by Hans Morgenthau some decades ago, should place the interests of his nation above the personal wishes and values of its statesmen and, of course, above the wishes and values of its less influential citizens. This

> concept of interest defined as power imposes intellectual discipline upon the observer, infuses rational order into the subject matter of politics, and thus makes the theoretical understanding of politics possible. On the side of the actor, it provides for rational discipline in action and creates that astounding continuity in foreign policy which makes American, British, or Russian foreign policy appear as an intelligible, rational continuum, by and large consistent within itself, regardless of the different motives, preferences and intellectual and moral qualities of successive statesmen. A realist theory of international politics, then, will guard against two popular fallacies: the concern with motives and the concern with ideological preferences.[2]

1. The Limited Rationality
of Governments and Nations

The following reflections present an alternative starting point. The *raison d'état* model seems inadequate for two reasons. First, it presupposes a higher degree of continuity in the foreign policy of great powers than can in fact be observed. During the decades between 1900 and today the U.S.A., Great Britain, Germany and other Western states have all changed the fundamental objectives of their foreign policy, both in respect of their principal methods and strategies and also with regard to individual goals. The former Soviet Union likewise later replaced its original sworn political goals by the official recognition of the doctrine of peaceful coexistence, including the assertion that world wars were avoidable in future, even though two-thirds of mankind were living under capitalist economic systems. This kind of empirically observed discontinuity is usually ignored in the *raison d'état* model.

A second objection is even more far-reaching in its implications: states act a lot less rationally than claimed by theory. The rationalist model presupposes a greater frequency of correct prognoses on the part of governments concerning the consequences of their own foreign-political actions than can be observed in practice. The frequency of mistakes and miscalculations was high especially for those decisions on the basis of which governments initiated or escalated major warlike actions. Of all state-made decisions that resulted in the outbreak of major wars since 1910 about three-fifths proved wrong, both in the assessment of the capabilities and intentions of the other big states at the time of the beginning of the war and with regard to the actual consequences at the end of the war:[3] Austria-Hungary's decision in 1914 to declare war on Serbia, Germany's decision to go to war against Russia and France and to invade Belgium, the decision by the Ottoman empire to fight on the side of the Central Powers instead of remaining neutral, and Austria-Hungary's decision to fight for Trieste and South Tyrol instead of ceding these territories to ensure Italy's neutrality – all these turned out to be wrong decisions that largely contributed to the annihilation of the governments (including the government systems!) that made those decisions. Germany's decision to attack Poland in 1939 and Russia in 1941, the Russian decision not to expect a German attack in July 1941 and the Japanese decision to attack the United States in September 1941 – all these proved to have been mistakes. In the cases of Japan and Germany they resulted in the annihilation of their governments and in the case of Russia Stalin's mistake demanded an additional high price for the eventual survival of his state.

2. The Search for Rational
Models for Irrational Behaviour

Purposeful rationality seems to be much more infrequent in crucial decisions by states than we might expect on the basis of a rationalist theory of interests.[4] Something similar has long been observed in the lives of individuals. In moments of critical decisions they, too, act far less frequently in accordance with objective purposeful rationality and far more frequently in a way that is harmful and destructive for themselves and their supreme values – certainly far more than, proceeding from any kind of rationalist theory of enlightened self-interest, one would have to suppose. Moreover, it is clear in the case of individuals that, if they are supplied with additional information on the consequences to be expected from their behaviour, they frequently do not believe such information or reject it on other grounds. In short: cognitive information often plays a lesser role in the decisions actually made by individuals at critical moments than any rationalist theory of interests would normally predict. Conventional thinking explains the difference between what purposefully rational individuals would do and what individuals actually do by the 'irrationality' of human nature. Such thinking tends to label counterproductive behaviour as irrational, as a fact not to be justified by anything. Modern depth psychology and psychiatry, however, endeavour to reproduce the processes step by step that make people act in a way that leads to results they do not consciously desire or would even prefer to avoid altogether. Scientists like Sigmund Freud have, in the course of their therapeutic practice, tried to develop formally rational models for the irrational behaviour of their patients – in the hope that such models might eventually lead doctors to therapeutic procedures that would cure, or mitigate, the self-destructive behaviour of their patients.

Something similar has been more recently attempted with examinations of the decision structure of big organisations. Examinations of modern economic organisations have shown that purposefully rational action cannot always be assumed as a matter of course. Economic organisations are less often guided by market forces, government authorities are less often guided by voter approval or parliamentary majorities, political parties are less often guided by voter reaction than might be expected on the basis of a simple rationalist interest theory. More recent research has tried to explain in a comprehensible and transparent way why such organisations behave in such an irrational manner (from the viewpoint of purposeful rationality) that they arrive at results that contradict both the objectives of the organisation in question and the wishes of its managing staff. Comparable problems may arise in the planning of big computers and of complex self-governing mechanical and/or electronic systems. In such cases the planners have before them a particular category of results that seem to them desirable; they try to design comprehensive control and communications systems working on the feedback principle; they are designed to guide the system in the direction of the desired goals or results. Such complex systems, however, also include a multitude of feedback circuits that are often arranged in subsystems and hierarchies. Such subsystems and feedbacks on a lower level can then bring about decisions preventing the overall system from reaching its goals; it can also happen that the overall system, even in the absence of such internal difficulties, receives inadequate or misleading information from the even bigger suprasystem within which it has to function. In both cases the result can be a behaviour that is counterproductive with regard to the objectives of the original overall plan. Problems of this kind are being studied by communications and control specialists and in many cases have proved to be soluble only with great difficulties.

It seems therefore that individuals, large organisations of people and certain communications and control systems not relating to humans have certain problems in common. With all of them a difference can arise between target-aimed purposeful rationality and actual behaviour; and all of them may find it difficult to coordinate feedback systems at the level of the entire self-governing systems, as well as on the plane of its constituent subsystems and the supra-system in which they are embedded.

In the field of peace-cause research examinations of this kind are needed in order to explain the frequency and the causes of such irrational behaviour – irrational from the point of view of purposeful rationality – by governments and nations with regard to decisions that might have a crucial effect on their stability and chances of survival.

A possible access to these problems is found, with a generalising perspective, in the work of Sigmund Freud.

3. A Structural Interpretation of Freud's Model for Individual Decision Systems

Freud's fundamental theories resulted from his attempt to derive universally applicable patterns from his clinical experience. Although he was largely concerned with questions of the biological bases and developmental phases both of the individual and of the whole species of man, the basic model that he eventually developed has a relatively simple structure. What we shall deal with here is not so much Freud's ideas on the possible genesis, but rather the structure, of his model of the human personality system.

Such a comparison of structures will be based on the deliberate use of incomplete analogies. Analogies that have proved useful in science have often been incomplete in the sense that they bracketed out many important aspects; yet the very limited aspects with regard to which the two systems were comparable were significant within each separate system and their comparison proved fruitful for further work. Harvey, for instance, in comparing blood circulation with a system of mechanical valves and pumps, disregarded the very factors that are essential for the real functioning of the blood supply of the human body. In comparing the structure of our circulation system with the structure of a hydraulic system Harvey disregarded, or missed, the role of the red and white blood corpuscles and their chemical and biological properties, the mechanisms that maintain the blood temperature, the existence of blood groups and much else. From these and many other points of view, human blood in a living body was indeed 'not comparable' with water in a pump. But with regard to its reaction to the functioning of valves and pumps it was comparable. Seeing this comparability and effectively developing the comparison was an essential part of Harvey's scientific achievement.[5]

We shall here put forward a similarly limited comparison of certain structural features of Freud's model of the individual psyche with certain structural features of national states, of interest groups within a nation and of the international system. In doing so we shall inevitably move to and fro between the level of the individual and that of the state, without losing sight of the limits of similarities to be analytically explored. The reader should bear in mind that all comparisons of this kind will disregard many important aspects of Freud's model (e.g. his views on personality development), or deal with them only partially, such as Freud's concept of libido and its distribution to the various actions and objects of the conscious mind. All that matters is that the limited structures that are compared with one another prove comparable within their relatively narrow limitations and that their comparison contributes to the elucidation of the above-described problems and therefore is analytically fruitful.

Freud himself would perhaps have taken the view that such an endeavour did not run entirely counter to the spirit of some of his works. In 1915 he published an article entitled *Zeitgemäßes über Krieg und Tod* (Timely thoughts on war and death), in which he discussed 'the mega-individuals of mankind, the nations'. In it he observed how these 'mega-individuals' in war drop their mutual inhibitions, taking this as an opportunity to escape the existing pressure of culture for a while in order to give transient satisfaction to their until then held-back drives – probably, he added, without damaging the relatively high measure of morality within their national community. 'The nations,' he concluded, 'at present obey their passions far more than their interests. At most they use their interests to rationalise their passions; they pretend their interests in order to find reasons for the satisfaction of their passions.'[6]

In passages like these Freud treated the communities of human mega-individuals as social systems, comparing limited, but important, aspects of their behaviour with the behaviour of the systems of 'micro-individuals'.

With the aim of further exploring the possibilities of such a kind of comparison, the relevant aspects of the structure of the Freudian model of the individual personality will be set out. This will be done rather extensively because Freud's theorems, viewed in general terms, are of great importance to peace research. Later the Freudian model will be compared with relevant aspects of the structure within which the peace-policy behaviour takes place.

3.1 Drives and the Id

Proceeding from the behaviour of infants, Freud viewed human behaviour as determined by a series of fundamental drives, which he called instinctive, i.e. inborn and not learned, based on the physical, neurological and biochemical constitution of the human organism. Breathing, thirst, hunger and love – the last-named by no means only in the form of sexuality – were to him examples of such basic drives. A multiplicity of such drives, he believed, exists in the human organism and, by way of the nervous system, triggers a series of behaviour patterns leading to a transient state of satisfaction, or at least tending in that direction. We know today that these assumptions need making more precise, or indeed revising, as the relation between drive and object in humans is relatively open, or structured by socialisation, which has an effect on the drive activity itself.

The 'region' or the 'psychic province' of the human personality that unites all these drives was called by Freud the id. To Freud, therefore, the id was a collection of nervous and psychological processes. He explained emphatically that the id was not an organisation, that it required no consistency and that it was not subject to the law of excluded contradictions as known in the classic form of logic. The id knows neither logic nor morality nor fear. Its individual drives or subsystems blindly urge, or demand, satisfaction. That satisfaction was experienced by the organism as pleasure, and the search for that pleasure – which Freud called the pleasure principle – was the only principle that the id obeyed. The id in its totality, as the sum of all these drives, was for Freud the source of all 'psychic energy' and was therefore the basis of all human motivation, inclusive of motivation conveyed by reality and experience, that, resembling repetition constraints, acts from the unconscious.

Although Freud defined the id as the sum of a multitude of diverse and potentially contradictory drives, in reality he devoted most attention in his writings to one of the drives, which he called libido. In his own words he described as libido 'the energy of such drives that concern everything one can sum up as love, viewed as a quantitative magnitude, though at present not actually measurable'.[7] Nevertheless Freud never denied the significance of other basic human drives, though he devoted less attention to them –

possibly because he had the impression that in the middle-class milieu of his contemporary Vienna they were less often neglected or suppressed.[8] (An exception is the aggression and death drive in Freud's later writings.)

3.2 Reality and the Ego

The other extreme of the Freudian model was his biggest and most comprehensive system, which he called 'reality' or the 'real world'. This, according to Freud, includes not only the physical world of rock and stone and day and night, but also the entire human and social environment of the individual, such as family, neighbours, government, society and culture. Every person has to seek the satisfaction of his various drives in this real world, which exists mostly outside his own body and independently of his own inclinations and perceptions; but even a broken leg can function as part of that reality. Man can process this reality and even change it slightly so that it satisfies some of the needs of his drives; he can, according to Freud, cultivate a field and grow his food to satisfy his hunger. However, reality, whether in the form of restrictions or favourable opportunities, confronts man with the reality principle, which demands that every individual be aware of the conditions imposed on him by the outside world and of the consequences of his actions in that world.

The id (and with it also all drives), on the other hand, is blind to the greater part of that reality. A certain drive can react to a certain signal that is relevant to it, for instance when a choking man gasps for breath or a thirsty man reaches for water. Yet the overwhelming part of human perception of the outside world is not part of the id. Instead, perceptions belong to the perception system through which alone the id receives information on the outside world and thus, in a sense, mediates between the drives and reality.

In the course of human evolution, Freud believed, this perception system and its mediation function developed a good deal further. It was enriched by memories and made progress with its coordination and decision capabilities. Eventually it became a fully developed autonomous system, a mediator between the great system of the external world and the weakly organised pluralist chaotic system of the id, which was largely blind to the external world, which only had 'its own world of perceptions' and which obeyed the 'inexorable pleasure principle', which, however, lacked the internal organisation to ensure consistency in its separate and competing drives.

Freud called this mediating organisation the ego. It was in fact an organisation as he described it:

> The principal characters of the ego. As a result of the preformed relationship between sensual perception and muscular action the ego has control of deliberate movements. Its task is self-assertion, discharged by coming to know

external stimuli, storing experience of them (in the memory), avoiding excessive stimuli (by escape), facing moderate stimuli (by adaptation) and by ultimately learning to change the external world purposefully to its advantage (activity); internally against the id by gaining control over the demands of drives, deciding whether they are to be admitted for satisfaction, by postponing such satisfaction to times and circumstances favourable in the external world, or by suppressing its excitements altogether. In its activity it is guided by taking notice of arousal tension existing in it or introduced into it. Their increase is generally felt as unpleasure, their reduction as pleasure. Probably, however, it is not the absolute degree of these arousal tensions, but something in the rhythm of their change that is perceived as pleasure and unpleasure. The ego strives for pleasure and tries to avoid unpleasure. An expected, predicted increase of unpleasure is responded to by the anxiety signal, its cause, whether from outside or inside, is called danger. From time to time the ego dissolves its link with the external world and withdraws into the state of sleep, in which it extensively transforms its organisation.[9]

For every individual, Freud argues, his ego is the organised part of his personality, which allows him to adapt to the outside world, while at the same time preserving a certain compatibility and consistency in his behaviour. No one, however, was born with such a fully developed ego. Most elements of his ego are derived from the individual's experiences and are, in the course of his personal development, built up into an organised system. Many of these experiences differ from person to person; some indeed are accidental. From these diverse elements, acquired over different time spans, each individual builds up his own ego, which differs in some points from every other ego.

3.3 Society, Morality and the Superego

A category of experiences that, according to Freud, enter into the ego of practically all persons is the rules and prohibitions that every child receives from his parents or other persons involved in his education. Many of these prescriptions and prohibitions are norms of the specific culture, religion or ideology in which the individual has grown up. Associated with them are tender or painful recollections of his parents, recollections of childish fears and of the authority that provided protection or made those fears worse. The totality of these prescriptions and prohibitions with their associated feelings of love or fear become, according to Freud, a coherent autonomous subsystem within the ego. This part was called by Freud the Superego or the ego ideal. Its commandments are what is commonly called the voice of one's conscience.

A part of the ego might therefore split off from the ego and, in a sense, confront it. Its commandments might contradict the actions chosen by the ego; actions that the ego had conducted and controlled might encounter serious disapproval on the part of the superego, which would then symbolise the disapproval that the parents or persons in authority, remembered by the individual from his past, might have voiced about that behaviour had it come to their knowledge.

While Freud's contemporaries were predominantly captivated by his concept of the id and its unconscious way of function, it is the ego that occupies a central position in the structure of his model. That is why, over the past few decades, psychiatrists have devoted more attention to the ego; it is the ego and its way of functioning that, from structural points of view, makes Freud's general model especially relevant to the analysis of international politics within the meaning of our analogy procedure.

3.4 The Tasks of the Ego: Perception, Mediation and Control

Freud's description of the relationship between ego and id is stimulating:

> Perception plays the part for the ego that drive does for the id. The ego represents what one might call reason and prudence, in contrast to the id, which contains the passions ... The functional importance of the ego emerges from the fact that it normally governs the accesses to motility. In its relation to the id it therefore resembles the horseman who is supposed to control the superior strength of the horse, with the difference that the rider tries to do so with his own strength, but the id with loaned strength. This analogy goes a little further. Just as the rider, if he does not wish to be separated from his horse, often has no choice but to guide it where it wishes to go, so the ego usually translates the will of the id into action as though it were its own will.[10]

In its relationship with the external world the ego has the task of perception and adaptation (perception understood in the autoplastic and alloplastic sense). In allowing for the dangers and obstacles of the external world its performance criteria could be caution and purposefulness, as well as far-sightedness and resolution.

However, in its relation with the superego it may happen that, in the assessment of the existing outside world, caution and purposefulness clash with the remembered commandments of tradition and persons of authority. These commandments of the superego can have the more weighty consequences as both their effects and their sources have probably become subconscious, so that the counter-commands of the ego no longer have access to the superego. In most persons the superego speaks out, though it cannot itself be addressed.

Much the same applies to the id. The contents of the id are likewise largely subconscious. A large part of our motivation is subconscious, just as are most of its details and the recollections and reactions we have associated with them in the course of our psychological and emotional development. That is why they are, as a rule, inaccessible to criticism by the ego, or only accessible with difficulty as far as their inappropriateness or incompatibility with each other or with one of the other systems are concerned. Normally their sources cannot be managed by reason. One can only watch them carefully, resist them, accept them or suppress them. And because the id is the source of psychic energy and of motivation (including mediated motivation as in the case of repetition constraints), the efforts of the ego to resist the id are very serious indeed.

Freud describes the conflict between the ego and the id as follows:

> There are two roads by which the contents of the id can penetrate into the ego. One is the direct road, the other leads via the ego ideal and many psychological actions may depend on which of the two roads is chosen. The ego develops from drive perception to drive control, from drive obedience to drive inhibition. In this achievement the ego ideal, which is partly a reaction to the drive processes of the id, has a major share ... But on the other side we see the same ego as a poor thing that is under three kinds of subservience and in consequence endures three kinds of dangers: from the outer world, from the libido of the id, and from the severity of the superego. Three kinds of anxiety correspond to these dangers, because anxiety is the expression of a retreat from danger. As a borderline creature the ego wants to mediate between the id and the world, make the id compliant with the world, and make the world meet the wish of the id through its muscular actions. It actually behaves like a physician during an analytical treatment: with its consideration for the real world it recommends itself to the id as a libido object by trying to attract its libido to itself. It is not only a helpmate of the id, but also its submissive slave wooing for its master's love. It attempts, wherever possible, to remain in agreement with the id, it overlays its subconscious commandments with its pre-conscious rationalisations, feigns obedience by the id to the admonitions of reality even where the id has remained rigid and unyielding, it glosses over the conflicts of the id with reality and, where possible, also those with the superego. In its intermediate position between id and reality it all too often yields to the temptation to become sycophantic, opportunist and deceitful, rather like a statesman who, despite good insight, wishes to maintain himself in public favour.[11]

As this passage reveals, Freud emphasised the permanent possibility of three kinds of conflict: between the ego and reality, between the ego and the id, and between the ego and the superego. At a different place he deals with a fourth kind of conflict, namely, between reality and the id. In such a conflict, he says, the ego must side with reality. If, however, it does so in an unsuitable manner, a neurosis will develop in the individual. Such a neurosis, according to Freud, arises from a conflict between an

> ego that is inhibited in its synthesis and an id in which individual drives have made themselves independent, pursue their objectives with no consideration for the interests of the individual as a whole ... that the ego has made the attempt

to suppress certain parts of the id in an unsuitable manner … and the id has revenged itself for this. The neurosis, therefore, is the consequence of a conflict between the ego and the id, a conflict into which the ego enters because it … wants at all costs to hang on to its compliance towards the external world. The conflict is between the external world and the id, and because the ego, faithful to its innermost nature, sides with the external world, it gets into conflict with the id. But note carefully that it is not the fact of this conflict that causes the condition of sickness – because such conflicts between reality and the id are unavoidable and mediating about them is part of the constant tasks of the ego – but the circumstance that the ego has used the inadequate means of repression for settling the conflict. This is due to the fact that, at the time when the task arose for it, the ego was undeveloped and impotent.[12]

Elsewhere in his writings Freud mentions other types of conflicts. If one systematically orders the main types of possible conflicts contained in Freud's scheme, one arrives at ten possible conflict types; it is these ten types that can have their counterparts in types of potential conflict on a sub-national, national and international plane.

4. A Simple Typology of Possible Conflicts in Freud's Structural Model

In a large part of his writings Freud was especially concerned with conflicts between the ego and the other three system levels in his model. These conflicts were: id versus reality, id versus superego. and id versus ego, as well as conflicts between some sub-systems that make up the id. In addition to these four possible types of conflict there can be a fifth type of conflict between the ego and the superego; Freud devoted a great deal of attention to such conflicts. But even a sixth type of conflict is possible, namely, between the ego and reality. Physical or social reality can be so complex, can change so quickly, or can be so threatening that the ego is unable to form an adequate picture of its surroundings, or else is unable to find an adequate apparatus of behaviour reactions to cope with its surroundings. Karl Mannheim came close to the first of these possibilities with his idea of the non-transparency of modern industrial societies.[13] The second possibility, that of overwhelming demands on the self-reflection ability from an intolerable environment, is one of the aspects that Bruno Bettelheim in his study of the behaviour of prisoners in the Nazi concentration camps has discussed; it plays a part also in the exploration of the psychological reactions of individuals to disaster situations.[14]

A seventh type of conflict situation might arise between the superego and reality, especially when reality is of slight relevance to the superego, or when reality is such that the commandments of the superego cannot be followed under its conditions. In such situations, presumably, either reality or the superego has to be changed. But by the time this happens the conflict may have become aggravated. Conflicts of this type often play a part in disturbances among juveniles and students; they can also be observed with social and political leaders anxious to reshape both their own superego and part of their contemporary world order. Possible examples are Martin Luther and Mahatma Gandhi, whose cases have been studied by Erik H. Erikson.[15] Freud himself concerned himself rather rarely with conflicts of the sixth or seventh type, but some of the more sociologically-oriented psychiatrists and psychologists did so later.[16]

Three further types of conflict similarly received little attention from Freud, even though they are logically contained in his scheme. First and foremost, reality itself is not free from serious conflicts, contradictions and incompatibilities. In social reality, in particular, there is neither a culture nor any political or economic system whatever in which some of its human components, its prevailing practices or the conditions of its physical environment, are not involved in internal conflicts and contradictions. The history of social conflicts, of population growth and of exhaustion of resources offers a multitude of examples.

Secondly, it is improbable that the recollections and commandments that make up the superego are free from contradictions and internal conflicts. It is difficult to construct a system of commandments or logical statements or electrical switches or synapses between nerve cells in such a way that, even for a short space of time, it would be entirely free from contradictions and paradoxes. According to the mathematician Kurt Goedel the immunity of any such systems from contradictions can never be demonstrated in the long run. The history of philosophical and religious systems shows that, sooner or later, all of them have produced opposing and in themselves contradictory commandments. The resulting conflicts of conscience and loyalty are a regularly recurring theme in literature, philosophy and politics.

Third and last, it is improbable, for the same reasons, that the ego system itself would be free from internal contradictions and conflicts. Certainly the task of the ego consists of searching for consistency and synthesis; but it continues to be a system. No matter how logical its structure, it is still subject to the Goedel theorem. Internal conflicts in the ego – the conscious part of a personality – have interested psychologists and psychiatrists, writers and thinkers of all times.

Freud himself was concerned less with these conflicts within each of the system levels of his model: the conflicts within the superego and the ego system. On the other hand, philosophical traditions from Kant via Hegel and Marx, all the way to the modern existentialists, have long been emphasising their importance.

Altogether there arise ten types of possible conflicts from Freud's model (see Table 3.1).[17] Four of them are conflicts within the system levels, while there are six conflicts that reach across the levels. In this context it is

Table 3.1: A scheme of possible conflicts in the Freudian model

	I Reality	II Superego	III Ego	IV Id	Conflict types
I Reality	Conflicts between components of reality (e.g. class antagonism, role conflicts)	Reality vs. superego (e.g. prejudice)	Reality vs. ego (e.g. demand for symbol-creating ability)	Reality vs. id (restriction of primary narcissism)	Reality conflicts
II Superego	Superego vs. reality (e.g. outrage)	Conflicts between components of the superego (e.g. loyalty conflicts)	Superego vs. ego (guilt, encouragement to reach an ideal)	Superego vs. id (e.g. repression, defence and symptom formation)	Superego conflicts
III Ego	Ego vs. reality (e.g. denial or processing of reality)	Ego vs. superego (e.g. awareness of historicity of values)	Conflicts between components of the ego (e.g. role conflicts, overcome consciously or by defence)	Ego vs. id (e.g. repression, or rationalisation, realisation of imperatives of reality)	Ego conflicts
IV Id	Id vs. reality (e.g. projection or autism mediated through the ego)	Id vs. superego (according to ego mediation: psychotic or neurotic solutions)	Id vs. ego (e.g. fear of drives: psychotic behaviour or compulsive neurotic symptoms)	Conflicts between components of the id (e.g. contradictory drive impulses)	Id conflicts

assumed that the sequence of initial and reaction unit within each separate conflict pair is irrelevant, so that a conflict between ego and id is treated as equivalent to a conflict between id and ego. If one were to dispense with this simplifying assumption – e.g. if one attempted to distinguish between the subsystem in which a conflict arises and the subsystem in which the effects of the conflict subsequently emerge – then the number of possible types of conflicts between the systems would rise to twelve and the total of potential conflict types to sixteen.

5. Ego Stress and Ego Performance

Every one of the ten types of potential conflicts represents a potential stress for the ego. According to Freud, man has no other mechanism for mastering any kind of conflict than the ego system. Even with regard to its own internal conflicts the ego has to achieve its own stability.

Freud's model thus provides a clear indication of the wide scope and the difficulty of the communication and decision burden that every ego has to bear if it wishes to be up to its control function. Freud did not explicitly formulate the concept of the ego burden, but it is implicit in the concepts ego strength and ego performance – concepts that occur in his writings and that have met with unchanging and great attention on the part of his contemporary social philosophers.[18]

To the extent that man's relevant environment becomes much more complex, and that the social systems in which he lives become more complex and full of contradictions, the burden or stress on his ego inevitably increases; equally the demands made by life on his ego performance become greater. To the extent that his ego-performance grows more difficult, his failures become more frequent and more dangerous.

6. Defence Mechanisms of the Ego: Repression, Projection, Denial and Autism

This scheme clearly suggests that the stress on the ego can be great and the ego performance demanded from the individual very high indeed. Frequently, Freud says, the overstressed ego cannot master its task. In its failure it can become the blind servant of one system level, moreover at the expense of profound frustration and disadvantage of the other. The ego, for instance, can entirely submit to the superego by repressing, or sidelining, the needs of the id and by depriving the individual of substantial sources of pleasure and motivation. In the service of the superego it can blindly deny reality to the point of self-destruction. Or else, on the contrary, it can become a submissive servant of the id by meeting its demands for pleasure and 'rationalising' any claim in a language it has borrowed from reality or from the superego, without paying serious attention to reality or the superego.

Even if the ego places itself entirely in the service of a subsystem, the other subsystems do not disappear. Whether ignored or repressed, their information is blocked from access to consciousness; yet it remains part of the subsystem – with indirect but far-reaching consequences.[19]

The repressed desires of the id, as well as socially transmitted drives, can associate with other psychological contents that accept the ego and the superego. but they can also attach to these seemingly more harmless or more objective demands a stronger charge of pleasure or unpleasure deriving from the concealed demands of the id. It can therefore happen, as Freud points out, that thoughts of morality and punishment expressly approved by the superego may associate with concealed but powerful associations of self-castigation, with neurotic feelings of guilt, with ominous forebodings, and even with a secret desire for these.

Repression is but one of the defence mechanisms of the ego against the temptations of pleasure, as well as against the prohibitions of reality and of the conscious mind. A further defence mechanism – or a further defence procedure – is called projection. Here the ego does not seriously admit to itself that a forbidden desire of the id could exist in his own person. But because the desire is felt so strongly that its existence cannot be denied, it is projected on to some other actor, who quite clearly is not the self and against whom the repressive wrath of the superego can safely turn. Thus, as Freud has shown, one's own desires for spontaneity, laziness, disorder, uncleanliness, sexual freedom, etc., are often projected to the images of those who are socially below us, or to people of foreign nations or other races. The poor, the working class, the ethnic minorities, the blacks or foreigners are then credited in one's imagination with a certain inclination or some special courage for that kind of forbidden behaviour. Once our perceptions are distorted in this manner, our superego and our ego can, with a mixture of moral outrage and hatred and concealed envy, drive us to persecuting, or even killing, the persons or groups upon whom the repressed desires of our id have been projected. According to Freud, psychological processes of this kind take place automatically in many individuals.[20] Political movements and national governments often deliberately attempt to create such conditions for political or war purposes. If the instruments of governance and the mass media are used by them for the deliberate propagation of hatred, the consequences of an initial projection can extend and intensify to a great degree.[21]

A further defence process of the ego is directed against reality. Information from the real world that is incompatible with powerful desires of the id or with severe prohibitions of the superego can simply be denied. By means of such a denial the ego persuades itself that this unacceptable information from reality has not reached it at all, or that the conditions of the real world described by that information do not exist or else are irrelevant.

Such processes of denial can serve to shut off such information as seems to be incompatible with other cognitive recollections or ideas of the ego. While psychiatrists supporting Freud particularly emphasise man's inclination to deny information that is associated with powerful affect, other psychiatrists stress our inclination to deny such information as is incompatible with cognitive consonance of what we believe we know.[22] In practice the process of denial in individuals frequently contains a mixture of emotional and cognitive elements. Thus, for instance, the National Socialist government in 1944 denied the relevance of the truth of the Allied plans for the invasion of Normandy, sent from Ankara by Ambassador Franz von Papen after they had been stolen there by Nazi agents. The information revealed by these plans about the strength and capabilities of the Allies were not compatible with earlier estimates of the Nazi leaders and did not fit into the self-image of these leaders, which attributed to them prudence and far-sightedness. As a result they ignored this new information with disastrous consequences for them.[23] Generally it seems that denial, rejection, cognitive consonance and consistency play an important part in most major mistakes made by governments with their espionage services in peacetime and in wartime.

Repression, projection and denial have one thing in common – the tendency to weaken, or exclude, control of information from reality through the actions of the ego. However, to the extent that effective control is excluded by means of the reality principle, the ego will proceed towards autistically preformed actions. Autism is a state of communication in which information from the inner self has clear priority over information from the wider neighbourhood of the individual. 'Psychism' – to use Robert J. Lifton's term – is a related reaction. Here the actor believes that the outer world can be changed by a mere effort of the psyche or the will.[24] In both cases information from the external world is roundly rejected or else formally accepted without, however, being considered in the decision-making processes of the ego. The actor turns blind and deaf to the world around him and increasingly listens only to the result of his inner voices.[25]

Autism – understood here in terms of communications theory – is a last desperate defence of the overcharged ego against the unbearable conflict between the external world's reality as a whole and the partial inner realities of its own id and superego. To the extent that external reality actually becomes more hostile, harder or inaccessible, its conflicts with the inner needs and strivings of the id and superego will probably be tolerated less; in consequence the probability of autistic behaviour will increase. Partly, of course, autistic behaviour may consist in depicting reality as more hostile than in fact it is and in projecting the individual's own emotions of anxiety, anger and aggression on to other individuals and groups. Autistic behaviour will then develop a dynamic of its own. As this is a self-aggravating process, a vicious circle, this may lead, in individual persons or groups, to a growing isolation from reality and other actors, as well as to ever sharper conflicts with them.[26]

7. Foreign Policy and Defence Mechanisms: 'Schumpeter Effects'

From the pressure weighing upon them, national governments resort to defence mechanisms that, in their communication aspects, greatly resemble the defence of the id of individuals. In defending their cognitive consonance they use the mechanisms of projection, repression and denial; this produces 'autistic milieux'. The process of increasingly autistic communication and corresponding behaviour in individuals, as described by Freud and his followers, shows striking parallels with the development of militarism, as described, for instance, by Joseph Schumpeter.[27] If one follows Schumpeter, nations or states can experience a certain real, albeit limited or temporary, military threat from the world around them. Most probably they will react to this threat by developing military skills and social institutions, castes or classes, which might help them to stand up to the threat successfully. However, when they have survived the external threat the strong violence-inclined and war-inclined social classes, institutions, interest groups, as well as a culture moulded by war continue to exist in their society. Individuals who have become accustomed to expectation of war and acts of war will be inclined to act out their habits or, at least, to seek an opportunity for doing so. Those classes and interest groups for whom war was profitable in the past will continue to seek similar 'profit'. Information from the outside world suggesting a need for the continuation of war preparations and wars will be eagerly chosen, accepted, emphatically confirmed and will be rewarded by such 'defence-minded' or 'war-accustomed' individuals or groups. Information about the outside world testifying to the opposite will be rejected, or not believed, and anyone acting in line with them will be punished in a great variety of ways. In consequence, warlike behaviour will increasingly be determined by processes unrolling within the violence-prone or war-prone state. Its rulers and soldiers will find ever new reasons why precautionary measures should be taken, additional weapons provided, alliances concluded, military bases set up, allies subjected, foreign governments overthrown and new border provinces conquered.

Expansion of dominated regions, even more so of empires, is therefore, according to Schumpeter, driven mainly from within, especially through a sociologically or interest-motivated process of cognitive distortion. Schumpeter wrote his study in 1918, his examples from history reaching from ancient Egypt and Rome to the First World War. More recent empirical research supports Schumpeter's general thesis, but does not completely confirm his specific conclusion that such autistic warlike behaviour is confined primarily to aristocratic or large landowning societies or that it eventually crumbles to the extent that commercial and capitalist economic and social orders are developing; these, Schumpeter believed, would rather cling to reality, rational behaviour and peace. Recent research shows that the autistic form of hostility in foreign policy clearly predominated in the foreign policy of the modern great powers both before 1914 and since.[28]

8. The Freudian Concept of the 'Death Drive': Burden and Failure of the Control Performance

The ego processes as a rule include the testing of reality. This therefore implies self-criticism, self-correction and frequent revision of earlier impulses and earlier behaviour. Facing up to earlier behaviour and changing it often mean a temporary increase of internal disequilibrium, called inner tension. Such an increase is felt as unpleasure, similar to the sense of unpleasure that causes pain.

With other ego processes, too, including the mediation of the sixteen kinds of conflicts, there is a probability of a temporary increase of the internal disequilibrium. This increase of inner tension is likewise experienced as unpleasure; such unpleasure can reach a degree that is just as hard to bear as pain. The less the ego overcomes such conflicts, the worse the ego burden becomes and the more the ego performance will be associated with unpleasure.

According to Freud such psychological processes seek their own automatic ways, which result in release of tension and hence the creation of pleasure or a reduction or avoidance of pain.[29] If this is so, then strategies are pursued that lead away from the full ego burden and the associated nagging or tormenting self-awareness. Simultaneously, ideas of such actions and personality states that are felt, in a sense, to oppose the ego burden are associated with pleasure. Under such conditions it may happen that ideas of intoxication, sleep or even death are charged with pleasure and libido. They become the more tempting and attractive – at times almost overwhelmingly tempting and attractive – the greater and more frustrating the ego burden has become.

What Freud has called the death drive will, according to the hypothesis here offered, grow to the extent that the ego's overload grows. This hypothesis predicts an increase in the frequency and/or intensity of death symbols in the communication and in the dream reports of persons suffering from an overload of the ego. It also predicts that social conditions that place intolerable demands on the ego performance and subject the ego to extreme internal tensions will produce many death-associated symbols of this kind and death-related behaviour patterns. Finally, death-associated works of art and literature, as well as death-related cultural and political symbols, will infect many groups, more particularly those to which such conditions apply. The first prediction can be tested with the aid of a contents analysis of the relevant materials, while the second can be tested by the frequency of murder, suicide and other forms of destructive fury; the third can be tested by observing the frequency of the emergence and spread of death-related expressions in art, politics and culture.[30]

If this argument is acceptable as a provisional working hypothesis, then it follows that the death drive is not an innate inclination or drive, as Freud primarily saw it.[31] Instead it now appears as a function of a system, perhaps more particularly as a concomitant phenomenon of system overload. In the movement towards death the ego *load* – the burden of painful decisions, anxieties and inner conflicts – is cast off. A single behaviour determinant can, with a grandiose disregard for the manifold demands and restrictions of reality, outweigh all the rest: the heroes of the *Edda* or the *Nibelungenlied* go calmly to their death; centuries later Oswald Spengler advises the Western nations to acquire the same heroic behaviour with regard to their inevitable ruin. Or else all behaviour determinants are devalued equally down to insignificance and life then ends in the nirvana of the Buddhists or in the resignation sought by Schopenhauer.

Freud himself described his own concept of the death drive as no more than a hypothesis; he could offer no proof of it; the hypothesis, he said, had been developed on the basis of theoretical, biologically supported, considerations.[32] This drive, however, differed from other drives as other behaviour researchers and sometimes Freud himself understood them. As in the case of Eros, it was also assumed of the death drive that it was 'active in every piece of living substance'. But, whereas Eros was believed to be relatively strongly concentrated in certain parts 'so that some one substance could be the principal representative of Eros', Freud gave no indication that any definite substance might be the principal bearer of the death drive. Nor did the 'death drive' seem to have any survival value for the human species. Contrary to other drives the death drive was neither conserved nor favoured by natural selection.

In short, Freud's 'death drive' was an abstract principle, the diminution of differences and tension down to the conceptual zero point. Freud's concept of Eros was more concrete. But by being placed alongside the death drive, it was, by definition, also a general principle, whose aim it was 'to render life more complex by a steadily more far-reaching concentration of living substance dispersed into particles, and of course to preserve it'.[33] The concept of the death drive thus practically becomes another name for the general entropy principle: the tendency that all differences in form and energy become blurred until a state of weak 'random noise' is attained. And Eros aims at the opposite principle: at a negative entropy (negentropy) or the accumulation of increasing information and order applied to living substances.

In spite of its abstract nature, Freud's concept of the 'death drive', as well as his statement that the actor turns this drive outwards in the form of aggression, represent an important cognitive element from the viewpoint of general system theory. His approach contains an indication that behaviour patterns directed towards aggression or even towards death can be understood as the result of the deconstruction or dismantling of more complex order patterns. In the most striking cases of destructive or death-seeking behaviour the norms of control and of the ego performance are deconstructed.

According to this reflection the death drive is one of the phenomena of regression, linked to the loss of the ego performances, or with escape from them. Thus the exhausted victim of a snowstorm eventually sits down to fall asleep and never wake up again, and suicide represents the last decision, i.e. it lifts off all other decisions. In all such cases the painful duty of continual reality-related self-control is surrendered.[34]

Freud's fundamental system model, as sporadically hinted at above, is in many respects instructive for the behaviour of national states. In the following paragraphs we will try to examine what processes at the level of national states correspond to the conflicts of the pleasure principle, the reality principle and the superego. as developed in Freud's model; also to what extent the performance of a government in a nation resembles the ego performance in the ego and in what way national states may regress to destructive and self-destructive action just like mentally sick individuals.

9. Interest Groups, Reality Testing and Supra-national Morality at the Level of National States

From the above reflections it follows that the basic structure of the Freudian model can certainly be applied to the analysis of the behaviour of states and nations. A few limited, though specific, similarities are observable (see Table 3.2 compared with Table 3.1 above), Many modern interest groups behave, in certain respects, similarly to the partial mechanisms of the id. Each individual interest group through its behaviour expresses its intention of approaching its own particular objective or of promoting its own particular claims without much, or without any, consideration for the efforts of other groups. Just as an action is not pleasing to an individual unless it satisfies his

Table 3.2: Potential Conflicts in the National and International Political System

	World system	Ethical values and tradition	Governmental system	Interest groups	Conflict types
World system	Conflict within the world system	World system vs. ethical values and tradition	World system vs. governmental system	World system vs. interest groups	World system conflicts
Ethical values and tradition	Ethical values and tradition vs. World system	Conflicts between ethical values and components of tradition	Ethical values and tradition vs. governmental system	Ethical values and tradition vs. interest groups	Ethical values and tradition conflicts
Governmental system	Governmental system vs. world system	Governmental system vs. ethical values and tradition	Conflicts within governmental system	Governmental system vs. interest groups	Governmental conflicts
Interest groups	Interest groups vs. world system	Interest groups vs. ethical values and tradition	Interest groups vs. governmental system	Conflicts between components of interest groups	Interest group conflicts

id, so a political action will hardly find much consent unless it can gain the support of a certain interest group. In this sense interests are the basis of the pleasure principle in politics.

From the point of view of the politics of interest groups it is probable that, for instance, advances in the direction of increasing armaments and even limited wars may, in this sense, be felt to be politically 'pleasurable'. In many locations and regions new armament plants, defence installations or defence decrees will certainly be popular, seeing that they will give rise to a higher level of employment, of sales figures and of land prices. A closure of a state armaments depot or a naval dockyard, no matter how out of date, almost inevitably triggers protest. Members of Parliament from districts enjoying a maximum of special orders in the armaments industry are the principal champions of greater armament expenditure. Specific interest groups, such as the space vehicle industry and individual firms such as the Boeing Company are actively engaged in strengthening the public's defence awareness. In a certain way such firms and branches of industry demand higher allocations from the defence budget with the same blindness and ruthlessness as the hunger reflex in the human body ultimately leads to a stabilisation of our blood sugar level.[35]

However, just as information from the world of external reality can act against the drives of the id and its various subsystems, so information from the international system can attempt to halt or counteract the blind strivings of interest groups for an enlargement of the military or industrial defence apparatus. Such information from outside could, for instance, reveal the technical limitations of a nation's weapons systems and the capabilities of rival nations. Or it could point to the dangers of an arms race and the escalation in the international arena, or to the probability of a minor war unexpectedly proving to be greater and more frustrating. Or it might point to the social and political limitations of an expansionist foreign policy: the probable loss of international sympathies, the crumbling of alliances, the expenditure in human lives and financial resources, the possible decline of the purchasing power of one's own currency. If this happens, then the information from the external reality will collide with the demands of the interest groups.

Similarly to individual personality systems, national communication systems may contain elements that fulfil the function of the superego. Abraham Lincoln urgently asked his fellow countrymen to worry less about whether God was on their side than whether they stood on his. A hundred years later, during the Cuban crisis, John and Robert Kennedy resisted the urgings of some top-level advisers to deal the first strike against Cuba; this would have cost that country about 25,000 human lives and involved the risk of a major war with the then Soviet Union. 'My brother has no desire to become the Tojo of the Third World War', Robert Kennedy said on that occasion.[36] Thus something like a superego had preserved a minimum of effectiveness. Comparable elements of a superego can also be seen in the decision processes of other nations, including such countries as Russia and China, where commandments were for a long time clothed in the language of Marxism-Leninism. Deliberate rejection of a superego existing outside the national state was a characteristic of the fascist regimes of Hitler and Mussolini, which fortunately proved to be short-lived.

On the international plane not only individuals are bearers of the superego; it can be more or less strongly represented also in the communication structures and memories of social groups and institutions, such as churches, universities, humanitarian associations, sometimes even in the medical profession and in certain ideologically aligned political parties. As experience of past wars teaches, any one of these groups can be swept away by national fervour and special interests; however, some elements resembling a superego or world conscience are preserved. Such memory-moulded group values of the type of a superego should not be equated with the behaviour of economically, sociologically or power-politically oriented interest groups which, as is known, are guided more by immediate feedback signals of momentary successes.

Just as in the individual the ego has the triple task of mediating between id, superego and reality, so at the international level the government has to mediate between the ephemeral demands of limited interest groups, the internalised claims of national and supranational culture, as well as the reality constraints of the external world and the competing actors in the international system.

10. The Ego Weakness of the National State

The ego performance that this situation demands from a national government is at least as difficult as the comparable ego performance of most individuals, although the national governments are not nearly as well equipped for meeting these demands. The degree of attention devoted to external reality is much higher in individuals than in national states. This is true of the executive and, even more so, of the legislature, the mass media and the electorate. Even where a government action is defined as a foreign-policy step and as a necessary reaction to the international situation, closer examination frequently shows that its decisive determinants were narrow-minded domestic-policy interests.

For these and other reasons there is a far greater probability that the behaviour of national states, especially big ones, will become autistic than there is for individuals.[37] With individuals the process of reality testing proceeds constantly and simultaneously through different channels of sensual perception. We not only hear a meal being described as edible, but can also see it, smell it, touch it and taste it. The feedback cycles in reality testing by individuals are short and, at the same time, multiple; they return additional data to the actor – both about reality and the results of his own earlier actions. Self-correction is therefore rapid and relatively reliable. By way of contrast, reality testing in the foreign and military policy of national states is temporarily suspended; it is circular rather than interactive, it is slow and rare. It passes through only a few channels, sometimes through just one. Moreover, it provides relatively little information on the results of earlier measures in the policy in question. Self-correction of a national foreign policy is therefore much more difficult.

Finally, misperceptions of reality rarely have any consequences for the individual, even when they occur in cases of id-influenced perceptions, as Freud has described them, or in the relatively rare instances of purely chemical or physiologically based addictions, or in cases of reality distortion, when addiction-based and psychological processes are combined. Unlike individuals, national states are far more prone to addictive behaviour, especially in international politics: misperceptions of international reality may be quite profitable for individual interest groups and even for governments. It is therefore possible that, continually repeated, they settle firmly in memory, in communication practices and in social institutions, even taking root and moulding appropriate learning processes.[38] For all these reasons the 'state of mind' of national states is far more fragile and precarious than that of individuals.

If these theses are correct and if the basic structure of the Freudian model is relevant to the analysis of national states, then certain predictions arise for the real world: in international politics one might expect nations to act irrationally – in the sense of not purposefully and in a counterproductive manner; moreover so frequently that one cannot any longer speak of an accident. And rivalries and conflicts would presumably intensify beyond the interests of each nation concerned. Moreover, one would expect the frequency and effect of such failure to increase whenever the ego burden of national governments grows more rapidly than their capability for ego performance. Increasing participation of the masses in politics and growing strength of the interest groups within a country would therefore aggravate the burden of the government concerned. A further increase in the burden on a government would result from increasingly acute reality constraints.

All these processes characterise the international politics of the century now past. In many countries there has been a marked increase in mass participation and in the pressure from interest groups. At the same time an enormous increase in the efficacy of modern weapons and production systems has magnified the real dangers and constraints of foreign policy. There is, however, no sign of a simultaneous corresponding increase in the 'intelligence quotient' of national governments or political systems, i.e. an increase of their ability to evaluate information *sine ira et studio* and to take appropriate decisions. We must therefore expect an increasing frequency of intelligence failures and wrong decisions, as well as foreign-political steps proving counterproductive in the international arena.

11. Summary and Concluding Remarks

Our considerations proceeded from an empirical fact – the growing failure, since the beginning of the twentieth century, of national governments with regard to decisions that led to the exacerbation of conflicts, to war and even to defeat and removal of the governments that triggered a war of major or even lesser proportions. The search for a rational explanation of such counterproductive and hence *irrational* behaviour led to Sigmund Freud's theories of the structure model of a decision system, which provides an insight into ten types of conflict and the corresponding information flows, as well as the resulting proneness of individuals to irrational, destructive and self-destructive behaviour. It was then found that this Freudian model of the individual's personality system revealed many significant analogies with the decision system of national states.

Just like individuals, so governments have to meet great demands on performance. But they are poorly equipped for this task. They have to mediate both between the demands of interest groups within their borders and the external world of ecology, technology and international politics, and between each of these two worlds and the supranational ethical values and memories. In this respect their tasks resemble the performance demanded from the ego of the individual, which has to mediate between the pleasure principle of the id, the restrictions of the reality principle of the external world and the demands of the internalised supra-individual morality in the shape of the superego. Compared with their tasks, however, the information flow of governments on the state level is worse and less balanced; their means are less effective than those of the ego in the individual, while their power potentials are (fatally) far greater.[39] Changes in national and world politics since the beginning of the twentieth century have intensified this unbalance.[40] In consequence irrational behaviour, wrong decisions and escape to destructive and self-destructive behaviour at the level of national states are more frequent than on the level of the individual. One need only think of the history of Germany during that period. It is advisable to proceed from the assumption that, under the conditions of the late twentieth and the beginning twenty-first centuries, the 'state of mind' of the states is more precarious than that of individuals. Is this going to change in the course of the twenty-first century? Or will structure-determined problems contribute to the symptoms of the twentieth and twenty-first centuries, simply repeating themselves or even aggravating? It is not difficult to predict that the constituent conditions for peace policy reasoning and a reasonable peace policy will be no easier than in the recent past or today.[41]

Notes

1. Classic formulations of *raison d'état* can be found in Niccolo Macchiavelli, *Il Principe* and Carl von Clausewitz, *Vom Kriege*. An important critical survey is offered by Friedrich Meinecke, *Die Idee der Staatsraison in der Neueren Geschichte*, in *Werke*, vol. 1, Munich 1957; and Hans Morgenthau, *Politics Among Nations*, New York 1964, pp. 4–11. From these early reflections to the 'rationalist paradigm', as has repeatedly been propagated in the analysis of international relations since the 1950s in order finally to assert that it has found the master key of the analysis, the intellectual road is shorter than the above-named champions realised. See, Walter Carlsnaes et al., *Handbook of International Relations*, London 2002, Chapters 3 and 4.

2. Morgenthau, *Politics Among Nations*, p. 5.

3. Calculated from data about fifty international wars, 1815–1965, collected by J. David Singer and Melvin Small, published in *The Wages of War*, New York 1973. See Dieter Senghaas, 'Politische und militärische Dimensionen der gegenwärtigen Kriegs- und Friedensproblematik', in idem (ed.), *Friedensforschung und Gesellschaftskritik*, Munich 1970, pp. 39–57, esp. pp. 39–44.

4. Purposeful rationality describes a behaviour that actually has a high degree of probability of leading to the result wished by the actor. His wish for this result is, of course, subjective, but the probabuility that his behaviour will in fact lead to that result is a question of objective facts. According to Max Weber and Karl Mannheim this purposeful rationality should be distinguished from formal rationality, which consists of the retraceability of the sequence of steps through which a result or a decision has come about. The methods of formal logic, mathematics or accountancy are examples of formal rationality. If each step in such a procedure can lead only to one single result, we describe that procedure not only as formally rational, but also as rigorous.

 Purposefully rational procedures need not necessarily be formally rational. They can achieve the desired results also if the steps leading to them cannot be repeated. Formally rational procedures need not necessarily be purposefully rational: although repeatable in every step, it can happen that they do not lead to the desired result, especially when they proceed from incomplete or unrealistic premises. Coincidence of formal and purposeful rationality is therefore again a question of the empirical facts in every individual case. Simple everyday understanding of the concept of rationality leads one to expect such coincidence; experience, however, teaches that it cannot be assumed as a matter of course.

5. See James B. Conant, *Science and Common Sense*, New Haven 1951, pp. 221–222.

6. Sigmund Freud, 'Zeitgemäßes über Krieg und Tod', in *Gesammelte Werke* (London/Frankfurt/M. edition), vol. X. pp. 339–340.

7. Sigmund Freud, 'Massenpsychologie und Ich-Analyse', in *Gesammelte Werke*, vol. XIII, p. 98.

8. See also Alfred Lorenzer et al., *Psychoanalyse als Sozialwissenschaft*, Frankfurt/M. 1971.

9. Sigmund Freud, 'Abriß der Psychoanalyse', in *Gesammelte Werke*, vol. XVII, pp. 68–69.

10. Sigmund Freud, 'Das Ich und das Es', in *Gesammelte Werke*, vol. XIII, pp. 252–253.

11. *Ibid.*, pp. 286–287.

12. Sigmund Freud, 'Die Frage der Laienanalyse', in *Gesammelte Werke*, vol. XIV, p. 231.

13. Karl Mannheim, *Mensch und Gesellschaft im Zeitalter des Umbaus*, Darmstadt 1958.

14. See Bruno Bettelheim, *Aufstand gegen die Masse*, Munich 1965; Allen H. Barton, *Communities in Disaster. A Sociological Analysis of Collective Stress Situations*, New York 1970.

15. Erik H. Erikson, *Der junge Mann Luther*, Munich 1965, and idem, *Gandhi's Truth*, New York 1969.

16. See especially Alexander Mitscherlich, *Auf dem Wege zur vaterlosen Gesellschaft*, Munich 1963; Alexander and Margarete Mitscherlich, *Die Unfähigkeit zu trauern*, Munich 1968; Theodor W. Adorno, 'Zum Verhältnis von Soziologie und Psychologie', in *Sociologika I*, Frankfurt/M. 1955, pp. 11–45; Klaus Horn: Politische Psychologie, in Gisela Kress and Dieter Senghaas (eds), *Politikwissenschaft*, Frankfurt/M. 1969, pp. 215–268.

17. A central problem of the presentation in Table 3.1 is the difficulty of making the dual aspects of the listed structure concepts visible. Thus the function of the ego consists, for one thing, in the formation of reality-compliant symbols (synthesising and organisatory function); this is the ego that the id is to become. On the other hand, the ego is the location of the defence mechanisms. Self-awareness and reality understanding are not being created in a reality-conforming manner (defence function). Within the concept of the ego there is a tension between its authoritative, sanctioning, and indeed punishing, function and its function of being a role model and ego ideal. The id contains both archaic dynamic elements, as well as what has, in conjunction with it, been repressed. These selected and hinted-at dual aspects of the structural concepts can be separated here analytically; in the life story of people, however, they are closely intertwined and as such are parts of the identity of personality.

18. See the literature quoted in note 16.

19. On the relationship of Freud's general theories to the analysis of war and peace see Alix Strachey, *The Unconscious Motives of War*, London 1957. On the interpretation of the mediation of subconscious motives for social actions see Klaus Horn, 'Insgeheime kulturistische Tendenzen der modernen psychoanalytischen Orthodoxie', in idem, *Psychoanalyse und gesellschaftliche Widersprüche (Schriften*, vol. 4), Gießen 1998, pp. 41–74.

20. See Daniel J. Levinson, 'Authoritarian Personality and Foreign Policy', *Journal of Conflict Resolution*, vol. 1, 1957, pp. 37–47, as well as the summarising report by William Eckhardt and Theo Lentz, 'Factors of War/Peace Attitudes', *Peace Research Review*, vol. 1, no. 4, 1967 (special issue).

21. See Gordon Allport, 'The Role of Expectancy', in Hadley Cantril (ed.), *Tensions that Cause War*, Urbana 1950, pp. 43–78.

22. A collection of these theories can be found in Robert Abelson et al. (eds), *Theories of Cognitive Consistency*, Chicago 1969.

23. L.C. Moyzisch, *Operation Cicero*, New York 1969.

24. See Robert J. Lifton, *Revolutionary Immortality: Mao Tse Tung and the Chinese Cultural Revolution*, New York 1968.

25. For an earlier discussion on autism see Theodore M. Newcomb, 'Autistic Hostility and Social Reality', *Human Relations*, vol. 1, 1947, pp. 69–86. See also E.M. Lemert, 'Paranoia and the Dynamics of Exclusion', *Sociometry*, vol. 25, 1962, pp. 2–20.

26. For an interpretation of deterrence policy in the framework of the model of autistic communication and behaviour resulting from it see Dieter Senghaas, *Abschreckung und Frieden. Studien zur Kritik organisierter Friedlosigkeit*, Frankfurt/M. 1981, 3rd edn., pp. 185–203.

27. Joseph Schumpeter, 'Zur Soziologie der Imperialismen' in *Aufsätze zur Soziologie*, Tübingen 1953, pp. 72–146.

28. For a survey of such literature see Robert Jervis, *Perception and Misperception in International Politics*, Princeton 1976.

29. Sigmund Freud, 'Jenseits des Lustprinzips', in *Gesammelte Werke*, vol. XIII, pp. 1ff.

30. Some examples of death-related political symbols are quoted, in a somewhat different context, by Karl W. Deutsch, *Nationalism and Social Communication*, Cambridge 1968, 2nd edn., pp. 182–183, 306. Such internally produced interest in death – internally from the viewpoint of the actor – should be distinguished from reactions to death symbols that emerged through external events, e.g. after the plague in the Middle Ages or the nuclear explosions of Hiroshima and Nagasaki. On the latter see Robert J. Lifton, *Death in Life*, New York 1967. On internal concern with death as an alternative to endless decision

problems and frustrations see the description of death in Friedrich Hebbel's *Die Nibelungen* and Richard Wagner's musical tetralogy *Der Ring des Nibelungen*, which enjoyed enormous popularity from 1870 to the end of the National Socialist era. See also Robert J. Lifton, *History and Human Survival*, New York 1970, Part II, pp. 114–207.

31. Freud, 'Das Ich und das Es', pp. 237ff., and 'Jenseits des Lustprinzips', ibid., pp. 40ff.
32. 'Das Ich und das Es', pp. 268–269. Freud stated that he had 'supposed' the death drive, whose task it was to bring organic life back into the lifeless state.
33. Ibid., p. 269.
34. An impressive example of just this state of affairs is found in the autobiography of the composer Hans Werner Henze, *Reiselieder mit böhmischen Quinten*, Frankfurt/M. 2001, 2nd edn.:

> It must have been at a moment of particular psychological exhaustion, amidst the pain and defiance of parting, in a depression. Maybe too much bad news had come at the same time, too many personal difficulties for which I no longer knew a solution; maybe there was too much darkness. At any rate it so happened that one Sunday morning I took a dose of sleeping powder in order, as I hoped, to settle the matter once and for all. Twenty-four hours later I awoke in the Westend Hospital ... Overcome and swallowed up by the metropolis! Forced to the knees by mental deficiency! (p. 112)

35. See, comprehensively, Dieter Senghaas, *Rüstung und Militarismus*, Frankfurt/M. 1982, 2nd edn., Part III.
36. See Robert Kennedy, *Thirteen Days*, New York 1969.
37. Further reasons are discussed in Dieter Senghaas, 'Zur Analyse von Drohpolitik in den internationalen Beziehungen', in *Rüstung und Militarismus*, Part II, pp. 28–93; idem, 'Towards an Analysis of Threat Policy in International Relations', in: *German Political Studies*, vol. 1, 1974, pp. 59–103.
38. This set of problems is central to Karl W. Deutsch, *The Nerves of Government. Models of Political Communication and Control*, New York 1966, 3rd edn., esp. Parts II and III. See also Dieter Senghaas, 'Politik mit wachen Sinnen betreiben. Eine Erinnerung an Karl W. Deutsch (1912–1992)', Science Centre Berlin (WZB): *WZB-Vorlesungen*, no. 4, 2003, pp. 11–25.
39. For a systematic analysis of this contrast see Senghaas, *Rüstung und Militarismus*, pp. 63–84.
40. See also Ernst-Otto Czempiel, *Kluge Macht. Außenpolitik fur das 21. Jahrhundert*, Munich 1999 – a book in which the peace problem of the present is examined in a complex manner and with an appropriate sense of configurative analysis.
41. A study of the intervention of the former Soviet Union in Afghanistan after Christmas 1979, which turned into total disaster, Pierre Allan and Dieter Kläy, *Zwischen Bürokratie und Ideologie. Entscheidungsprozesse in Moskaus Afghanistankonflikt*, Berne 1999, reads like a detailed confirmation of the reflections presented here systematically. In an analysis of the reasons for the war of the U.S.A. against Iraq in the spring of 2003 Thomas Powers, solely on the basis of officially accessible documents, observes dramatic misassessments. In 'The Vanishing Case for War', *The New York Review of Books*, vol. 50, no. 19, 4 December 2003, pp. 12–17, the author, a specialist in the analysis of secret services, diagnoses a series of total misjudgments, mistakes and lies. He says that the evaluations in the US Administration were wrong in every single detail and especially 'at the heart'. These misjudgments evidently correlate with the real or presumed fullness of power ('superpower'/'hyperpower') from which they sprang.

Chapter 4

FOURTH SECTION

Commenting on Critiques
of the 'Civilisatory Hexagon'

Ever since the earliest expositions in the 1990s, the 'civilisatory hexagon' as a peace-theory and peace-policy perspective has been the subject of critical objections. In the following section these will be translated into questions; the answers to them are attempts at dealing with the critiques substantially. Both the objections in the form of bundled questions and the answers are central arguments, by no means trivialities.

1. Questions

The questions asked have always been and still are roughly as follows.

1. *Was the process of the development of the civilisatory hexagon not one of violence (power monopoly) and is this violence not a constitutive element of the corresponding reality, and will it not remain so, and hence also an element of the peace operationally articulated in the civilisatory hexagon?*

The answer can only be 'yes, but ...' Historically seen, the constitution of the monopoly of force was, as a rule, entirely marked by violence: it was the result of prolonged power-politically motivated elimination struggles. But the concessions and compromises that the power monopolists, always only temporarily victorious, i.e. the warlords with absolutist aspirations to dominance, were compelled to enter into with mostly not entirely vanquished, or not entirely defeated or defeatable, political forces in the short, medium and long term cannot be described by the label of 'violence', but much more accurately by that of 'reluctant power control' (see the pre-modern or early modern history for the frequent political-constitutional concessions made by royal houses that became the central power towards the clergy, an oppositional landowning aristocracy, the cities and even sometimes the peasants). And the more society emancipated itself – first the bourgeoisie against the *ancien régime*, then the proletariat against the bourgeoisie, etc. – the more power control established itself as a social force, eventually on a broad basis. The process (in retrospect) reaches from prominent conflicts like the one in thirteenth-century England around Magna Carta (1215) and comparable early events in the south-west of Germany to the revolutions in Europe in 1989/90 and it was, especially regarding the recent experiences, invariably driven by a societal impulse. Force, therefore, played a central role in the development of the power monopoly, and also in the political conflicts around control of just that power monopoly. However, where these conflicts, governed by power patterns translated into historical compromises, the rule of law was born; its initially narrowly limited principles (e.g. protection against arbitrary arrest) became more and more differentiated over the centuries, in parallel with the emancipation of now socially mobile societies. Not without historical logic the relevant newest politically prominent 'Magna Carta' of this secular development was drawn up shortly after the 1989/90 revolutions in Europe: the *Document on the Meeting of the Conference on the Human Dimension of the CSCE in Copenhagen* of 29 June 1990. This contains a comprehensive and detailed enumeration of all those principles and mechanisms that are conceptually associated with 'rule of law', or today, conceptually extended, with the 'democratic constitutional state'.

In this context – the reflection on the monopoly of power – it is advantageous to think in the categories of the civilisatory hexagon because, configuratively thinking, the hexagon draws attention to the diverse components and differentiated framework conditions that are necessary in modern societies to ensure that (for instance) the rule-of-law control of the power monopoly is durable (stabilisation through feedback with other corners of the hexagon).

At this point it may be useful to repeat again what has always been emphasised in the original exposition of the 'civilisatory hexagon': the monopoly of power is beneficial only if it is controlled by judicial institutions, principles and mechanisms of the rule-of-law state, i.e. by the democratic constitutional state. If the concept 'monopoly of power' had not established itself, it might have been more correctly described as monopoly of rules. Only the monopoly of power and rule-of-law control and democratic participation combined ensure, in conditions of a socially mobile society, that legal community, i.e. the 'rule of law' in contrast to the 'rule of the stronger' who, in the past, simply had greater means of force at his disposal. If anyone does not agree with concretely formulated law, as it has arisen within that specific institutional arrangement, then he has at his disposal not the mobilisation of force for enforcing his own beliefs, identities and interests – i.e. not the rule of power, 'personal violence or personally ensured justice, but the opinion-forming, will-shaping and decision-making process of modern pluralist democracy.

It may be a banal observation, but it cannot be repeated too often: the entire arrangement of the democratic constitutional state is not conceivable without a monopoly of power, i.e. without the fundamental prohibition, applicable to everybody, of resorting to violent self-help in a machiavellian selfish intent in the event of political dissent. There is usually not much comment on this elementary state of affairs in the critiques of the power monopoly, both within and outside hexagonal discussions. This is all the more surprising as a critique of the power monopoly is often voiced even by scholars who should be well informed on the subject, but obviously are not or else do not want to be for political or patent 'regime-critical' reasons.

Another variant of the critique emphasises that the power monopoly should be viewed dialectically: while it may have satisfactory results at the intra-state level, it facilitates – so it is claimed – power concentrations externally, concentrations of uncontrollable nature that, if so desired, could easily be translated into warlike actions. This observation, too, is correct only on the surface, because it is evident (and there is an intensive debate proceeding on this issue, with an almost unanimous conclusion) that hexagonal societies do not wage wars against one another. More especially, they do not do so if their economies are symmetrically positioned (exchange on the basis of substitutive division of labour) and if, moreover, they are mutually so networked through common international regimes, organisations and institutions that they must continually reciprocally coordinate and concert their external behaviour. The debate on 'peace zones' in the international system has identified the crucial factors that are constitutive for international peace with regard to hexagonal societies.

So a frequently asked question is: where is the military in the hexagon? Is it not, in hexagonal societies vis-à-vis other societies (especially those not hexagonally constituted), a factor representing the problematical unrestricted reverse of the constitutionally ring-fenced power monopoly, i.e. the pacified internal rule-of-law community? These questions are, at least conceptually, easily answered by the international law at present valid, as expressed in the United Nations Charter. Viewed from today's international law, personal force, i.e. the politically motivated employment of the military for the enforcement of one's own interests is forbidden in principle. Only one exception is provided for the individual state – that of individual or collective self-defence (Article 51 of the UN Charter). Yet even this exception is viewed restrictively: self-defence is possible only until the instruments of collective security envisaged in the Charter go into action. When this occurs, self-defence loses its temporary legitimacy.

Transferring the civilisatory hexagon to the international level we might find the following: at this level, at least as the presently valid international law is concerned, there already exists a prohibition of violence in principle, ruling out therefore the arbitrary use of force by individual states. This is conceptually an important (albeit from the hexagonal perspective still inadequate) building block of an international rule-of-law community – genuine progress compared with the classic international law, which viewed war and peace as two equal states of affairs in international law. International law as a result became international peace law; this, conceptually also implies a police function for the military in dealing with breaches of international law. It is regrettable that these fundamental facts are generally not, or not adequately, realised; it is also regrettable that states behave as though the modern international law (and in this respect chiefly the UN Charter) did not exist. The much quoted 'community of nations' still acts like a classic power-politically defined 'world of states' and not, especially with regard to elementary policing functions, as an international rule-of-law union. This shortfall cannot be blamed on modern international law as such, or on those reflections with which the civilisatory hexagon is transferred to the international plane. If one were to pursue these last-mentioned reflections, then legal institutions analogous to rule-of-law states would have to be established on that level. Only then would a monopoly of power (ring-fenced analogously to a rule-of-law state) legitimately assert itself also on that plane. Not only would a prohibition of force then apply; the Security Council of the United Nations would also be bound by existing and further developing law with regard to its essential decisions. Power-political decisions driven by particular interests and chosen à la carte would then no longer be possible.

2. Do experiences of the civilisatory relapse remain extraneous to the hexagon or can they be understood as immanent from the analytical construct?

The relapse problem is immanent in the civilisatory hexagon. Apart from historical experience, it also follows from the logic of the analytical construct. The civilisatory hexagon is built up from components, but it does not, in the real-historical process, come together as a self-stabilising structure as a matter of course. This fitting together is itself part of a civilisatory accomplishment; the result always remains a fragile artefact. That is why the idea of ultra-stability is alien to the thinking about the hexagon, just as such ultra-stability does not exist in reality. If it ever came about, then such a state of affairs would most probably have to be understood as an exceptional case. Nevertheless, it makes sense to reflect on an optimisation of the unshakeability of hexagonal societies in order to strengthen their resistance to the threat of regression.

On the grounds of systematic as well as historical reflections it is therefore advisable to remember the fundamental brittleness of the construct. However, unlike in accepted reflections – e.g. those in *The Malaise of Culture* (see Sigmund Freud: 'compulsive passions are stronger than rational interests. Culture must make an all-out effort to set limits to men's aggressive drives') – reflections on the civilisatory hexagon consider all of the six components as well as their feedbacks. In the light of this approach any purely psychologising and sociopsychologising suppositions and assumptions, e.g. about 'civilisation as varnish', seem insufficiently deep as analysis, the more so as the emancipatory process and the opportunities resulting from it for civilisatory reinsurance are not adequately allowed for. An analytical price has to be paid in this connection because the argument is not differentiatedly configurative, but ultimately monothematic (or, formulated in the context of the civilisatory hexagon: 'shrunk-theoretical') because a really existing complexity is, in the limiting case, reduced to a single factor.

A more far-reaching critical argument assumes in this context that in modern, functionally differentiated societies that reproduce themselves according to a specific system logic affect control might possibly come about, but only at the expense of pathologising drive repression and a resulting emotional damming up that acts against self-reflexive drive regulation. From compulsive self-suppression a proneness to violence and corresponding behaviour patterns would result with greater likelihood than an assumed civilisatorily positive affect control. Relapses therefore are not, it is claimed, 'special ways' but predictable products of the civilisatory process itself: barbarism and civilisation, viewed from that perspective, are more or less a symbiotic unit, the recto and verso of one and the same state of affairs.

If one regards the phenomena postulated in this argument as an expression of collective behaviour and not as instances of deviant behaviour in a few individuals, then of course the argument collapses in the light of experience: after the Second World War there was no widespread mass regression in the suggested direction in any of the more or less 'mature' hexagonal societies. This does not mean that it would have to be ruled out for all time. An important historical fact in this context is also that only in societies that before the Second World War were not yet hexagonally structured were the production locations for barbarism localised: historians and social scientists have for decades pinpointed the relevant aspects in the history of Germany after 1871 and the history of Japan since the mid-nineteenth century, as well as the various variants of south-European and southeast-European fascism during the inter-war years of the twentieth century, as well as of Stalinism, not to mention appropriate experience in post-colonial states. All these societies, viewed from the 'civilisatory hexagon' and judged by the advanced hexagonal societies, show extremely high deficits. Also the problems marked by the cue 'Hiroshima' (first use of atomic weapons) sprang from an arcane area of American decision-finding (one that characterised the US foreign policy scene all the way to the debacle of the Vietnam war). Besides: thinking in categories of affect control does not, as is often assumed, mean support for an anti-emotional, anti-needs and anti-pleasure anthropology. On the contrary, one might argue the other way: it is just when needs, drives, pleasure and emotions are anthropologically assumed, what relevant critique calls the 'sensuous person', that affect control is called for, because such an emotional equipment, to be assumed as very real, might on the collective plane translate into a higher degree of conflict-proneness than if an opposite type of person were used as the basis of argument. It should be remembered that, in the configuration of the civilisatory hexagon, affect control and democratic participation are in a reciprocal relationship: affect control is an instance of self-moderation and deliberate self-control, while democratic participation is a downright action-activating instance, hence an opposite pole.

3. Does the problem of the civilisatory hexagon not consist of an explicit or implicit 'claim to cultural superiority'?

Superiority, or even missionary thinking and action, is totally alien to the construct. Admittedly, hexagonal societies are civilisational accomplishments because the bulk of those in them have an opportunity of becoming capable of mature judgment and because this state of affairs is no longer reversible – and also because these societies, as a result of much political dispute and many developmental processes, have more or less learned to deal with the multiple conflicts of interest and identity, which inevitably arise in advanced societies, in an essentially civilised manner. For those that are not, or not yet, hexagonal societies this state of affairs implies no more than an offer: how to deal now and in future with comparable problems they can find out only as the result of collective learning processes, and only they can find suitable institutional measures resulting from such localised experience. With regard to extra-Western cultural spheres it is important to remember that even in Western history the civilisatory hexagon was a very late product in a historical development that was by no means deterministically preordained. This state of affairs cannot be emphasised enough, because it makes debates on cultural differences between a Western-oriented civilisational model and other models appear questionable on double grounds: first with regard to the western development as such and secondly with regard to statically ontological or culture-essentialist assumptions about the 'culture genes' of cultures and civilisations.

The 'civilisatory hexagon' is, of course, Eurocentric. How else could it have been formulated seeing that it articulates a set of problems that, for the first time in world history, became virulent on a broad scale in the north-western part of Europe? Yet this state of affairs has nothing to do with occidental 'self-hypostasis' or 'Eurocentrism'. As shown above, we find here a rather opposite perspective – i.e. a fundamental openness for others, for innovative answers to what may be a similar set of secular problems in other parts of the world.

The yardsticks for 'civilisation' are not culture-genetically prescribed. Instead they are everywhere the product of multiple conflict-rich historical experience, i.e. conflict histories. For that reason the hexagon cannot simply be implanted elsewhere. If one were to attempt this, failure would as a rule be as predictable as with the transfer of advanced technologies to developing countries. What remains, as has happened often enough in the last case, is investment ruins, except that in this context they are 'soft technology' ruins, i.e. not functioning regulatory mechanisms and institutions of public order.

4. In view of, mainly, the ecology problems (but also other sets of problems), does the civilisatory hexagon not have to be expanded into a 'heptagon'?

This question suggests a fundamental misunderstanding of the hexagon. The hexagon is a historically grown framework for the civilised treatment of politically relevant identity and interest conflicts in socially mobile politicised societies. It is based on the assumption that the six components formulated in it (and their feedbacks) are necessary to lend endurance to this platform, to the civilised handling of publicly relevant conflicts. The six components are therefore constitutive for the handling of conflicts referred to, not because they represent an important state of affairs, but because without them no civilised conflict treatment *in any areas* could come about in such societies. Illustrated by an example this means: the component 'social justice' figures in the hexagon not because the social problem is important in itself, but because the treatment of this issue has acquired central importance for the historically positive assessment of the democratic constitutional state as a politically legitimate institutional arrangement for the dealing with public conflicts. The weight of this component is the result of an historical process that, in the societies that became hexagonal, began in the second half of the nineteenth century; the assignment of such parts is not the result of an arbitrary choice.

If the ecology issue were to acquire a position comparable to that of the social issue with a view to the general politically institutional framework for the civilised handling of conflicts, i.e. if 'sustainable development' were to acquire an emergent significance comparable to 'social justice' for the legitimation of the democratic constitutional state, then – logically viewed

– the hexagon would indeed have to be widened into a heptagon: the place of the present sixth component would be taken by 'enduring development', and 'conflict culture' would move on to become the seventh component, because, with such an assumption, the legitimacy of the democratic constitutional state and the hexagon generally (and within it chiefly conflict culture) could be stabilised only by serious endeavours for enduring development.

What matters in the question 'hexagon or heptagon' is not whether the ecology problems are objectively important today or are becoming more acute, nor whether they are being correctly perceived. What matters, with regard to the civilisatory hexagon, is solely the question whether the ecology problems can, in the given hexagonal framework, be politically handled or whether, because of inappropriate treatment, they are creating a problem pressure that is apt to delegitimise the hexagonal arrangement of a civilised conflict treatment and letting it break up. If the latter were the case, then the hexagon would have to be extended into a heptagon for systematic reasons. If the latter is not the case, then it would make just as much sense to replace the ecology problems by, for instance, the foreseeable transport congestion problem. In other words, it would be analytically unjustified to proceed in such a way because our argument would miss the issue of the constituent conditions for a civilised treatment of any publicly relevant conflict. The objective, or subjectively perceived, significance of a specific range of problems for politics is one thing; the significance of the same problem for the constituent conditions for civilised treatment of it, or of any other politically relevant problem is something entirely different. This fundamental distinction results equally from historical experience and from the logic of the hexagon. A 'political framework assessment' today suggests that, with regard to the fundamental conditions for the civilised treatment of conflicts, the ecology problem does not (or not yet) occupy a position comparable to that of the social question, so that, while displaying a well-meaning attitude to ecology politics, it would be an analytical mistake to enlarge the hexagon into a heptagon.

The systematic problems were thematised here by the ecology problem, as an illustration, because the hexagon is usually criticised in this specific respect as being in need of enlargement. But any other range of political problems should be viewed similarly: transport policy no differently from the generation conflict, the 'ageing society' and its consequences no differently from the problem of multiculturalism, etc.

Conclusion: the hexagon is urgently in need of enlargement if it has to be enlarged for systematic reasons to ensure civilised conflict handling in all specific spheres of politics. For analytical and practical reasons it is not open to just any problem assignments or corresponding enlargements of components.

5. *Can the 'civilisatory hexagon' be unambiguously characterised in terms of scientific logic?*

The question seems obvious if one considers the complexity of the 'civilisatory hexagon'. Seen historically, the hexagon reconstructs a building process. In the West European context (later in the OECD world) one building block, metaphorically, followed upon another. However, the feedback mechanisms, viewed from the provisional final result, also offer a reproduction perspective. The question is then: how do the emergent building blocks support each other in the sense of positive feedback? Another question, however, is: what critical signals are built into these feedbacks, triggering timely learning, amendment and adjustment processes (negative feedback)? The only consistent thing in this context is the collapse perspective that the hexagon, spelled out negatively, provides. We are faced therefore, in scientific-logical terms, with a historical-genetic paradigm that, the more pronounced it is, not through the individual factors and building blocks, the more it is characterised by its configuration, in the strict sense by structural causality, because the overall construct, over time, is redundantly caused through multiple feedback processes.

Nothing therefore prevents us from using the 'civilisatory hexagon' in totally distinct ways: heuristically or with empirical study (historically, genetically, structurally, comparatively) or also praxeologically (normatively). Its methodological attraction is due to just that multiplicity, which cannot be reduced to a single dimension (e.g. 'normatively'). The civilisatory hexagon makes it possible to turn the light on real-history processes – with a comparative approach as the royal road of analysis. Why has Scandinavia developed differently, with regard to the civilisatory hexagon, from the Iberian peninsula? Why did, albeit predictably and predicted, the real-socialist countries collapse? What is happening in a country like China, which in political respects is constituted like a real socialist country, while at the same time, though not covering the entire area, it is experiencing a fulminant socio-economic modernisation process? Why are hexagonal societies successfully developing in East Asia ('emerging hexagon'), while in South America once promising 'emerging industrialising countries' (for instance Argentina) have failed, since the 1920s, to cross the threshold to durable hexagonality? What happens in societies like the black African ones, in which important features of the hexagon were not yet pronounced and where meanwhile, in many places, even the first building block, the power monopoly (never yet reliably ring-fenced by the rule of law), collapses? What constructive work would have to be performed in failed states in order to render an initially civilised conflict settlement more or less possible again in the public area? Another question is: how does hexagonality become marked in a political multi-level system such as the EU, and is such hexagonality relevant on the world plane?

This is not to say that the civilisatory hexagon is a key to everything. But, as the ongoing discussion and the analytical application to specific cases have shown, it does open up prospects that have proved fruitful.

6. Is the 'civilisatory hexagon' a contribution to civilisation theory or to civilising theory?

The answer can be outlined as follows. From the beginning the 'civilisatory hexagon' was conceived as a contribution to peace theory. Unlike its broadly diversified medieval claim ('ordo') the centre of hexagonal theory is held not by reflection on the 'good society' as such, nor on the 'good international society', but by the question: How and through what does peace constitute itself – peace being understood as the constructive non-violent treatment of unavoidable collective conflicts in the relevant public sphere, which today is mostly characterised by broadly effective politicisation. The reflection on civilising (the process of civilisation) is therefore a much more modest enterprise than that on 'good civilisation'. That there can be, and indeed must be, transitions between the two is a matter of course because 'good civilisation' today cannot be imagined without civilising the modern conflict. The question, however, whether any dimension of such a civilisation becomes a requirement, or indeed an indispensable prerequisite, of the civilising of the modern social conflict, needs to be clarified before it is simply postulated.

2. Conclusion

Thinking in categories of the civilisatory hexagon has a number of analytical advantages in view of the fundamental politicisation in discussions of the prerequisites and conditions of civilised conflict handling: the framework of successful or unsuccessful civilised conflict management is logically analysed as a multidimensional construct on the basis of an empirical study. The differentiations thematised in this process – six components and their feedbacks – make it possible to identify variable paths of development and forms on the basis of historically comparative findings. A comparative analysis, more than anything else, emphasises the need for configurative consideration. From a practical point of view, too, thinking in categories of the civilisatory hexagon is instructive with regard to hexagon variations: optimisations become equally imaginable as threatening regressions that call for repulse. The analytically broken-down construct inspires measures with regard to its 'overall architecture' as well as localised interventions. The prospect of medium and long-term success of short-term measures of conflict management can only be assessed if, in the specific instance, they are linked by feedback with situation evaluations in the light of findings arrived at with the civilisatory hexagon.

As the fundamental politicisation of the world progresses, it would be advisable to keep civilised conflict management conceptually at the level of the political virulence resulting from such politicisation: civilised conflict management must be equal and live up to the complex bundle of problems to be mastered. That is the real context within which the civilisatory hexagon finds its analytical status.

Part II

SUPPLEMENTS

Chapter 5

FIRST SUPPLEMENT

Peace – a Multiple Complex Programme for Durably Successful Community Creation

The creation of political communities is a process requiring a great number of preconditions, especially in modern, i.e. socially mobile and thoroughly politicised societies, where, not only in the political class but on a mass basis, all essential social disputes present themselves as political and all political conflicts present themselves as social. Such societies split by interests and identities – the result of developments over centuries – are apt to give rise not only to conflicts but also to violence. That is why, in present-day conditions, the emergence of durable self-regulatory political communities is a remarkable civilisatory achievement. One might define this achievement as peaceful coexistence despite fundamental politicisation.[1]

This state of affairs points to historical, topical and future problems; it is equally relevant at a low level (region), at a medium level (state/nation) and at a higher level (Europe/other macroregions/world). The same question poses itself at all levels: what are the premises of successful political community creation? Assuming the peaceful attainment of successful community creation, this question could also be formulated as: what are the constitutive conditions of lasting peace?

These questions are of immediate topical relevance; they are also politically virulent. They can refer equally to disintegrating societies and to societies that wish to create communities with others, i.e. to integrate. Thus it applies equally to disintegration and to integration processes.

Disintegration testifies to the erosion of an evidently not viable community; often also, as in the case of nationalistically secessionist movements, a search for a new community; integration processes reveal that the spatial range of previous community creation is being exceeded. These processes, which in one direction or the other can today be observed in many parts of the world, are based on circumstances that can be examined by well-tested analytical instruments.[2] These are to be discussed constructively with regard to integration; the signs of the argument, however, could – as will be shown at the end – be easily reversed, in which case disintegration would be the analytical point of reference.

The question therefore is: what does scholarship say about successful community-creating processes or about the conditions of durable peace?

The state of affairs is complex, which rules out simple answers. It is therefore useful to recall those lines of argument that, as a tendency, reflected the complexity of the analysis. What is needed therefore is not a monocausal or mono-thematic argumentation, but a differentiated or configurative line of argument: hence complex thinking and complex conclusions on complex states of affairs. In terms of practical politics, what is needed is complex programmes about the emergence of a political community capable of peace no matter at which level.

Set out below are four such complex programmes based equally on scholarly analysis of experience and on peace-theory reflections. The first complex programme outlines the characteristics of a structure, or architecture, of durable peace – a structure in which the extent of integrating community creation is still small, but peace prevails. In the second complex programme the preconditions of intensive community creation (and thus actual integration processes) are set out. Both programmes, as a rule, refer to frontier-transcending processes of community creation between already existing communities (such as states). Their preconditions within the frontiers, i.e. among the decisive actors at low or medium level, are reflected in the third complex programme. The fourth complex programme may be understood as a kind of synthesising guidance perspective.

For illustration reference will be made chiefly to Europe – Western Europe and Europe as a whole. However, the following observations are transferable in respect of the levels to which they can refer, both downward (region) and upward (other continents/the world). They have been tested against historical material and, moreover, are not without the temptation of prognostic forecasts.

1. Complex Programme I:
Elements of a Peace Structure

'Zones of stable peace', as Kenneth Boulding called a structure of reliably durable peace between autonomously operating groupings or states,[3] are, according to the first complex programme, characterised by at least five structural features:[4]

1. Positive interdependence: Relations between the collective actors (today still mostly states) must reach an order of magnitude of high reciprocal relevance in the crucial dimensions of economy, communication and contacts in order that a potentially confrontational attitude of one actor would result not only, as intended, in damage to the other side, but also in considerable self-damage.

   To ensure that such a positively interdependent structure is durable a second characteristic is necessary:

2. Approximating symmetry: Interdependences are very diversely located: they can be symmetrical, asymmetrical, confrontational and otherwise. For a structure of durable peace symmetrical interdependence is of crucial importance, especially in an economic respect. In this area it is not difficult to make it operational: if both sides have comparable competences and opportunities of value creation in the production and marketing of know-how and merchandise and, above all, if goods of high value creation are exchanged on both sides, i.e. in the presence of substitutive division of labour, symmetry exists. The exact opposite would be a colonial exchange structure as a result of complementary division of labour, such as exists in an extreme form in the exchange of capital-intensive and know-how-intensive goods against raw materials and/or goods of a low degree of processing.

   Positive interdependence with symmetrical signs suggests a further characteristic of a peace structure:

3. Homology. More than a hundred years ago Lorenz von Stein acutely formulated this state of affairs as follows:

   > Only when, along with the acknowledgement of itself as an independent power, the acknowledgement and validity of its own laws of life has truly taken place also *within* the other parts of the system of states can genuine peace emerge. Only then is the condition of universal peace, the total similarity of the general social and political conditions, really present.[5]

From this point of view the situation in Europe prior to 1989/90 was the very opposite – a situation of incompatibility of general political and social conditions. Homology therefore means comparable political, social or economic structures that are significant mainly in a pragmatic respect. For in conditions of comparable structures everyone finds on the other side – in the other state, in the other society, in the other economy – its comparable counterpart. This tends greatly to facilitate flexible relationships. The significance of such comparable structures for a peace policy can be realised in retrospect – *ex negativo* – by recalling the situation in Europe before 1989/90, when entrepreneurs, trade unionists, scientists, sportsmen, etc., of the West had to deal with party and state functionaries on the other side, the East, and variegated non-manipulated and beneficial relations, especially at the civic level, were not achieved.

The characteristic of homology suggests a further, in some respects related, category:

4. Entropy. What does this mean? Again we may go back to an old observation. In 1667 Samuel Pufendorf in his treatise *De statu imperii Germanici* interpreted the Holy Roman Empire of the German nation as an 'irregulare aliquod corpus et monstro simile', as a structure characterised by a lack of hierarchy and centralisation, by, as we would say today, clear-cut subsidiarity, by all kinds of overlapping competences, by a lack of institutional synchronisation, in short by 'muddle' and hence a need of the political skill of mutual arrangement.[6] In the political-institutional reality this was an anticipation of the entropy idea, which today is of considerable importance in reflections on a viable peace structure. Entropy is understood here as multiple criss-cross references (the opposite of *Gleichschaltung*, of alignment) in frontier-transcending dealings, as free choice of partners, as a substantial measure of self-regulation without centralist, hierarchically graduated, patterns, as a network structure[7] – as the very opposite of a rigid bipolar system-antagonistic deterrence constellation like that before 1989/90, which, throughout forty years, was incomparably 'tidy'.

Of course such a loose structure is always apt to tip over into chaos – which is why some authors since the 1990s have spoken of the danger of a 'nouveau moyen âge' (A. Minc). But peace theoreticians have thought through also this possible consequence and provided for, or empirically proved, the existence of a fifth characteristic of a structure of durable peace:

5. Common institutions, i.e. an institutional form which – although the theoreticians' ideas are rather cautious and pussyfooting – would act upon overall happenings in a directing, regulating and controlling manner, with the result that the danger of chaos has no real virulence and that, as provided for in the theories of international regimes,[8] an institutional reinsurance exists for expectation reliability and hence

expectation stability. On the interaction plane such institutions are fences around any potentially threatening or actually existing counterproductive group dynamics ('security dilemma').

In all configurative thinking and in every practical complex programme the listed characteristics, though enumerated sequentially, must of course be thought of configuratively as present together. Where they evolve and eventually are present, positive feedback comes about. They reinforce each other reciprocally – in which case the security dilemma disappears. And the so-called development dilemma, resulting in an interlocking world from the development gradient or the competence gradient between individual economies, would be levelled down or largely overcome.[9]

What then, looking at examples and illustrations, is the reality in Europe regarding this complex programme? The Europe of the fifteen (EU), as well as the Europe of the European Economic Community (EEC = EU plus rest-European Free Trade Association, EFTA), largely meets the criteria mentioned. These parts of Europe are characterised by high interdependence, by symmetric-substitutive division of labour, by homologous internal structures, by institutionally cushioned entropically structured relations and by the existence of common institutions. With regard to the whole of Europe the situation concerning some criteria and their sum total is still somewhat problematical. The west of the continent is far more important for the life of the east than the other way round. The division of labour between west and east continues to be complementary and only in exceptional cases (such as relations with the Czech Republic) is it at the very beginning of being substitutive, and then only in segments; homologous social structures are only in a nascent state in the East (the ongoing debate on the 'civil society' lacking there is an indication). Entropy in the above sense does not therefore exist as yet; such common institutions as do exist (e.g. the OSCE) often still suffer from weakness of competence and, especially, efficiency.

Whereas the situation in Europe as a whole seems, with regard to the above-mentioned five characteristics, capable of positive development over the coming decades (see the ongoing process of step-by-step enlargement of the EU), the starting situation in many parts of the rest of the world is far more problematical because none of the required characteristics is present there as yet in clear outline, with the result that an appropriate peace-favouring structure-creating process is lacking. It is possible though that East and South-East Asia will prove an exception because the networking of their economies and the symmetrisation of their trade structures – for which the necessary domestic-economy competences either exist or are being rapidly developed – are beginning to emerge.

2. Complex Programme II:
Peace as a Collective Learning
Process of Community Creation

A second complex theoretical approach by scholars endeavours to work out analytically the preconditions of more far-reaching community-creation processes. This approach is the result of historical comparative studies of the processes of political community creation, i.e. studies of unification efforts (integration, association, community-building), as well as of processes that could, if the promoting factors flip over and become explosive, lead to disintegration, collapse, dissociation and community decay).[10] Hard findings and softer insights point to ten substantive issues with regard to supportive conditions for frontier-transcending community-creation processes.

1. Compatibility of essential values. Conditions with regard to Europe as a whole can be viewed, in model terms, as follows. The slogan 'Return to Europe', as heard before and after 1989/90 by influential agents of radical change (V. Havel and others), revealed a political will to orient their own political and social systems along the accomplishments of the constitutional democracies of the West. Simultaneously, national-chauvinist and ethnically radical endeavours were pointing in the opposite direction. Which way Europe will develop will essentially depend on which option the societies in the eastern half will adopt. As gradations are to be expected (eastern central Europe will very probably follow the Havel option; as for really eastern and south-eastern Europe one cannot be sure), the future Europe will be graduated, in a system-political respect, from west to east. This gradation is now obvious in the EU's step-by-step enlargement towards the east.

2. Extension of frontier-transcending communication and transaction processes that become important for both sides. This situation was described as positive symmetrical interdependence in complex programme I above. With regard to eastern Europe this means specifically: Will eastern Europe repeat the 'East Asian road' of the past 40 years, i.e. choose a development beginning with relatively simple economic and merchandise structures and go, step by step, through an 'upgrading' all the way to capital-intensive and technology-intensive production, or will Western Europe (the EU of fifteen) be the centre and eastern Europe its quasi-colonial periphery? If in eastern Europe (certainly in eastern central Europe rather than in eastern Europe beyond eastern central Europe) a 'peripheralisation' can be avoided, then there would be a chance of its gradual integration in the club of highly industrialised West European societies and economies. If this

happened, the fact that eastern Europe would become a real, highly qualified competitor to western Europe, would, in the long run, lead to increased integration rather than to disintegration.

Not the quantity of exchange, but its qualitative 'upgrading' would be of significance in that case. But since 'upgrading' equals a prolonged process of reduction of asymmetry, a further point is of importance during the period of transition:

3. 'Responsiveness', i.e. the openness of stronger partners to the concerns of others, especially their readiness to concern themselves with the needs of the weaker ones. 'Responsiveness' is the opposite of power, competence, economic and cultural arrogance and of the insensitivities characterising them. Experience, however, teaches that 'responsiveness' as a political attitude arises more readily if economic substance is found on the part of those who have to act sensitively. For this reason a fourth condition is of major importance for a community-building process:

4. Accentuated growth and expectation of mutual advantages. The facts are banal: if the cake gets bigger, more can be shared out, more transfer performances can be executed. This makes it easier for the pack donkey to assume such a role, especially if the beneficiaries of the transfer performances become 'useful' in a foreseeable time. i.e. if the unilateral transfer performances are gradually replaced by structures of mutual advantage ('joint rewards'), so that the roles of the pack donkey on the one hand and of the beneficiary on the other are not permanently fixed. More economic substance also means more opportunities of problem solving. And this is the fifth point.

5. Increased ability to resolve problems. Such ability, of course, is not only based on economic conditions, but is of importance in all relevant political areas. The perspective of this point is immediately obvious. If coalescing political communities prove capable of jointly resolving problems jointly perceived, new loyalties arise to those institutions of problem solving that become reliable agencies of coordinated political action. Where incapability is found, as is still the case at the OSCE level regarding peaceful settlement of conflicts and collective security, both old and new institutions lose respect, giving rise – if an historical example may be quoted – to the 'Abyssinia syndrome', when fascist Italy in the 1930s demonstrated the League of Nations to be a powerless body, just as the former Yugoslavia, i.e. Serbia, did vis-à-vis the CSCE/OSCE, the EU, NATO and the United Nations in the final decade of the twentieth century.

The crucial importance of this point will also become obvious in the European Union. If, for instance, it failed to have any success in checking the growing structural unemployment, opposing the frontier-transcending economic criminality, controlling migration, containing terrorism and managing other similarly grave problems in its catchment area, the European integration process would lose the support that it is still more or less enjoying today.

6. Core areas with draught-horse function. Wherever a number of collective players intend to (or should) move towards a common denominator in perception and behaviour, experience teaches that there is a need of certain action poles with strong radiation. Theoretical discussion, in this context, speaks of 'core areas', political discussion speaks of 'core Europe' as a driving force of the community-building process.

   There is a need therefore for political leadership because without such leadership drifting may occur. Needless to say, such political leadership, assumed by a single agent, or by a few for a time, contains the danger of resistance-provoking hegemonic centre formation, or the development of an oligopolitical power concern. For that reason a further factor has, in historical experience, proved of importance:

7. Role rotation. In a major community it is important that the same player does not always take on the same role, that there is a change of roles, that the individual players or political units play in groups – at one time in the majority situation, another in a minority situation without being subject to, or following, rigidly assigned roles: in other words, a rotation of roles. Such role change brings flexibility into an emerging political community; it creates a political manoeuvring mass for the bargaining processes indispensable in the political area. Similar experience applies also to the eighth point:

8. Enlargement of the elites in the sense of a chance for upward mobility. Obviously an emerging political community has to create fresh spaces for cooptation, spaces into which the new and young elites can grow, just as frontier-transcending mobility by the citizens is important for the cohesion of such a structure. In place of encapsulation and restriction there should be opening and eventual upward mobility into the new greater social body. This enhances life opportunities and creates new loyalties at a new level. This also leads to a ninth point:

9. Chances of a new/alternative lifestyle. This becomes the daily experience of a newly forming political community. The new environment (e.g. Europe) becomes a self-evident setting for socialisation processes. In consequence there is a marked difference between being part of such an emergent community and standing outside it. The demand frequently heard in the eastern half of Europe

since 1989/90 not to be cut off from developments at the all-European level, to participate in them, to get into their stream and thereby to share in their desirable accomplishments, suggested and still suggests that living inside or outside the European integration process makes a considerable difference to the life of the individual. Such a perception, which translates into a sense of belonging, is, at the affective and emotional level, a kind of litmus test of community building.

10. Predictability of motivations and behaviour (expectation stability). One of the chronic problems of state anarchy is uncertainty and insecurity concerning the behaviour of the other side, which, for its part, has the same problem. The security dilemma is therefore regarded as a core syndrome of state anarchy. Expectation stability or expectation reliability is the result of the contrast programme to state anarchy, namely, political community building. This does not mean that there would be no clashes of interest or other conflicts in such an environment. They are indeed present, but they do not translate into potentially autistic escalatory conflict dynamics. This makes a fundamental difference, especially with regard to the violence-proneness of conflicts; this is in practice eliminated as a result of successful community building. In which case we would, in the above-mentioned sense, find 'stable or durable peace' as a structure of a kind of its own.

Complex programme II – a constructive peace policy programme – thus resembles a broad-spectrum collective learning process with normative, institutional, material and emotional dimensions of such community building. The ten points formulated above show how many preconditions such a constructive process has.[11]

The preceding exposition, however, has failed to address one core problem. The ten-point programme presupposes action-capable players in the sense of states or societies. This precondition applies even when the community building is to be limited, i.e. when the result of the community-building process is not going to be, in Karl Deutsch's terms, an amalgamated integrated new political entity (the way the U.S.A. developed from the British colonies in North America), but only a limited confederative or 'pluralist security community'[12] or some structure in between. Historical comparison has shown that such a community, limited in scope, can be attained if at least three of the above-listed ten factors are jointly present – compatibility of fundamental values, predictability of motivation and behaviour, as well as ability to allow for the concerns of the partners ('responsiveness'). But even in this limited case, which will be the most common by far for community creation at the international level, more or less consolidated political players are necessary. In conditions of weak leadership and ungovernability even limited programmes, such as a confederatively oriented 'pluralist security community', are improbable.

Ability to act by the collective players concerned was therefore, in the above exposition, an unspoken condition of successful frontier-transcending community-building processes. This premise, however, is questionable in view of a fundamental politicisation observed not only in some parts of Europe but worldwide, a politicisation that – as set out above – consists in the fact that all essential societal conflicts present themselves as political ones, and all political ones as societal; socially mobile societies become politicised with regard to interests, identities, and also passions, so that the inner coexistence potential is accentuated and, often enough, the problem of ungovernability arises.

In the western part of Europe the above problems, viewed from an all-European or even worldwide perspective, are only mildly acute; in the rest of Europe and in many parts of the extra-European world, they are often of dramatic virulence. For this reason we have to refer to a third theoretical proposition of scholarship.

3. Complex Programme III:
the Civilisation of Conflict Management

This third complex programme concerns, above all, the consolidation of societies with regard to their internal political system, which – viewed worldwide – often enough faces collapse today, or just about survives, or is in a (new) construction process. The situation in many ways resembles the system-political problems in north-western Europe in the early phase of the modern period. The task is to find an internal peace formula with the help of which the 'Hobbesian situation', i.e. a chronic political state in which civil wars threaten or erupt, can be overcome. Admittedly the difference from the beginning of the modern age is that the Hobbesian solution, i.e. the Leviathan pure and simple, is no longer viable today. Admittedly, the Hobbesian formula, the compact power monopoly embodied in the 'Leviathan', is still a partial answer, though only one of six, one that, moreover, is being qualitatively rearranged within the six reciprocally intertwined answers. These six answers, the 'civilisatory hexagon', represent the third complex programme; this was set out in detail in the main chapter of this book (Chapter 2) and is here only briefly outlined:

1. Without a monopoly of power no civilising of public conflicts, i.e. no reliable non-violent management is possible. At the same time, however:
2. Without rule-of-law control of the monopoly of power the monopoly of power itself is not tolerable. It is only from the combination of power monopoly and rule-of-law control that the rule-of-law state, perceived

as legitimate, the quintessence of all rules for the management of publicly relevant conflicts, arises.

3. Useful for the consolidation of potentially conflict- and violence-prone societies is the evolvement of a division-of-labour-differentiated social body, especially of an appropriately labour-division economy that helps produce the 'homo sociologicus', i.e. a multiple role player bound into differentiated interdependence structures and capable of survival only with considerable affect control.
4. The transformation of traditional societies into socially mobile ones represents a major restructuring process resulting in the emergence of new social strata, classes and lifestyles with differentiated specific interests and identities. This emancipation process makes democratisation steps, or democratisation, irrefutable in the medium and long term; with a time delay also:
5. The tackling of social equity, the more so as in societies modernising themselves the natural result of a competitive economy is inequality rather than equality.
6. If all goes well, such developments give rise to a political culture of conflict management that is reflected in appropriate in-depth links – 'ligatures'.

This so-called 'civilisatory hexagon' is, in socially mobile societies, formulated in abbreviated form, a complex programme for internal peace: 'rendre la paix interne perpétuelle' – a project that, in the western half of Europe, began, if not before, with the struggle for Magna Carta (1215). In this western Europe the complex programme passed through a centuries-long developmental phase and still it achieved only preliminary results or intermediate steps: even in later phases the hexagon remained prone to erosion and collapse, moreover beginning from all its six components. One gains the impression that, even in the western part of Europe, this structure acquired stability only after 1950; at any rate it seems to be less threatened by collapse than in the preceding decades. However, this impression may be deceptive if, in future, important components were to break off, for instance as a result of globalisation with respect to failures of serious endeavours for social justice.

It is often argued that this complex programme, shaped and steeped in a western mould, cannot be successfully transferred even to the neighbouring eastern half of Europe or that, even if it were transferable, there is not enough time for it. This statement about eastern Europe, however, is refuted by the most recent East Asian experience: especially in the East Asian threshold countries of Korea and Taiwan we see that a dictatorial monopoly of power in combination with a developing efficient economy provokes inescapable democratisation processes that, in turn, lead – through violent political conflicts – to the emergence of the rule of law and hence to a domestication of the power monopoly. Moreover, shortage in the labour markets and democratisation make fairness of distribution a political issue of the first order. And successful development compels even Confucian conflict-avoiding cultures towards the evolution of a modern political culture in which conflicts are seen as unavoidable, in which they are openly fought and managed in a constitutionally fixed institutional framework.

Although the East Asian experience need not be repeated in the eastern half of Europe or anywhere else, the fundamental argument that the West European experience is not transferable is being refuted, especially with regard to societal, political and also cultural transformation processes (and not only, as is obvious by now, with regard to economic change).

4. Complex Programme IV: Synthesising Guiding Perspective with Praxeological Implications

In the thirteenth chapter of the *Leviathan* (1651) Thomas Hobbes wrote: 'The nature of war consisteth not in actual fighting, but in the known disposition thereto, during all the time there is no assurance to the contrary. All other time is PEACE.' Peace to Thomas Hobbes (as centuries later for Kenneth Boulding) therefore meant that the institution of war has been abolished and that a war-facilitating or war-inclined structure has been replaced by a peace structure, in which even the 'disposition to fight' has been reliably eliminated. Peace therefore reigns when irrefutable conflicts, institutionally made safe and hence durably managed without the threat, let alone the use, of organised military force, are managed in a reliably non-violent manner. In the international system, therefore, peace is a totally different state from a state that knows the threat of force, or even its use. Peace, understood here as a process model of non-war, institutionalised in the international system, has at least six preconditions in the fourth core programme to be discussed below, a programme that within itself subsumes the core aspects of the above-quoted three complex programmes:[13]

1. Elimination of anarchy in the international system through cooperation of states in system-wide international organisations.
2. Equalisation of the power figure through greater fairness of distribution of societal chances of development and enhancement.
3. Democratisation of the systems of governance to ensure that society's demands enter unfalsified into the decisions of the political system and can there be translated.
4. It is necessary for interest groups to be made transparent and for their access to the foreign-policy decision process to be controlled.

5. Facilities for controlling complex interactions of regional or global scope have to be improved (global governance, creation of international regimes); representatives of civil society have to participate in the modern forms of government.
6. The strategic competence of the players has to be improved, their training has to be modernised and professionalised.

This complex guiding perspective combines experience and consequential imperatives at the international (interstate and inter-societal) level with the experiences and imperatives resulting with regard to the new constitutional character (order) of states and societies.

5. Outlook

The complex programmes listed represent, as otherwise theoretically unthinkable, ideas about the optimum. Nothing, however, can prevent us, in the light of the experience-based and theoretically definable optimum, from also reflecting on the practically realisable sufficient minimum. Yet scholarship should not, from praxeological points of view, content itself too readily with the minimum: the optimum in the conception of a peace programme leading to durable political community-building can be understood as a regulatory idea with a practice-relevant perspective. Or, as Kant formulated it in his *Rechtslehre*: 'We must act in a way as if the thing, that perhaps is not, is.'

Nor can anything stop us from reversing these constructive perspectives into a reflection of disintegration and decay processes: all one has to do is rehearse the quoted complex programmes negatively point for point in order to grasp the decisive factors that cause decay and loss of the political community. Developments such as in former Yugoslavia after 1990, as well as elsewhere, then become more or less comprehensible. Moreover, the much quoted thesis of the non-transparency of the world situation then loses plausibility.

Villages become 'landscapes', landscapes become regions. regions become countries, countries become states and states become frontier-transcending political communities of various degree of integration – all these are, with regard to the establishment of internal and international peace, entirely transparent processes. They are a mixture of cognitive, material, institutional, emotional and also constitution-political dimensions. Successful political community building, reflected in reliably non-violent constructive conflict management, being the result of a collective learning process, invariably remains an artificial civilisatory product and therefore fragile and in danger of collapse. This civilisatory achievement should be protected and looked after. The fact that such constructs, being political communities based on so many preconditions, do in fact often collapse is, in the light of the above exposition, hardly surprising. However, the causes of their jeopardy are known – and so are the points at which constructive countermeasures should be aimed.

Notes

1. Striking explanatory attempts can be found in Dieter Senghaas (ed.), *Den Frieden denken. Si vis pacem, para pacem*, Frankfurt/M. 1995.
2. See Richard Merritt and Bruce Russert (eds), *From National Development to Global Community* (Festschrift for Karl W. Deutsch), London 1981.
3. Kenneth Boulding, *Stable Peace*, Austin 1978.
4. The following categories have been taken from a peace-theory debate on Europe in the early 1970s. See Johan Galtung (ed.), *Co-operation in Europe*, New York 1970, Chapter 2, in which the categories are outlined ('A Theory of Peaceful Co-operation'), pp. 9–21. See also idem, 'Europa – bipolar, bizentrisch oder kooperativ?', in Johan Galtung and Dieter Senghaas (eds), *Kann Europe abrüsten?*, Munich 1973, pp. 9–61, as well as idem, *The True Worlds. A Transnational Perspective*, New York 1980.
5. Christian Count Krockow, in his book *Soziologie des Friedens*, Gütersloh 1962, has formulated appropriate reflections in connection with Lorenz von Stein (Part II, Chapter 5).
6. Samuel Pufendorf, *Die Verfassung des Deutschen Reiches (1667)*, Stuttgart 1976. Linking up with Pufendorf is Tilman Evers, 'Supranationale Staatlichkeit am Beispiel der Europäischen Union. Civitas civitatum oder Monstrum?' *Leviathan*, vol. 22, no.1, 1994, pp. 115–134.
7. See Johan Galtung, *Entropy and the General Theory of Peace. Essays in Peace Research*, vol. 1, Copenhagen 1975, pp. 47–75.
8. See, for a summary, Michael Zürn, 'Vom Nutzen internationaler Regime für eine Friedensordnung', in: Dieter Senghaas (ed.), *Frieden machen*, Frankfurt/M. 1997, pp. 465–481.
9. On this and other dilemmas see Dieter Senghaas, *Wohin driftet die Welt? Über die Zukunft friedlicher Koexistenz*, Frankfurt/M. 1994, pp. 121 ff., as well as Chapters 7 and 9 of the present book.
10. The classic study of this direction of argument is Karl W. Deutsch et al., *Political Community and the North Atlantic Area. International Organization in the Light of Historical Experience*, Princeton 1957. Building upon this, see Michael Zielinski, *Friedensursachen. Genese und konstituierende Bedingungen von Friedensgemeinschaften am Beispiel der Bundesrepublik Deutschland und der Entwicklung ihrer Beziehungen zu den U.S.A., Frankreich und den Niederlanden*, Baden-Baden 1995; Emanuel Adler and Michael Barnett (eds), *Security Communities*, Cambridge 1998.
11. With regard to Europe I proposed a suitably detailed plan after the historic transformation of 1989/90. See Dieter Senghaas, *Friedensprojekt Europa*, Frankfurt/M. 1992. The book justifies in detail a peace plan for Europe as a whole, which I conceived directly during the historic turn of 1989/90, *Europa 2000. Ein Friedensplan*, Frankfurt/M. 2000.

12. This concept was introduced in the 1950s by Karl W. Deutsch and has become current since (see note 10). A summarising exposition is found in Karl W. Deutsch, 'Frieden und die Problematik politischer Gemainschaftsbildung auf internationaler Ebene', in Senghaas (ed.), *Den Frieden denken*, pp. 363–382.

13. See Ernst-Otto Czempiel, *Friedensstrategien*, Opladen 1998, esp. Chapter 1. The list quoted is found in idem, 'Der Friedensbegriff der Friedensforschung', in Benjamin Ziemann (ed.), *Perspektiven der Historischen Friedensforschung*, Essen 2002, pp. 43–56.

Chapter 6

SECOND SUPPLEMENT

Peace Zones – No Chimera

'Peace zones' is the name given in the present-day international system to those areas or reference models and action patterns in which 'stable peace' reigns. Stable peace, according to Kenneth Boulding who created the concept, is a situation in which the probability of a war is so slight that it no longer plays a part in the considerations of political decision makers or nations.[1] Stable peace therefore exists wherever existing conflicts of interests are brought to a regulation or resolution in a non-violent manner, i.e. without the classical instruments of extreme power politics, hence without the threat or use of military force. This state of affairs is also described as a reliably constructive, i.e. durably civilised, conflict management.[2]

Stable peace in the sense of the above definition – reliable absence of even the expectation of war and, of course, of war itself – is found today mainly in the so-called OECD world. This means the democratic market-economy Western industrial countries with high revenue that represent the centre of gravity of the present-day world economy. Although the OECD world can be described as one peace zone, it is based on clearly identifiable and by no means identically structured components, which is why the concept in the plural, peace zones, makes sense. These zones today include the North American continent (U.S.A.-Canada), that part of Europe which, even during the past decades, already consisted of West-oriented industrialised countries, i.e. the EU sphere, lately including the countries embraced through 'extension towards the east'; the 'transatlantic community' built upon its two pillars, the North American countries on the one hand and the EU members on the other. Stable peace exists also in relations between Australia and New Zealand, between Japan and these two Oceanian countries and finally, of especial importance, between North America and Japan. Despite geographical distance mention should also be made of relations between the EU and Japan – an extremely loose OECD component – since, in the past, distance was no obstacle among the main actors in international politics to the expectation of war, preparations for war or actual wars.

In these roughly thirty countries of the OECD world there live more than 900 million people, or about one-seventh of mankind. Viewed from the world overall, this is quite clearly a privileged minority, mainly because an ancient institution of humanity, war, has been abolished in the mutual relations of the participating nations. What developments have contributed to this?

1. The Origin of the OECD World

The OECD world and its components only developed as a peace zone, or as peace zones, after the Second World War. As with every historical process that crystallises into a new structure there were several favourable factors:

The first factor was the East–West conflict (1947–1989/92). This characterised the dominant political conflict constellation of the post-war period,[3] which came to an end with the collapse of the Communist regimes in eastern Europe and in the Soviet Union. While Communist regimes (until 1959 including China) were forming the originally more or less monolithic eastern components of this conflict, the intensification of this conflict also contributed to a resultant self-organization of the West: this based its political, ideological and military security on the principle of collective defence, reflected on the military plane in the transatlantic institution of NATO.

This process in the early phase of the East–West conflict has many parallels in practical life and is fairly familiar to general conflict theory: in escalating conflict relations the inclusion/exclusion mechanism intensifies in response to actual conflict attitudes or to an exaggerated perception of conflict, resulting in the formation of conflict parties which, as the outcome of conflict escalation, ultimately exhibit a greater degree of cohesion than at the beginning of the conflict.

While between East and West an aggravated security dilemma without parallel in history developed, a security dilemma reflected in a bipolar deterrence constellation, with a reciprocal threat of annihilation,[4] the security dilemma practically vanished within the Western world. Although there were persistent conflicts among the Western states about the specific modalities of security policy, chiefly about the possibility of credible nuclear and/or conventional deterrence and about burden sharing, these intra-Western conflicts were always governed by the restrictive conditions of the superior East–West conflict constellation.[5] They remained without political virulence.

Hence the East–West conflict has undoubtedly had a structure-creating effect also within its Western component. The security policy of the participating states was, in the individual case, more or less aligned towards a common platform, appropriate institutions were developed for concerting security-political actions, as well as a joint military infrastructure. Although formally still a domain of national policy, security policy in political practice became a community task without having been truly turned into a community matter. Community building that would mean more than mere intergovernmental cooperation is envisaged only in the context of the further evolution of the European Union.

A retrospective examination of this state of affairs is important because it was not infrequently argued that with the end of the East–West conflict the West would lose some of its security-policy cohesion and that the joint security-policy institutions (especially NATO) would therefore be in danger of crumbling, with the final result of renationalisation of security policy. In plain language such an assumption amounts to this thesis: the collapse of the East–West conflict will, in the long run, lead to sharper outlines of conflicting interests,[6] wherefore – it is often concluded – it is thinkable that, also in intra-Western relations, military power potential might once more gain in importance. This forecast is based on a reverse argument: external pressure enhances internal cohesion, less external pressure means less inner cohesion, no external pressure results in the break-up of cohesion.[7] The forty-year-long transatlantic structure-building processes have – at least until now – worked against that logic. Whether the clear political power gradient between the U.S.A. and the EU and the resulting differences in world-political interests will tend to dissolve the more or less existing political cohesion across the Atlantic is a question without – so far – an unambiguous answer (Iraq crisis 2002/3). But it remains unlikely that a political quarrel would lead to a militarily virulent situation.

A second factor that helped the formation of the OECD world is the towering economic position of the U.S.A. during the first two or three decades after the end of the Second World War.[8] At that time the U.S.A. had the greatest, most productive and internationally most competitive economy in the world. Only such an economy is able to assume the role of a lead economy and to develop and stabilise a global economy in its own interest. In this endeavour a free-trade orientation is the most obvious lead perspective of such an *économie dominante* with a hegemonic creation privilege.

To be able to operate as a reliable motor and stabiliser a dominant economy must pursue a policy that, while aiming at its own interests, nevertheless promises potential advantages to other parallel economies.

Thus it will temporarily have to assume the role of growth engine, for instance by having its imports stimulate a growth of exports in other, subordinate, economies; it will also transfer public means and, later, make direct investments outside its frontiers in order to provide in other countries the capital necessary for infrastructure and economic growth. This includes also the transfer of technology and the spreading of know-how, for instance knowledge of modern management of economies and firms. The need is, therefore, for a benevolent lead economy, which, out of its own interest, contributes to the development of an extending economic area and provides the material and institutional framework conditions required for this.

This took place in the post-war world mainly as a result of a world trade regime (GATT), aimed at free trade and progressively becoming a free-trade system, as well as of the world currency regime of Breton Woods. The former, which has since been succeeded by the World Trade Organisation (WTO), contributed to the liberalisation of world trade, while the latter contributed to the currency stabilisation of international economic relations.

The U.S.A. as the lead economy, the above-mentioned international regimes as the institutional framework and a historically unparalleled economic growth that triggered a further wide-range modernisation thrust, outside the U.S.A., chiefly in Western Europe and Japan (i.e. in countries fairly industrialised even before the Second World War), thus considerably contributed to the evolution of the OECD world. Just as in respect of the first-named factor, the East–West conflict, there was also, regarding the economic emergence of the OECD world, an intensive debate on whether the end of the U.S.A.'s global economic hegemony, the outlines of which became discernible since the early 1970s, must also lead to the end of the liberal global economic OECD structure. What is the durability of the OECD world 'after hegemony', i.e. after the end of the U.S.A.'s hegemony position in the world's economy?[9] Those who once formulated a sceptical answer, forecasting the collapse of the liberal international regime permeated and buttressed by the lead economy, have, despite all crisis-prone developments in the world's economy since the 1980s, been proved wrong.[10]

A third contributory factor in the development of the OECD world in its western European component was the political will, demonstrated in Western Europe in the immediate post-war period, to convert this historically chronic zone of war into a stable zone of peace. This was again promoted by the East–West conflict, but the European idea and the will to create peace were stronger. The painful lessons of not only the First but especially the Second World War should provide lessons with irreversible institutional consequences: what was envisaged was a Europe that would no longer relapse into disastrous warlike disputes, i.e. a 'united Europe' (whatever was meant by this term in detail). From the original 'peace project Western Europe' there developed, in the shape of the EEC, a long-term economy-based enterprise whose ultimate political finality under the present label of the EU continues to be unclear.[11] Yet also with regard to this 'project' the anxious question was often asked after 1989/90 whether the forces of cohesion would continue to be stronger than the tendencies towards disintegration. In this respect, too, the fears of aggravated renationalisation, i.e. a regression to a nationalistically determined policy, have proved exaggerated.

2. Structure-creating Consequences

The three above-listed starting constellations were of importance for the evolution of the OECD world. They moulded major political processes, such as the integration of Western Europe, transatlantic bridge-building and the American–Japanese security community including their gradually increasingly important economic dimension – processes that in turn had long-term new structural consequences. These need to be considered if one wishes to assess the durability of the OECD world as peace zone(s). The observations that are, for their part, significant for the characterisation of the OECD world as a structurally founded peace zone stand in the foreground of these reflections:

The first observation can be summed up as follows: the OECD world has become a world of democracies. This distinguishes it emphatically from the world of highly industrialised, though not yet fully or in-breadth modernised, countries of the 1920s and 1930s, which then was entirely heterogeneous in terms of political system. Today the OECD is marked by (in spite of all differences in detail) a common political order, the democratic constitutional state, with such essential components as rule of law, separation of powers, democratic pluralism and parliamentarianism. Historical experience teaches, in general and with regard to post-war development in particular, that the democratic constitutional state and an efficient economy that leaves space for distribution are closely linked. Only under such conditions can a stable political culture of constructive conflict management be expected in socially mobile politicised societies. Jointly present and mutually reinforcing each other, these components of a modern political order are the basis of internal peace. This state of affairs was, earlier in this book, illustrated with the concept of the 'civilisatory hexagon'.[12]

Democratic constitutional states of this type are moreover presumed, with regard to peace policy, to be peace-loving structures also in their foreign relations, at least among each other. Although the general theoretical controversy about this subject continues,[13] a second observation is undisputed: in the OECD world the reciprocal institutional networking has contributed to the evolution of what Kant called a 'peace alliance' (*foedus pacificum*) and Karl Deutsch a 'pluralist security community'. Among these states the so-called 'security dilemma' has been largely eliminated as a result of persistent concentration and coordination of policy. In consequence military power disappeared as a factor of strategic policy in the mutual relations within the OECD world, even though it can continue to be of isolated importance (especially in respect of the status of some countries as nuclear powers – a matter whose significance, however, is now only of an imagined symbolical value).

Such networks are today particularly dense in the area of the European Union. Across the Atlantic relations institutionalised by NATO are still relevant, though of clearly diminishing weight.[14] On the plane of the OECD world a certain measure of continuing foreign-trade coordination has been institutionalised by means of global economic summits, especially by their preparation and follow-up. In the OECD world, therefore, though graduated in detail in its components and with varying density, an in-breadth institutional interdependence has arisen.[15] It characterises the organisational superstructure, which, however – differently from the rest of the world and also from the history of the industrialised countries before the Second World War – rests upon an appropriate economic infrastructure.

This is what the third observation refers to: networking is not only institutional, but also material and economic; it is of considerable extent and of a specific quality (this last point is being largely ignored in theoretical and practical reflections). As is well known, some 75 per cent of the global gross domestic product arises within the OECD world. With a 70 per cent share of global trade about 50 per cent of global trade takes place between OECD countries themselves. If we take as a reference not the world but the OECD world (= 100 per cent), then intra-OECD trade amounts to about 75 per cent of the total OECD trade. The OECD countries invest predominantly in other OECD countries and technology transfer therefore takes place mainly among themselves. The OECD world is therefore characterised by a high degree of economic and geographical self-reference.

Moreover – and this is a special, so far neglected, quality of the exchange – trade within the OECD is chiefly an intra-industrial or substitutional exchange. Exchanges are mainly of comparable high-value finished goods, with the result that in large parts of the OECD world there is a symmetrical interdependence of economic exchange conditions. This presupposes mature market economies, i.e. economies with a tendency to display competitive ability in all important fields. This specifically qualified profile can be measured with economic aggregates: 5:30:65. This means that 5 per cent of the OECD populations in work produce in the agricultural sector 5 per cent of the gross domestic product (with a clearly declining trend); the same process is found in the industrial sector (30 per cent, clearly declining trend) and in the services sector (65 per cent, trend clearly rising). Variations in individual cases amount to only a few percentage points, with the secular development (*longue durée*) aiming at an average of 2:23:75. There exists therefore a considerable degree of homogeneity and coherence of the economies,[16] the so-called OECD profile. In consequence of that profile we encounter the at first seemingly paradoxical phenomenon of economies, capable, against the background of such a parallel highly qualified economic structure, of a replacement competition embracing all fields, of in fact mutually permeating one another to an incomparable degree and, by way of this replacement competition, achieving a high degree of economic interdependence on a symmetrical basis.

Only this qualitatively high-level symmetrical (= substitutively oriented) replacement competition is, in its nature, peace-favouring because, unlike a competition on the basis of asymmetrical complementary division of labour, it most probably does not trigger an in-breadth marginalisation pressure, but instead in-breadth durable innovation stimuli. Resulting from these is competition 'with a level playing field', which might be described as symmetrical replacement competition. The danger that this type of replacement competition in the global economy might lead to some kind of peripheralisation or marginalisation is exceedingly slight. First of all, it exists only in specific branches or sub-branches of an economy and not on a broad front. Secondly, the forces of self-assertion through innovation in production processes and products usually work against such localised danger (even if present in several sub-branches) so that there is no threat of an in-breadth in-depth comprehensive regression. Economies with an OECD profile continually rotate around the profit-oriented presentation of innovation and it is this (on a broad basis observed) state of affairs that makes them immune, if not always in the short run (two to five years), then in the medium and long term, to any disastrous substitution competition with the consequence of regression (loss of branches without ensuing compensation within challenged or even within entirely new branches). This state of affairs (and only this) permits efficient OECD economies to be free-trade open economies. Hence not any kind of exchange, but only this specific type, in which, faced with symmetrical replacement competition, old or new influential economic actors have to prove themselves continually, and are in fact doing so successfully, is peace-supporting.[17]

The above state of affairs – substitutive division of labour – is well advanced for the past three decades in the European economic area (EU/rest–EFTA), as well as in transatlantic relations. Admittedly there are chronic deficits in quantity and quality in American–Japanese exchange trade and in European–Japanese relations; these have resulted in considerable trade balance deficits for the U.S.A. and Europe, and more particularly in serious branch-specific consequences (motor car and electronic industries) of a, for a time, extremely successful replacement competition between Japan and the old industrialised countries.[18]

Regardless of these temporary deficits and consequences a specific profile of the political economy of the OECD world can be confirmed. Production and trade take place in a frontier-transcending area that – on a global comparison – is characterised by secure rule of law, by good infrastructure and training (human capital), by high productivity and readiness for innovation in all categories and by high-demand internal markets, in turn the result of the above-mentioned conditions and resulting relatively high remuneration.

In the OECD world as a whole, and especially in its European component, the original structure impulses – all of them expressly developed from the framework conditions of the East–West conflict and from the global economic hegemony of the U.S.A. – have since given rise to independent structures with their own weight: system-political profiles of the democratic constitutional state in combination with efficient economies, which do not exist quasi-nomadically side by side with one another, but are closely networked with each other politically, economically and increasingly also on the social plane ('transnationalisation'). This state of affairs was characterised once by Ernst-Otto Czempiel with two new, but now current, concepts: by way of complement to the still significant, but by no means exclusive, relations among states, the 'state world', he argued, there now exists in this segment of the international system a 'societal world' based on parties, associations, social movements and other groupings, as well as an 'economic world' shaped by multinational firms.[19] One might add that the North American, European and transatlantic peace zones are also linked by a common cultural horizon ('cultural world'). Whether or not this will, as the result of further modernisation steps, extend also to the East and South-East Asian components has been, and continues to be, a controversial question.

3. General Structural Characteristics

It is interesting that the development of the OECD world, especially in its North American, European and transatlantic components, is largely in line with the peace-theory criteria formulated in the more recent discussion regarding the existence of a structure of durable peace. According to these reflections, briefly listed here again,[20] such a structure or architecture is marked by five specific features:

1. Positive interdependence. Relations between the collective actors must, in the essential dimensions of economy, communication and contacts, reach an order of magnitude of high mutual relevance so that a potentially confrontational attitude of one side does not only lead to damage to the other side but also to considerable self-damage. There should therefore be symbiotic relations. Just these conditions are easy enough to prove in large parts of the OECD world.

2. Approximating symmetry: Interdependences are, generally speaking, very diverse: they can be symmetrical, asymmetrical, confrontational, etc. For a structure of durable peace a symmetrical interdependence is of crucial importance, especially in the economic respect. There it is also easily made operational: if both sides have at their disposal equally high and innovation-supporting competences in the production and marketing of commodities and in know-how, and if qualitatively comparable commodities are exchanged, i.e. substitutive division of labour exists, then there is symmetry. The direct opposite of this would be a colonial exchange culture, as for instance in the case of capital-intensive and know-how-intensive goods being exchanged for raw materials. Substitutive or intra-industrial division of labour has meanwhile become a general feature of exchange processes in the EU and across the Atlantic. In American–Japanese and in European–Japanese relations, however, there still exist qualitative asymmetries in this respect, which, as is known, give rise to long-term foreign-trade and diplomatic conflicts (admittedly of slight vehemence) which are settled bilaterally or within the framework of the World Trade Organisation (WTO).

3. Homology. Relations are facilitated by comparable structures among all exchange partners. As a result of such structures everyone finds a partner on the opposite side – the entrepreneur an entrepreneur, the trade unionist a trade unionist, the independent artist other independent artists, the party member other like-minded partners, etc. The evolution of open pluralist societies – the result of various modernisation thrusts in the OECD world over the past fifty years – played a major part in enabling such liberal relationships to develop across frontiers between actors in comparable structures ('transnationalisation', 'societal world', 'economic world').

4. Entropy. A peace structure should be marked by a multiplicity of criss-cross relationships, i.e. by the opposite of *Gleichschaltung*; moreover by a free choice of partners in frontier-transcending dealings, as well as by a considerable measure of self-regulation of decentralised or privately acting agents. Such a construct is, if one wants to put it this way, the direct opposite of the bipolar system-antagonistic deterrence constellation familiar from the post-war order, a constellation that was characterised by 'order', i.e. hierarchical and centralised patterns and by *Gleichschaltung* from the top downwards. Entropy in this context

therefore means that in a peace structure there must be a certain degree of 'disorder': subsidiarity instead of predetermined scopes of action, a certain overlapping of responsibilities, a lack of institutional synchronisation and comparable phenomena rendering flexibility possible – all of these can play a useful part. In such conditions there is a large measure of self-control; problem situations are more easily cushioned than in conditions of rigid hierarchical relations. Maybe, to quote an example, the scepticism of an overcentralised 'Brussels' reflects an instinctive understanding that, under modern conditions, non-hierarchical political systems with permanent local roots, i.e. network systems and systems presented under the private–public partnership label, are, even on the superstate level, more viable and efficient than overcentralised systems out of touch with life.

5. Joint institutions. These are understood as an institutional roof from which, in line with theory, overall events are, mutedly rather than brashly, being influenced in a regulatory and directing manner; this prepares the way for problem solutions and counteracts the danger of chaos.

Proceeding from these five characteristics of a peace structure, the OECD world – disregarding the American–Japanese and the European–Japanese components – continues to present itself as a structure or architecture in a reasonably favourable light. Momentary political turbulences should not disguise this fact. Likewise from the perspective of the theory of a pluralist security community, as formulated by Karl W. Deutsch decades ago, the state of development of the OECD world is rather encouraging.[21] In this theory three factors were named as the result of historical comparative research as a basis for the development of durable peaceful relationships: compatibility of fundamental values, predictability of motivations and attitudes (calculability) and ability to address the concerns of partners ('responsiveness'). Once more, these criteria seem to have been largely met in the European and transatlantic context.[22] though not in American–Japanese or the European–Japanese relations. Both these relationships exhibit deficits that might lead to chronic stresses. Anyway, enlargement opportunities will have to be weighed up, with regard to the OECD world, against dangers of collapse.

4. Enlargement Opportunities and Dangers of Collapse

Enlargement opportunities with regard to the OECD world exist at present in parts of the eastern half of Europe, as well as in east Asia.

The revolution in eastern central Europe after 1989/90 was characterised by the system-political slogan of 'Return to Europe'. This means that the political revolution was to lead to integration in the Europe of the democratic rule-of-law state and the market-economy system. This declaration of intent met an important criterion for accession to the OECD world (agreement on fundamental values). However, this did not yet guarantee the translation of this intention into reliable political and economic structures on the spot. The developmental road necessary for this is beset by considerable problems, chiefly the 'dilemma of simultaneity', i.e. the double task of, on the one hand, newly, perhaps for the first time, institutionalising the democratic constitutional state and, on the other, simultaneously accomplishing an economic reconstruction in the direction of the market[23] – both in conditions of politicised societies as well as a considerable productivity and competence gradient between the OECD world and the integration-desiring revolutionary societies.

East Asia has the advantage over eastern central Europe that the evolution of the rule of law and democracy is becoming a more or less inevitable consequence of a previous, exceedingly successful economic modernisation process, which, however, took place under dictatorial conditions. For that reason the dilemma of simultaneity does not exist there: an efficient, i.e. globally competitive, economy that opens up the domestic market with in-depth efficiency already exists; democratisation is overdue and follows. In both cases, eastern central Europe and east Asia, democratisation has its opportunity (oddly enough perhaps faster and more reliably in East Asia than in the eastern half of Europe). As a result of this process, as indeed also in the event of a corresponding economic success of eastern Europe, the number of those states and economies that, at least in their mutual relations, act like 'trading states' would increase. These, as is known, are aligned towards commercially motivated compromises; they pursue a political management of economic interdependence with the object of using multilateral arrangements to attain profit opportunities; consistently selfish and nationalist behaviour tends to be the exception. Needless to say, power politics can be observed also among trading states. But this remains fenced in by the fact that the interests of trading states have always largely been symbiotically interwoven interests.[24]

The open question, of long-term importance, regarding such a prospect of self-enlargement of the OECD world is whether powerful states of the old type, like Russia in the eastern half of Europe and China in East Asia, will join such a development emerging in their immediate neighbourhood or not.

These prospects, however, are also faced by dangers of collapse. These arise mainly from the partial weaknesses and limited problematic conditions of the OECD world. As for the weaknesses of the OECD world, the American–Japanese and the European–Japanese economic relations, a future aggravation of the competitive situation[25] and the resulting larger trade deficits (further magnified by continuing uneven investment opportunities) might increase the political conflict-proneness of the relevant relations and lead to one kind or another of – put in exaggerated form – 'economic warfare'. In the U.S.A. and Japan such a conflict has been termed a 'geo-economic conflict', but without any military component having been predicted as yet.[26] It is highly probable that this danger has always been dramatically exaggerated as the Japanese economy in the final decade of the past century lost its formerly astonishing vitality and got into a permanent crisis. Different developments in competitiveness could make even previously symmetrical relations, such as those in the EU and in the transatlantic area, begin to appear problematical if an asymmetrical replacement competition were to arise. In that case upwardly mobile economies would, as the strength of their economic position might suggest, remain oriented towards free-trade and multilateral positions, while downwardly mobile economies would tend to become protectionist. At the least, economic interdependence management would be more difficult under such conditions. That, of course, would also happen if there were another collapse of the global economy, caused perhaps by financial speculation. Although concerted action would then be more necessary than ever, there might well be a collapse of common regulations (regimes) and of the necessary interdependence management.

A growing economic cake facilitates, as is known, the evolution and the self-stabilisation of democratic constitutional states. If the scope of share-out shrinks as a result of economic crises and the loss of competitive positions, there might easily arise a legitimacy crisis of the democratic system, especially if the social issue were again to become more virulent. In individual cases, where the democratic culture is not deeply rooted, such a process could even jeopardise the constitutional state.

Dangers therefore exist even in the OECD world, both from outside and from within. These dangers of collapse must be opposed by a solid global interdependence management. In the event of problems in the club of the OECD world concerted joint action would be the premise of successful assistance. Without such interdependence management there is a danger that economically threatened states might drift away in foreign-trade policy and perhaps in system policy. If this happened in several places, then the cohesion, until now useful to all participants, could no longer be ensured.[27]

In other words, today the OECD world is a peace zone or a composite of peace zones, but it is not ultra-stable, i.e. it is not unshakeable or protected against regression under all external and internal conditions. Yet it also has the opportunity of self-enlargement.[28] This opportunity, however, can be utilised only if other parts of the world, today mainly the eastern half of Europe, are given the trade opportunities needed to promote increases in performance ('upgrading') beyond one's own frontiers. If one is prepared to do this, then structural change within the OECD must also be promoted. Otherwise the zero-sum logic applies, when the one gains what the other loses. Circumspect handling of this problem affects not only the economic future of the OECD world, but also the future of democracy.[29] The twenty-first century will be concerned not just with 'OECD peace', i.e. with peace in one's own neighbourhood, but with a global peace system in the full sense of this concept, that is real worldwide peace.[30]

Ever since the beginning of the early modern age the peace plans of European philosophers and political advisers – for example the Abbé de St. Pierre – have been aimed at the establishment of regional zones of stable peace. Every one of these plans was met at the time by the objection of this being a utopian chimera, a fantasy. Such a reaction is found in scholarship and in the political public to this day.[31] History, however, has meanwhile shown that just such regional peace zones are no chimeras: they are realisable under specific conditions and they exist in reality: peace is therefore achievable.[32]

Naturally enough, the suggestion that they attempt to achieve the impossible still applies to plans for global peace. The realisation of such plans globally in the real world admittedly encounters a great many difficulties. But now that there exist regional peace zones in the real world and now that their conditions of existence have been identified by experience-based scholarship and hence made transparent, the traditional objection, relating to the world as a whole, is no longer as convincing as it used to be in the centuries when many a plan for regional peace was found inspiring but remained without results in Realpolitik. In view of the problems diagnosed in this book this may be no more than slight consolation – but neither is the situation totally hopeless.

Notes

1. Stable peace is therefore a system status with a tendency towards self-stabilisation. See Kenneth Boulding, *Stable Peace*, Austin 1978; Ernst-Otto Czempiel, *Friedensstrategien*, Opladen 1998; Dieter Senghaas (ed.), *Den Frieden denken*, Frankfurt/M. 1995.
2. See Chapter 2 of the present book.
3. See fundamentally Werner Link, *Der Ost-West-Konflikt*, Stuttgart 1980; Dieter Senghaas, *Konfliktformationen im internationalen System*, Frankfurt/M. 1988, chapters II and III.
4. See Dieter Senghaas, *Abschreckung und Frieden. Studien zur Kritik organisierter Friedlosigkeit*, Frankfurt/M. 1981, 3rd edn..
5. See Dieter Senghaas, *Die Zukunft Europas*, Frankfurt/M. 1986, Chapter 4.
6. Cautiously formulated assumptions on these lines are found in Hans-Peter Schwarz, *Die Zentralmacht Europas. Deutschlands Rückkehr auf die Weltbühne*, Berlin 1994.
7. An early forecast along these lines, by now to be called classic, is found in John J. Mearsheimer, 'Back to the Future. Instability in Europe after the Cold War', *International Security*, vol. 15, no. 1, 1990, pp. 5–56.
8. See Senghaas, *Konfliktformationen*, Chapter V.
9. See Robert O. Keohane, *After Hegemony. Cooperation and Discord in the World Political Economy*, Princeton 1984. See also Dieter Senghaas, 'Die ungleichen Partner der Triade. U.S.A. – Japan – Deutschland', *Blätter für deutsche und internationale Politik*, no. 9, 1993,

pp. 1080–1085, as well as now especially Ralf Rudolf, *Europa, Amerika und Asien zwischen Globalisierung und Regionalisierung*, Paderborn 2001.

10. A detailed analysis of this is in Stefan Robel, 'Hegemonie in den internationalen Beziehungen. Lehren aus dem Scheitern der 'Theorie hegemonialer Stabilität', *Dresdner Arbeitspapiere. Internationale Beziehungen*, no. 2, Dresden 2001.

11. Still fundamentally on this see Heinrich Schneider, *Rückblick für die Zukunft. Konzeptionelle Weichenstellung für die europäische Einigung*, Bonn 1986.

12. See Chapter 2 of the present book.

13. See comprehensively and fundamentally Harald Müller, 'Antinomien des demokratischen Friedens', *Politische Vierteljahresschrift*, vol. 43, no. 1, 2002, pp. 46–81.

14. See Thomas Risse-Kappen, *Cooperation among Democracies*, Princeton 1995.

15. See Reinhard Rode, *Weltregieren durch internationale Wirtschaftsorganisationen*, Halle 2001, as well as, on the peace-theory foundation of this state of affairs, Wade L. Huntley, 'Kant's Third Image. Systemic Sources of Liberal Peace', *International Studies Quarterly*, vol. 40, no. 1, 1996, pp. 45–76.

16. On the categories of homogeneity and congruence see Ulrich Menzel and Dieter Senghaas, *Europas Entwicklung und die Dritte Welt. Eine Bestandsaufnahme*, Frankfurt/M. 1986, Chapter 6.

17. The state of affairs described cannot be overemphasised since it remained totally disregarded in the extensive debate on so-called 'democratic peace'. This is true even for a complex or configuratively argued study such as that by Bruce Russett and John Oneal, *Triangulating Peace. Democracy, Interdependence, and International Organization*, New York 2001. Even in this excellent study there is no qualification of economic exchange (interdependence) and therefore no qualification concerning peace-beneficial and peace-non-beneficial interdependence. The reason for this disregard of the state of affairs described is the total absence of expertise in systematic-historical developmental research in the debate on 'democratic peace'.

18. See Senghaas, 'Die ungleichen Partner der Triade'.

19. Ernst-Otto Czempiel, *Weltpolitik im Umbruch*, Munich 1993, 2nd edn. As for the heuristic consequences for the analysis of political processes of an internationalising policy, these are explained by Czempiel in *Internationale Politik*, Paderborn 1981.

20. See Chapter 5 of the present book.

21. Ibid.

22. For the West-European region see the detailed study by Michael Zielinski, *Friedensursachen. Genese und konstituierende Bedingugen von Friedensgemeinschaften am Beispiel der Bundesrepublik Deutschland und der Entwicklung ihrer Beziehungen zu den U.S.A., Frankreich und den Niederlanden*, Baden-Baden 1991. See also idem, 'Gesamteuropa als Friedensgemeinschaft', *Die Friedenswarte*, vol. 75, 2000, pp. 309–330.

23. See Claus Offe, *Der Tunnel am Ende des Lichts. Erkundungen der politischen Transformationen im Neuen Osten*, Frankfurt/M. 1994.

24. See Richard Rosecrance, *Der Handelsstaat*, Frankfurt/M. 1987.

25. This means, precisely, if asymmetrical displacement competition deepens and its opposing forces are no longer strong enough to achieve a symmetrisation of the displacement competition.

26. An example of this debate is Edward N. Luttwak, *Weltwirtschaftskrieg. Export als Waffe – aus Partnern werden Gegner*, Reinbek b. Hamburg 1994. On the specific American–Japanese problems see Hartmut Hummel, *Der neue Westen. Der Handelskonflikt zwichen den U.S.A. und Japan und die Integration der westlichen Gemeinschaft*, Münster 1999.

27. See Reinhard Rode, *Weltregieren*.

28. See Max Singer and Aaron Wildavsky, *The Real World Order. Zones of Peace/Zones of Turmoil*, Chatham 1993.

29. On this, fundamentally, now Ernst-Otto Czempiel, *Kluge Macht. Außenpolitik für das 21. Jahrhundert*, Munich 1999.

30. On this, fundamentally, Volker Bornschier, 'Zivilisierung der Weltgesellschaft trotz Hegemonie der Marktgesellschaft', in Dieter Senghaas (ed.), *Frieden machen*, Frankfurt/M. 1997, pp. 421–443.

31. Illuminating in this context is Wolfgang Burgdorf, *Chimäre Europa. Anti-europäische Diskurse in Deutschland (1648–1999)*, Bochum 1999, esp. Chapter 4.

32. See Senghaas (ed.), *Frieden machen*.

Part III

APPENDICES

Chapter 7

STRUCTURE-CONDITIONED DILEMMAS OF THE WORLD AND CONCLUSIONS FOR PEACE POLICY

If today's world is viewed from peace-policy angles, what central structural aspects need to be considered in an analysis and what practical implications result from such a situation assessment? Answers to these questions are to be outlined below.

1. Structural Conditions

1.1. Security Dilemma

The security dilemma has long been a familiar state of affairs for the analyst of international politics. Wherever territorially organised entities such as empires, states or differently structured political communities coexist without any superordinate political authority, there exists an 'anarchical' basic constellation marked by a considerable measure of uncertainty concerning the intentions and actions of all the others. If, moreover, in such a situation of non-existent mutual expectation–reliability the interests of the participants are incompatible, such uncertainty is actualised. Each entity, especially in the event of aggravated conflicts of interest, feels confined by the opposite side in its own freedom of action, or in the extreme case in its existence, and each believes that, in the absence of a superior conflict-mediating authority, it has to rely on its own strength, or ultimately on its own military potential. The efforts for existential self-assertion arising from such a situation then translate themselves into consequential defence strategies, though quite often into offensively interpreted assertion strategies and often enough into a mixture of the two, by which time the defensive and offensive components of such self-assertion strategies are frequently difficult to tell apart.

Since, as a rule, it is not just one side that thus tries to resolve the structure-conditioned security dilemma to its own advantage, but all participants proceed from the same logic, i.e. action on the basis of self-help, an aggravation of the dilemma results: appropriate measures, especially armament steps, outbid one another and translate themselves in an arms race that, in the extreme event, is driven forward by a self-releasing armament dynamics. However, that situation cannot always be correctly described as an 'arms race' since quite often one side's own dynamics are considerably superior for there not to be a race in the strict sense of the term.[1]

Most analyses of international politics would expect a skilful military power management as the usual resolution of the security dilemma. As, however, even the most sophisticated power management may founder, warlike conflicts cannot be ruled out from international politics. The security dilemma is therefore rightly credited with a potentially violence-prone character.

Alongside the mobilisation of one's own military strength there are other attempts of dealing with the security dilemma, such as alliances and balance of power systems, as well as imperial power deployment or order-creating hegemony structures. Collective security and, before it, modalities of peaceful conflict settlement are further possibilities of coping with the security dilemma. Confederative or integrational security communities actually serve the attempt to cushion, or overcome, the security dilemma reliably. Regional and international organisations are often seen as intermediate steps on the way to the 'elimination' of at least the virulence of the dilemma. Neutrality, non-alignment or non-participation in pacts or alliances were (and probably will still be in future) options for withdrawing from the dilemma.[2]

The security dilemma as a structural state of affairs is old, even older than the modern territorial state with which this dilemma is usually associated in thought. And in spite of many developments, which – as will be shown later – have led in the world to new and additional structural conditions, the security dilemma on the international scene has remained a fundamental fact to this day. Only in a few parts of the world has it been more or less reliably overcome ('peace zones'),[3] while in other parts it continues to be of great virulence. One need only compare the situation in Western Europe with, for instance, that in South Asia (there with particular reference to a truly classical security-dilemma situation, such as exists between India and Pakistan, including a nuclear component in an arms race on both sides). While in certain regions a previously virulent security dilemma seems, to some extent, to have been eliminated (for instance between Brazil and Argentina, where there were also the beginnings of a nuclear arms race) and while elsewhere there have been tentative but so far unsuccessful attempts along those lines (chiefly in the Middle East), there is a danger of potential dilemma situations (in the neighbourhood of North Korea and of China/Taiwan, as well as in the area of the transcaucasian and Asian republics), which could turn virulent at any moment. Some such situations seem to be chronic and insuperable without becoming really virulent (such as relations between Greece and Turkey – the Cyprus issue – where interestingly enough both countries are members of a joint military defence alliance, NATO).[4]

Alongside the classical interstate starting situation the security dilemma has experienced a kind of renaissance in the intra-state sphere – especially where states are collapsing and civil-war parties are clashing with more or less developed military formations and fighting against one another. In such situations all the problems of the classic security dilemma emerge: the lack of reliable expectation due to insecurity and uncertainty, anxiety of survival – as a rule much more acute in civil-war situations than in war situations – fear of identity loss, either as a result of cultural alienation or of enforced assimilation, or as a result of an extermination policy through ethnic cleansing.[5]

'Hobbesian situations' therefore exist not only, as discussed in the theory of international politics, in the interstate sphere but, as first thematised by Thomas Hobbes in the middle of the seventeenth century, renewed and multiplied also in civil-war situations, which fundamentally question the internal peace of political entities. This two-sided security dilemma should therefore be included in the first structural condition of the world as it presents itself today. Its traditional international dimensions could also be circumscribed by the ideologically or pragmatically stripped concept of geopolitics. This would apply chiefly to those geopolitical macroconstellations in which, in the absence of alternatives, no other means are available, or have evolved, for cushioning the security dilemma than the usual (military) power potentials (in this context these would include, for example, relations between China and India, between China and Japan, and indeed also between China and the U.S.A.).

1.2. Development Dilemma

The development dilemma arises in a relatively open global economy between societies and economies that practise trade exchange and between whom there exists a wide gap concerning know-how and organisational capabilities, as well as between technological and organisational innovations. A less productive economy is then confronted with a more productive economy. Between them a competence gradient develops. The consequence of such a competence gradient is a persistent structurally caused replacement competition between a lead economy and a catch-up economy.

Societies exposed to such a competence gradient are easily marginalised: they are subject to a peripheralisation pressure, i.e. there is a danger that in the global economy and hence in the international division of labour they are peripheralised or even marginalised. This *structural* problem has been virulent since at least the middle of the eighteenth century; it is discussed under the heading of 'catch-up development'. The core question is whether, despite the existence of a competence gradient between peak economies and lower-level economic areas, a catch-up development can come about.[6] If catch-up development actually takes place, an upward mobility arises; the development dilemma is de-dramatised. The lead economy is caught up with or even surpassed. In the latter event the replacement competition is then directed from the successful catcher-up against the former leader. This leader is then threatened by downward mobility and hence also by loss of status within the hierarchy of the international system in which states are assigned their status mainly according to their position in the international division of labour.

As a structural condition in the world, the development dilemma is of more recent date than the security dilemma. Today's observed upward mobilities and threatening downward mobilities have, as structural conditions, a prehistory of no more than 250 years. Contrary to suggestions by the development-policy discussion, the modern development dilemma is virulent at all levels of the world, not only between the so-called industrially developed countries (OECD) on the one side and the developing countries (what used to be the Second and Third, or even the Fourth, World) on the other, but also within these categories of countries – above all within the OECD world. Examining the development dilemma globally means therefore registering the state of affairs in the OECD world and, next, between the OECD world as the core of the global economy on the one hand and the developing countries on the other, and eventually also within the world of the developing countries, where upwardly mobile development situations (today East and South-East Asia) and downwardly mobile development situations (e.g. in large parts of Africa) exist.

The conflict potentials resulting from upward and downward mobility are nowadays, if they concern processes within the OECD club, often described as geoeconomic problems. This concept implies that upward or downward mobility leads to specific regional structures defined by international division of labour and its resultant competitive situations. That which takes place at the peak of the hierarchy of international division of labour (e.g. in the triad U.S.A.–Japan–EU) is repeated at lower levels. Ultimately no sphere in the world remains untouched by threatening or virulent replacement competition, especially if, as a result of the freed mobility of economic factors (goods, capital, technology, labour), global interdependences, which are mostly asymmetrically located, increase.

The conflict aspect of the development dilemma, however, shows marked differences according to whether the global economy is in a boom or decline phase. In boom phases new development opportunities open to catchers-up, especially if they attach themselves to peak economies as global-economy engines. But even then a catch-up economy is successful only under specific conditions. In global recession phases we find as a rule that protectionism prevails, directed at the maintenance of traditional production potentials, even though these are mostly not competitive in the long term. The present-day world is not conceivable without its continuous development dilemma since all its (largely asymmetrically interdependent) parts are subject to continual social change and, even in future, global homogeneity is far less probable than increased heterogeneity. A more far-reaching question for an analysis of the world, however, is whether the development dilemma will become the background of virulent security-policy dilemmas. In other words, can, or will, conflicting economic competition situations become charged in a security-policy sense, so that (at least at the top of the global hierarchy) geoeconomic problems also become geopolitical ones?[7] Or has the development dilemma – unlike, 100 years ago, the so-called 'inter-imperialist conflicts and rivalries' – meanwhile become immune to such a security-policy takeover, so that we can proceed not only from a terminological, but from a durably substantive differentiation between geo-economy and geopolitics?

1.3. Social Mobilisation as a Result of Politicisation

The precondition of the development dilemma is simultaneous unequal development processes, which are, in turn, the consequence of a varying degree of transformation from traditional to modernising, or modern, societies. This transformation consists of the evolution of subsistence economies for national economies, which give rise to an enormous broadening of people's horizon and scope of action; it further consists of an urbanisation leap with the result that most people in areas of denser communication become capable of organisation and aware of their interests; and, thirdly, it consists of a drive towards literacy, promoting the intellectual emancipation of major parts of the population. From the above transformation processes result enhancement of political co-determination as a consequence of prolonged chequered political conflicts stemming from the above socio-economic and cultural transformation processes.[8]

This process – starting in north-western Europe, i.e. on what was once the geographical 'periphery of world history' – has meanwhile become worldwide. It is still layered: it is most advanced in the OECD world and now also in East Asia; it is advancing in the rest of the world at dramatic transformation rates (especially in urbanisation). The demands of a growing number of people with regard to the political, social, economic and cultural order they regard as desirable are consistently increasing. The above transformation process is the objective basis of the politicisation of societies observed worldwide.

These demands will in all probability become even more diverse in the future than they are already or than they were in the past. Conflict-proneness in the world will therefore tend to increase further and with it the danger of conflict-proneness sliding into violence-proneness and into actual use of violence. It should therefore be remembered that social mobilisation, leading inescapably to politicisation, aggravates coexistence problems, which initially concern the internal order of societies. The fundamental question arising is faced with the fundamental politicisation of societies, according to which all social problems are political problems and all political problems are social ones, how does one avoid civil war?

The answers to the coexistence requirements found in that part of the world where social mobility first began are of an exceedingly complex nature. They were earlier, at least in respect of the history of Western Europe, described as the 'civilisatory hexagon', i.e. as the joint action of monopoly of power, rule of law, interdependences resulting in affect control, democratic participation, fairness of distribution and a political culture of constructive conflict management as the result of a collective learning process.[9] In some parts of East Asia we can today speak of comparable catch-up processes ('emerging hexagon'), while in other parts of the globe the transformation processes are continuing, although the constitutional, institutional, material and emotional safety nets, which would make coexistence possible, very often tend to collapse where they existed in a nascent form or are only laboriously, if at all, building up.

The internal and external attitudes of societies are today emphatically moulded by politicisable and politicised societies. Remote, oligarchically elitist politics, aloof from societal forces and groupings, is becoming increasingly dysfunctional: in the OECD societies it is no longer found; in the former Second World (real-socialism) it has been swept away by revolutionary upheavals; in extensive parts of the rest of the world, where it still exists (e.g. Saudi Arabia) it is untenable in the medium to long term, in spite of strong political repression. This state of affairs inevitably also affects the security dilemma and the development dilemma, which, in such circumstances, not only represent structural conditions between societies, but, being politicised conflict situations, are virulent within societies and are correspondingly politically instrumentalised. That has far-reaching detrimental consequences for the practice of a focused and systematic policy, domestically as well as towards the outside. Proceeding from this starting position, such a policy often has the rug pulled out from under it.

1.4. Globalisation

The transformation of traditional societies into self-modernising or modern societies is not a phenomenon identifiable only within individual societies. If this were the case there would be no development dilemma. The impact of briskly advancing societies characterised by higher productivity in the agricultural, industrial and services sectors upon lagging societies is a phenomenon observed at least since the agricultural–industrial revolution in England in the eighteenth century. It operated initially from England to continental Europe and North America, then from these three regions to the rest of the world – either through the so-called 'informal empire' or through colonialism, imperialism and neocolonialism. Thus the relationship systems of the world were internationalised, transnationalised and globalised. Over the past three decades, if not before, the process has become a truly global fundamental state of affairs, which is treated under the cue of 'global transformation'.[10]

The concepts of internationalisation, transnationalisation and globalisation mean processes of varying scale and varying scope on the international plane. The conditions referred to are no longer to be missed: growing interdependences not only at the inter-state level ('state world'), but above all also between societal agents ('societal world'), between transnationally and multinationally operating firms ('economic world') and between the world's cultural areas ('cultural world').[11]

Globalisation or internationalisation is found mainly in the world's economy, recently in particular with substantial growth in the service sector (insurance, advertising, tourism), as well as in the areas of information, communication and transport. But there are also internationalising problem situations, for instance in the area of a security policy no longer definable as being a national-state policy or in the framework of military alliances (proliferation of weapons of mass destruction, WMD, and related delivery technologies). Altogether, higher and more rapid mobility of frontier-transcending international transactions can be assumed. As a result, interdependence increases in the sense of Kant's venerable formulation: 'arrive at effective relationships with one another'.

Globalisation or internationalisation, however, is not an area-covering phenomenon since the international system is not marked by homogeneity but by layering and rifts (heterogeneity). It includes very diverse structural relations, such as: relatively symmetrical interdependencies in the relations between the highly industrialised Western societies (OECD), asymmetrical interdependence between this gravitational centre of the global economy or the international system and the world's 'developing regions' (West–East relations, West–South relations), confrontational interdependences (at present not in the sense of one great world-embracing conflict, but of many conflicts of lesser magnitude and range).[12]

Globalisation can be observed chiefly in the OECD context, the so-called triad. It should therefore be properly described as 'triadisation'. As, however, the situation in the world's developing regions is scarcely comprehensible without allowance for this triadic framework condition, a conceptually differentiated graduated concept of globalisation (and only such a one) makes good sense.

Sight should not be lost of yet another reference to the concept of globalisation, i.e. globalisation in the sense of the evolution of a global 'community of destiny'. Here mention should be made of the (meanwhile reduced) danger of nuclear war as well as of an aggravated worldwide ecology problem.

During global-economy boom phases globalisation intensifies relations between the core regions of the world (the centres), while during phases of recession the competitive situation is exacerbated. Yet even under favourable conditions a segmentation can occur in the societies concerned, i.e. chasms between successful or new core regions on the one hand and those areas on the other that now have only the status of subcontractors and suppliers, or those that are simply being unhitched from the general development trend.

Areas that hitch on to the upward mobility of the core regions will have no problems provided they utilise the opportunities opening for them for a diversification of their own production profiles and competences. Experience, however, shows that replacement competition between such old and new core regions and their lower-level peripheries can become so virulent that the latter are no longer up to the challenges. Unless straightforward recession occurs, politicised counter-trends become history-making conditions. Today these present themselves chiefly in a culturalisation of politics, staged with the objective not only of cultural but also of socio-economic and political self-assertion. Although culture-conditioned conflict fronts are improbable and although, more particularly, the thesis of the 'clash of cultures' has no basis in reality, we can, in the micro- and meso-sphere, observe numerous culturally charged defensive reactions against the detrimental consequences of globalisation in many places.[13]

These conditions represent an exacerbation of processes that have always been present in the context of the above-discussed development dilemma, except that today, in the face of real globalisation, they can be seen in every corner of the world.

1.5. Fragmentation

Whereas globalisation or internationalisation is obvious, a simultaneous and related marked tendency towards fragmentation can be observed.[14] The following conditions can be listed in cue form:

- State break-up (former Soviet Union, former Yugoslavia, several places in Africa, etc.) or threatening break-up (e.g. Indonesia).
- Fragmentation of existing societies; spread of ethno-nationalism and ethno-radicalism (and, as a result, secessions and separatist movements).
- New 'regionalism', 'provincialisation'; 'new tribalism' – foundation of new states, including a multiplicity of mini-states.

Such a fragmentation trend is inevitable in a world of unequal opportunities for upward mobility and a permanent threat of downward mobility. The resulting relations between centre and periphery are, in view of a universally observable politicisation, widely felt to be no longer tolerable. Hence the efforts for a new political basis for the maximisation of one's own life opportunities. In the resulting search for a new identity of one's own on the part of hitherto peripheralised and marginalised, and above all discriminated against, groups and ethnic entities, a potentially innovative political trend should be recognised.

As for the causes of fragmentation, one has to proceed, as a rule, from non-accomplished modernisation tasks. Modernisation that is not area-wide is bound, in conditions of fundamental politicisation, to trigger countermovements in order to counteract any threatening or already existing cumulation of disadvantages. In that lies the rational-innovative core of such movements.[15] They nevertheless display a considerable proneness to social learning pathologies. Attempts at self-reassurance in the sense of emancipation from the centre–periphery relationship might easily flip over into increasingly autistic patterns of perception and behaviour:

- Into ethnocentrism (in the sense of delimitation and exclusion), acutely reflected in chauvinisms and fundamentalisms.
- Into aggression-inclined escape movements.
- Into orientation along recognisable political and other salvation doctrines, etc.

Against such a background, fragmentation gives rise, naturally enough, to situations of confrontational interdependence, which, as experience teaches, can easily militarise themselves and often abruptly translate into military confrontation (civil war, war between states).

1.6. Heterotropy

Internationalisation, transnationalisation, globalisation – these concepts should not blind us to the fact that the intra-state or national relationships in which people live have grown denser or deeper, especially in the OECD context. More and more people are more and more dependent on 'their' state; they articulate their political demands with a view to their own state and expect specific services from it. The weight of the individual state, viewed over the centuries, has not diminished; on the contrary, it has grown in magnitude and importance, not least because requisite arrangements at the level of international politics can only be implemented through the individual state.

Hence a paradoxical situation arises: the world is more internationally structured than before ('globalisation'), yet at the same time it is more national. As for the relative weight of internationality and national orientation, the individual state, at least in the OECD area in the twentieth century and due to the development of the infrastructure and welfare state, and indeed also during and as a result of two world wars and economic crises, as well as during the reconstruction phase after 1950, has in all essential fields experienced a comparatively greater increase in importance than international interweaving. Only since the 1980s has there been an opposite development in the OECD world, described by Michael Zürn as 'denationalisation': in relation to the overall activities of the individual OECD states, their foreign activities have since increased in nearly all spheres – not dramatically but relatively.[16] In other words, international interlocking has meanwhile reached a significant absolute and relative order of magnitude; this is the decisive objective reason for a universally perceptible and ultimately irrefutable international need for action. Nevertheless, the significance or the weight of intra-state processes is not about to simply evaporate.

If, compared with the past, the world were to appear merely as more interdependent or more 'globalised', there would be hope of a gradually prevailing cosmopolitanism. But as, simultaneously, the world has also become more national and, above all, more politicised, nationalism of whatever type continues to have a future (and probably on a growing scale), chiefly in the chronic problem zones of international politics outside the OECD world. This paradoxical situation – two different directions of development stemming from one and the same context (heterotropy) – is not easy to process. That is a further reason why coordinated action in the world is getting increasingly difficult. The reasons for this complication are to be found both in the internal sphere of societies and at the international level.

2. Practical Implications

2.1. Diminishing Control Opportunities

The transformation occurring throughout the world, since the middle of the eighteenth century and which has become global in the twentieth century, of traditional societies into modernising or modern societies results in politicisation. Wherever this was constitutionally, institutionally, materially and emotionally hemmed in, there eventually arose, after highly conflict-laden and often violent political clashes, more or less stable political communities ('hexagon communities'). Wherever the gap between progressing socio-economic and cultural transformation on the one hand and institutional cushioning of the transformation process on the other has remained wide, the societies in question are characterised by virulent, often chronic, rifts and instabilities. In either case (albeit for different reasons) the chances of successful control of foreign societies from outside are lost. Revolutionary societies in particular dispose of a kind of 'chaos power' against which, as the most recent history teaches, there is scarcely a hope of successful tackling from outside. This provides a protection against imperial or hegemonist alien control – but that is the only positive aspect of this starting position.

The transformation of the world therefore contributes to reliably depriving imperial or hegemonist policy of its foundation. Potential areas for such a policy, as they still existed in the nineteenth and in the first half of the twentieth century (albeit with a steadily growing resistance potential), are dramatically disappearing. If such a policy is nevertheless attempted it will as a rule be counterproductive. Today the possibly only surviving exception in the world is some parts of black Africa; but there, too, hegemonistic policy, though locally still practicable, produces no benefit.

Imperial or hegemonist policy therefore evidently presupposes, as a point of reference, the type of traditional society that has long been an outdated model in the world. Moreover, it presupposes leadership powers able and willing to practise such policy. Even if the will were still there, ability is waning. The reason is that, in view of the costs bound to arise in its practical application, such policy is prohibitively expensive. Ever since the Second World War, if not longer, the wars started and usually lost by the leading powers confirm this state of affairs in respect of peripheral states and societies, both in personal and in financial terms – not to mention the counterproductive consequence in the domestic policy of the leading powers concerned (Britain, France, the U.S.A., the former Soviet Union, Russia). In this way such policy is deprived of its foundation also from the side of the 'home front' of traditional hegemony policy. The U.S.A. will not be an exception in the long run, though only as a consequence of considerable learning costs.

What remains are economic control mechanisms whose significance is also on the wane as it is gradually being realised that economically relevant profits on a substantial scale cannot be made in economically peripheral regions of the world but only in its core regions. That this is indeed so is clearly confirmed by today's spatial structure of the global economy.[17]

Even though the consequences of the socio-economic, sociocultural and political transformation of the world are depriving hegemonist policy of its peak and its basis, this does not mean that it is not tried again and again. However, failure is then preprogrammed, lasting success is improbable. This state of affairs, moreover, also deprives geopolitical carbon copies of their basis, if indeed such attempts were made again.

2.2. Primacy of Domestic Policy

An inevitable result of the politicisation of modernising or modern societies is that the foreign or international policy pursued by such societies reflects intra-societal problems and power situations rather than the imperatives of an overdue international order. Not the interests of mankind, but narrow-minded lobbyist interests of groups capable of organisation and arguments determine intention-formation and decision processes. Deliberately or not, domestic policy determines action. Whether or not one admits the primacy of domestic policy conceptually makes no difference to the actual state of affairs. As a rule there is nothing left of a society-aloof primacy of foreign policy, characterised by étatist premises, especially in complex societies of the type of the OECD world. Only in aggravated conflict situations is such primacy briefly resurrected.

The situation is not difficult to understand: why should social groupings characterised by diverse identities and interests have identical action maxims concerning their attitudes towards the outside? One will have to get used to a situation when the domestic scene familiar in modern societies will mark also foreign-political opinions, intentions and decision processes. Their characteristic is a lurching course prescribed by domestic-policy conflicts.

This state of affairs has long been observable in the classic country of only weak étatiste shaping, the U.S.A. Its foreign policy has always been an extended domestic policy. This is well documented in its foreign-trade policy (trade, direct investments, raw materials, energy policy, environmental policy) and indeed also in its security policy. Added to this is the fact that in all large-population societies their external involvements, seen as a percentage of their overall activities, is anyway relatively slight – a fact particularly noticeable in modern societies of the type of the U.S.A. Small-population societies (for instance the Scandinavian states), on the other hand, have a high proportion of external to domestic activities; however, there too it can be seen that domestic policy affects their foreign-policy attitudes, even though such societies cannot afford to withdraw from the imperatives set by global economics. The practical problem facing not only modern, but also still modernising, societies is that of self-coordination.[18] This is difficult within societies because interests are rarely identical; as a rule conflicting interests have to be reduced to a common denominator. Moreover, it is rendered more difficult by the fact that, as a result of internationalisation, transnationalisation and globalisation, societal agents are active not only in the limited areas of their own political communities, but across the frontiers, i.e. in the above-quoted societal, economic and cultural worlds. Then the power groupings articulated and organised transnationally in their now boundary-less areas react back upon the domestic areas of the political communities concerned. This state of affairs is more than obvious in the classic areas of modern economics – in agriculture, industry and services – and it is also of growing relevance in frontier-transcending fields such as international environmental policy.

2.3. Growing Need for International Coordination

In view of politicisable or politicised societies not only is the demand for self-coordination remarkably great (nothing can simply be enforced by command from above, nor does it come by itself), but the demand for international coordination increases as well – the more so as the tendency towards internationalisation, transnationalisation and globalisation creates additional sets of problems because such processes frequently weaken or even undermine the ability to control individual societies. When, as in the OECD world, hierarchical structures are no longer always action-determining, though in fact there is a high degree of interlockings especially in the areas of economy, information and communication, there is a demand for continuous interdependence management, often taking place in networks. In view of the growing complexity of the world, this will always lag behind the actual problems since even international interdependence management is subject to the restrictive conditions of the primacy of domestic policy. It rarely achieves what would really be offered or demanded by the situation. This state of affairs is evident[19] in nearly all the spheres of policy – agriculture, energy, raw materials, trade, finance, development, population growth, environment, climate, migration, armament/disarmament, human rights, drug-related crime, economic crime, control of epidemics, etc. In all these areas there are understandable efforts for a unilateral maximisation of one's own particular gains of position or efforts to ward off losses of position. Not infrequently this leads politics into a trap, since such efforts prevent the actually needed policy of collective optimisation of positions. The central question is therefore: will the decision-making agents on the political scene try to achieve their own interest by uncoordinated, unilateral, usually lobbyist or nationalistically motivated measures or will there be a coordinated multilateral behaviour in the sense of enlightened self-interest oriented along long-term objectives? Will multilateralism prevail or will unilateralist policy follow narrow-minded interests against its own better knowledge? Will there be a political evolution in the direction of intergovernmental coordination, international regime establishment, international organisation or even an institutionally backed thrust towards planetary politics?

Interlockings, overlappings and entwinings create areas of friction, nuclei of collision and triggers of incompatible modes of behaviour even under the favourable conditions of a symmetrical starting situation. In such situations, however, there is also a constraint towards coordination and concerting. Most starting positions in the world, however, are of an asymmetrical nature, and hence far more problem-charged.[20]

2.4. Civilisatory Thrust

Finding forms and formulas of coexistence in socially mobile societies with self-assured and competent people in the face of conflicting identities and interests resembles the efforts for the civilisation of conflicts. Such a task arises, in a world of growing globalisation, also between states, societies and cultures. As for attempts at civilisation, the modern world is like a laboratory with many tested, many unsuccessful and many not yet thought-through experiments.

Considering the growing complexity and polarisation it is obvious that not only individual societies but the world as a whole is in need of a civilisatory thrust, the more so in view of a multiplicity of negative developments. Whether of not this will be achieved will depend, though not exclusively, on relevant intellectual efforts. Considering the future of mankind the need is for nothing less than the self-civilisation of the world – certainly not a negligible task in theory and practice.

Notes

1. On the problem as a whole see Dieter Senghaas, *Rüstung und Militarismus*, Frankfurt/M. 1982, 2nd edn., Chapter II; Barry Buzan, *People, States and Fear. An Agenda for International Security Studies in the Post-cold War Era*, New York 1991, 2nd edn.; Barry Buzan et al., *The Logic of Anarchy*, New York 1993.
2. See also Harald Müller, 'Security Cooperation', in Walter Carlsnaes et al. (eds), *Handbook of International Relations*, London 2001, Chapter 19.
3. See on this Chapter 6 of the present book.
4. On these problem situations see, for example, Mir A. Ferdowsi (ed.), *Internationale Politik im 21, Jahrhundert*, Munich 2002. On the above-mentioned regional conflicts, which were virulent even before the end of the East–West conflict, see Dieter Senghaas (ed.), *Regionalkonflikte in der Dritten Welt. Autonomie und Fremdbestimmung*, Baden-Baden 1989.
5. See Dieter Senghaas, *Friedensprojekt Europa*, Frankfurt/M. 1992, Chapter 4.
6. See Dieter Senghaas, *The European Experience*, Leamington Spa/Dover, New Hampshire, Berg Publishers 1985, Chapter 1; see now also Ha-Joon Chang, *Kicking away the Ladder. Development Strategy in Historical Perspective*, London 2002. Extensively on this subject, Chapter 9 of the present book.

7. Fundamentally on the analysis of this, Robert Gilpin, *War and Change in World Politics*, London 1981.

8. See Karl W. Deutsch, *Tides Among Nations*, New York 1979.

9. See Chapter 2 of the present book.

10. Fundamentally on this subject see David Held et al., *Global Transformations. Politics, Economics and Culture*, Oxford 1999.

11. See Ernst-Otto Czempiel, *Weltpolitik im Umbruch*, Munich 1995, 2nd edn.

12. See Chapter 8 of the present book.

13. See Dieter Senghaas, *The Clash Within Civilizations. Coming to Terms with Cultural Conflicts*, London/New York 2002.

14. See Ulrich Menzel, *Globalisierung versus Fragmentierung*, Frankfurt/M. 1998.

15. See Dieter Senghaas, *Wohin driftet die Welt?* Frankfurt/M. 1994, Chapters 2 and 3.

16. Michael Zürn, *Regieren jenseits des Nationalstaates. Globalisierung und Denationalisierung als Chance*, Frankfurt/M. 1998, as well as Marianne Beisheim, Sabine Dreher, Gregor Walter, Bernhard Zangl and Michael Zürn, *Im Zeitalter der Globalisierung? Thesen und Daten zur gesellschaftlichen und politischen Denationalisierung*, Baden-Baden 1999.

17. See Chapter 8 of the present book.

18. Fundamentally on this, Karl W. Deutsch, *The Nerves of Government*, New York 1963.

19. See Peter J. Opitz (ed.), *Weltprobleme*, Munich 2001.

20. See the contributions to Dieter Senghaas (ed.), *Frieden machen*, Frankfurt/M. 1997.

Chapter 8

INTERDEPENDENCES IN THE
INTERNATIONAL SYSTEM

As in all analyses relating to politics, society, economy and culture, there exist no unambiguous concepts in the discussions of international politics and international relations. Attempts to achieve such unambiguous concepts by way of narrow, precise and seemingly exclusive definitions do not as a rule meet with consensus and therefore remain unsuccessful.[1] By way of contrast, the attempt to define the diverse dimensions of ambiguous concepts is more promising. But that should be done only when such differentiations are justified by the object at issue, i.e. not primarily as the reflection of scholastic theses or terminological games. Differentiation of a concept motivated by facts, i.e. not by meta-theoretical controversies about alternative paradigms, could also be described as its contextualisation: the specific profile of a concept then arises not from abstract terminological reasoning, but with regard to specific action contexts establishable by an empirically grounded social science.

In the following section we shall deal with such a context-related differentiation in the concept of interdependence. Interdependences in international politics and in international relations are being discussed in topical political discourse just as they are in scholarship. The first intention in the reflections that follow is to examine international politics and international relations as to their specific 'interdependence content'. To do this we shall be using an empirical inductive approach, as the most appropriate one. The question is: What interdependence is present in the present-day international system. and where is it? And how can it be distinctly characterised on factual grounds?

Explicit statements on trends are often associated implicitly or explicitly with the concept of interdependence. Frequently a transition is forecast from the 'former world of states' to a 'global society' and to a 'global domestic policy' that characterises it. Interdependence is therefore equated with a growing and deepening networking at a regional, continental and especially a global level. Frequently use is made in the discussion of picturesque concepts describing the earth as a 'spacecraft' or as a 'global village'. 'Globalisation' – the catchphrase of these years – might then be understood as the sum total of all deepening relevant 'interdependences' on a worldwide plane.[2] Are such ideas promising for the future or are they merely deceptive rhetoric? In order to answer this question meaningfully it is necessary to examine the diverse interdependence contents of international politics and international relations in a concrete manner.

The result of the exposition below will be the empirical observation that, for a differentiated analysis of international interdependences, account must be taken of at least eight action contexts:

1. The symmetrical interdependence in West–West relations.
2. The asymmetrical interdependence between the OECD centre of gravitation and the world's developing regions.
3. The *confrontational* interdependence in the former East–West relations and today's incipient structurally comparable interdependences in confrontational situations elsewhere.
4. International economic interdependence.
5. International ecological interdependence.
6. Institutional interdependence on a worldwide plane.
7. Worldwide cooperative functional interdependence.
8. The internationalising normative moral interdependence.

The interdependence content of these eight taxonomically differentiable constellations of international relations will be examined below. Moreover, the reciprocal relations between the eight contexts will be demonstrated. Neither of these two is possible without agreement on fundamental facts on the levels described.[3] This chapter is to provide an impulse for such agreement in the hope that this will also facilitate the analysis of 'interdependence of interdependences' (Willy Brandt). Only then will it be clear what it is that structures the international system and holds it together.

1. Symmetrical Interdependence in West–West Relations

In the present international system the densest mutual networking exists among the Western industrialised societies (OECD sphere). These societies are the dynamic pole or the gravitational centre of the global economic system: about 70 per cent of the total value of global exports is accounted for by the OECD countries; indeed the proportion of trade among the OECD countries alone accounts for about 50 per cent of global trade. Weightier still is the fact that about 75 per cent of their total exports (OECD exports = 100 per cent) are internal trade; in other words, the OECD countries exchange up to three quarters of their exports among themselves. This proportion is even surpassed with regard to direct investments and technology transfer. A comparable economic networking does not exist in other sectors of the international system; it is therefore quantitatively exceptionally high.

Added to the absolute and relative order of magnitude is a qualitative aspect: trade among the OECD countries is substitutive. This means that they essentially exchange largely comparable products of high value creation: capital-intensively and technology-intensively produced agricultural products, high-value finished goods, especially durable consumer goods, engineering and electrical engineering items, vehicles, etc. The bulk of the export articles, about 80 per cent, are from the processing industry; almost the same order of magnitude is found on the import side.

This relationship structure is due to the specific economic profiles of the individual OECD countries, characterised as they are by high productivity in all economic fields (including agriculture). These conditions are proved by a parallel, only slightly varying, breakdown of the population in work and of the production structure regarding the primary, secondary and tertiary sector ($<5:<30:>65$).

Economic relations among the OECD countries are therefore not only incomparably dense, but also relatively symmetrical; above all, they are based on comparable socio-economic profiles. The concept 'symmetrical interdependence' therefore has a substantive basis. However, the strength of the Western industrial countries as a collective is due not only to their economic strength, but also to the fact that they are based on a comparable political structure, characterised by separation of powers, rule of law and parliamentary democracy.

Moreover, economic relations among the Western industrial countries are proceeding in a tense institutional network.[4] An exchange of the order of magnitude referred to tends to require free-trade regulations: these were striven for in the post-war period of 1945–47 by the General Agreement on Tariffs and Trade (GATT) and by the international monetary system of Bretton Woods. The trade regime laid down in GATT obliges all participants to a reciprocal abolition of tariffs and other trade barriers, with exchange to be governed by multilateralism and most-favoured-nation agreements; the world currency system envisaged fixed rates of exchange and the free exchangeability of currencies, i.e. convertibility. Admittedly, the GATT principles were not fully implemented, nor did the Bretton Woods system survive. But the expected collapse of the global economic system as a result of the crises of the 1970s and 1980s did not take place. On the contrary: in

1985 the World Trade Organisation (WTO) was institutionalised as a successor to the GATT agreement. As a substantially enlarged regulatory system it continues the work of GATT; the basis of WTO has expanded to become a negotiation forum. Considering the implementation mechanisms of the organisation (conflict settlement procedures) one can regard it as an institutional quality leap.

For many years a number of organisations have contributed to the overcoming of the above-mentioned crises of the 1970s and 1980s; their task consists in attuning relations among the Western industrial countries with each other ('concertation'). Mention should also be made of world economy summits (G7/G8) held regularly since the 1970s; their preparation and post-summit work by the relevant governmental authorities are more important than the spectacular event itself. The Organisation for Economic Cooperation and Development (OECD) works more silently; in regular reports it presents the economic development of its member states and formulates directives.

Of particular political weight are the European institutions in the framework of the European Union. One of its pillars, the European Community (EC) is by far the greatest economic unit participating in global trade, accounting for roughly 40 per cent of global trade turnover. Since 1 January 1993 a uniform internal EC market has been in existence, leading to an integration of the participating national economies. On 1 January 2002 a common currency (euro) was introduced in almost all the EU countries. A further enlargement of competences is moreover envisaged for the common political institutions: with it a transition takes place in the EU area from relatively dense cooperation to a subject-area-oriented graduated integration; this represents the highest possible degree of institutional interdependence in international relations, attaining as a result a high level of expectation stability. The Maastricht summit in December 1991 and other EU summits (e.g. in Amsterdam in June 1997) have taken course-setting decisions for this. The discussion of an overdue 'Constitution of the European Union', conducted ever since 2002 in the so-called constitutional convention, demonstrates, despite divergent premises in acute controversies and transitional setbacks, the dynamism of this integration process, in the long run, a dynamism mostly underrated even by well-meaning critics who demand greater and faster progress.

Since 1993 the internal EC market has had a remarkable new economic and political attraction effect on the rest of Europe and on extra-European countries. Such an effect was first seen in the successful negotiations concluded during the 1980s between the European industrial countries of Western character, organised since 1960 in EFTA (European Free Trade Association) and the EC, which led to agreement on the establishment of a European economic area (EEA = EC + EFTA). As, however, most EFTA countries (like Denmark and Britain in 1972, Portugal in 1986 and Austria,

Sweden and Finland in 1994) have become members of the EU, only the rest-EFTA, Switzerland, Liechtenstein, Norway and Iceland were left outside. As a result, EFTA lost weight as a strategically relevant organisation, as the EEA did in consequence, even though in the early 1990s this was still seen by some people as a recipient organisation for the societies of eastern Europe – a prospect that became irrelevant with the dramatic loss of importance of the EEA.

Against this once benevolent intention, which, however, met with no resonance in eastern Europe, a second attraction effect of the EC internal market became evident: this was documented in the EU's association or cooperation agreements with the countries of eastern Europe, their corresponding subsequent applications for membership and the process – not confined to eastern Europe – of a step-by-step enlargement of the EU during the first decade of this century.

In the Western sector of the international system the economy is oriented towards frontier-transcending competition, while international politics are oriented towards coordination. Neither competition nor coordination can be assumed to be problem-free. They require continuous interdependence management: at the economic level this consists of the continuous efforts to enlarge the world trade regime further and further (now in the framework of the World Trade Organisation WTO) and to find substitute solutions for the Bretton Woods system, i.e. a new international finance regime. Political attention is focused predominantly on repulsing a tendency, feared over the last twenty-five years but not actually arisen, towards the encapsulation of regional economic blocks (EU/NAFTA/East Asia) at the expense of global economic relations.[5]

Interdependence management is needed also with regard to East Asia's new position in the global economic system: the development of Japan and the East Asian threshold countries into a new dynamic pole of the global economy has resulted in considerable shifts of weight in the global economy and in imbalances. In past centuries such shifts provided the background to power rivalries and elimination struggles between rising powers and those which in consequence felt threatened in their – until then – leading global power position.[6] The question of whether Japan will attain a truly hegemonic position in the first half of the twenty-first century, paralleling that of Britain in the nineteenth and of the U.S.A. about the middle of the twentieth century, has proved premature. It is probable that three more or less equal dynamic poles – the U.S.A., Japan, the EU – will stand beside each other, in hard economic competition, but otherwise peacefully coexisting in durable trilateral coordination. The real question that will arise in the first half of the twenty-first century is how China and hence presently one-fifth of the world's population and India exceeding that share soon, can gradually be joined to that triad or integrated into it.

Only one thing appears to be certain: any policy that endangered the historically unparalleled interdependence in the OECD sphere would be counterproductive for all concerned, including its originator. This realisation, today widespread in the Western industrial countries, should surely help avoid such a policy. Warlike disputes of the kind of the inter-imperialist rivalries about the turn of the nineteenth and twentieth centuries are now improbable in this sector of the international system. But of course one cannot be entirely certain. Admittedly, the sphere of the OECD countries has become a 'zone of stable peace'. Open use of force no longer plays any part in it, not even the threat of force.[7] But is this part of the world, chiefly in an economic respect, reliably upheaval-proof? Is the level of 'civilisation' attained really beyond any danger of regression in all fields of politics? These questions have to be asked, if only to keep sensitivity for an early perception of potential threats at a high level.

2. Asymmetrical Interdependence between Centres and Developing Regions

Development problems have been among the great themes of international politics for the past forty years. Their importance is not going to diminish in the coming decades either since the failures of development policy over the past development decades cannot be overlooked. Development results mainly from intra-societal endeavours, though their success or failure is closely associated with global economic framework conditions.[8] It should be remembered in this connection that the developing countries, viewed collectively and quantitatively, have only just been able to maintain their positions and that a quantitative and qualitative improvement of their situation has only exceptionally taken place (in East Asia and a few newly industrialising countries). The share of all developing countries in world trade still amounts to some 30 per cent, with 60–65 per cent of the Third World's total exports (= 100 per cent) going to the industrial countries and the rest to other developing countries including the former state-trade countries. The world's developing countries are thus far more focused on the western industrial countries than the other way round. Only about 25 per cent of the industrial countries' exports go to the developing countries.

More serious is the asymmetry in the export product baskets: three quarters of the exports of all developing countries are agricultural products, commodities such as tea and coffee, raw materials and energy; only in the export of energy (crude oil and gas) do the developing countries achieve a substantial share (about 60 per cent) of the world market. As against this there are their imports of finished goods, machines and vehicles from the industrial countries. Their foreign trade relations are therefore asymmetrical also qualitatively. They should therefore be described as complementary or vertical – in contrast to the substitutive and horizontal division of labour prevailing among the Western industrial countries.

The same pattern as in their export structure is revealed also in other dimensions: developing countries are essentially recipients of direct investments and technology transfer; only a few threshold countries have begun to invest outside their own frontiers and to transfer technology. In the international information and communications system most developing countries similarly occupy only a marginal position. And political organisations with a temporary weight of their own (e.g. the Group of 77) remained without effective force in the long term, as did developing-countries-oriented international organisations such as UNCTAD.

It is therefore entirely appropriate to continue characterising the relations between industrial and developing countries as asymmetrical interdependence: interdependence exists because events in the OECD world produce immediate reactions. Asymmetry exists because of the above-named reasons. Only a few developing countries have succeeded in demolishing their traditional structures, in qualitatively 'horizontalising' their foreign-trade relations and thus taking decisive steps towards a substitutive division of labour. This state of affairs has been particularly marked in the East Asian newly industrialising countries whose economic profiles approach those of the classic OECD countries.[9]

As for North–South relations, the developing countries have striven since the mid-1960s, and increasingly as a result of the OPEC shock, to arrive at a new interdependence management. The goal was new international regimes that would overcome the marginalised position of the developing countries in the global economic system and bring relations up to a new qualitative level.[10] With the exception of the Law of the Sea Convention, which produced a compromise, these efforts have by and large been unsuccessful: a comprehensive international system of storage areas for agricultural, mineral and industrial raw materials designed to stabilise raw material prices did not come about, any more than did a Common Fund for the financing of such stores; major shares of global industrial production for the developing countries, as striven for by UNIDO in negotiations, could quite obviously not be imposed by international diplomacy; technology transfer continues to be a business of private enterprise; a resources transfer of 0.7 per cent of the gross social product from the OECD countries to developing countries is still not taking place, etc. Nor have new international bodies been created in the field of the 'new international information and communications order': without their own news agencies, media firms, trained journalists and communication capacities within their own societies and in contact with abroad, most Third World countries are being simply overwhelmed by the efficient communications carriers of the industrial countries. The few exceptions, as for instance India and Brazil, and more recently the Al Jazeera transmitter in the Arab area, merely confirm the rule. Besides, the Law of the Sea Convention (1982) came about only because the coastal states, both industrial and developing, enriched themselves by the extension of their national sovereignty to the sea ('terranisation' of the sea). Where such an extension of national utilisation rights was not envisaged, as for instance in deep-sea mining, an appropriate regime only came about with major difficulties and, most probably, without a long-term prospect of operational realisation.

In contrast to the comprehensive endeavours for a new interdependence management in North–South relations, bilateral and multilateral development work usually proceeded along traditional lines. Hardly anyone still supposes that global development problems can be successfully 'resolved' by it. The disillusionment that can be observed possibly gives rise to the realisation that asymmetrical interdependence cannot necessarily be made unproblematic by deepening interdependence and that it might instead be possible to counteract it by forms of temporary selective detachment or dissociation.[11] This developmentally inspired assumption, however, is being opposed by the now predominant spirit of a neoliberalism fixed abstractly and uncontextually at 'globalisation', with the result that alternative options will not gain political scope until the unrealistic neoliberal dogmatism, which refuses to acknowledge asymmetries, has led itself *ad absurdum* in developmental practice because of the politically virulent faults it has led to.

3. Confrontational Interdependence

The decades-long confrontation between East and West, i.e. the East–West conflict, which has meanwhile come to an end (1947–1989/92) can be described as an interdependence of a type of its own. This conflict was based on a mixture of ideological differences and power-political rivalries. It translated into a long-lasting arms race in which both sides were striving for politically instrumentable armaments potentials with the aim of optimising their own military options and neutralising or thwarting those of the adversary.[12] Such endeavours inevitably led to an armaments dynamic in which, due to the order of magnitude and differentiation of modern armaments, the arms race and armament dynamics developed a momentum of their own that was eventually difficult to control and that, as international politics ('détente policy') provided some scope for corrective intervention. This fixation of the confrontation of the adversaries, underpinned by a considerable armament effort, went hand in hand, for decades, with limited economic exchanges and with impaired information and communication. In the exacerbated phases of the Cold War even human contacts were impaired. Any institutional interlocking beyond normal diplomatic traffic remained marginal for a long time.

East–West relations in the post-war period therefore followed a conflict structure of a type of its own, one that from a communication-theory perspective could be described as 'autistic'. Interdependence undoubtedly existed since the actions of the conflicting parties acted directly upon one another. Interdependence was largely negative, albeit accompanied by a crisis management that – viewed in retrospect – was surprisingly effective. In that confrontational interdependence both sides feared being outmanoeuvred by the other. Only deconstruction of confrontation made it possible to take steps towards positive interdependence.

Even though East–West relations in the post-war period were marked by a repeated alternation of conflict exacerbation and striving for détente, an overcoming of that confrontation can only be recorded since the mid-1980s. This was essentially the consequence of Soviet reform policy, which eventually embraced also the East European countries: within a few years the political reorientation in the Soviet Union and Eastern Europe led to a marked diminution of ideological confrontation. While, in the CSCE process, efforts were dragging along for ten years to find common principles of behaviour that would be agreed to by everybody, the reform process made agreement on fundamental positions possible within a few years. The revolutionary upheavals in Eastern Europe (1989/90) eventually brought about a lasting breakthrough in this respect. This eliminated the basic cause of the East–West conflict, the political confrontation between the democratic rule-of-law state and the political dictatorship stemming from the monopoly claim of a single party. System-political premises such as the rule of law, the separation of powers, political pluralism, democratic multiplicity of opinions, etc., have meanwhile achieved recognition in Europe, a recognition that is no longer questioned.

With the deconstruction of ideological and system-political confrontation and the eventual collapse of the *Realsozialismus* system the abolition of the traditional arms race became imaginable. Since the early 1990s no one in Europe any longer proceeds from the possibility of a large-scale surprise attack or space-seizing offensive military actions. The question that poses itself is that of a comprehensive European security structure in which military apparatuses would have to be directed towards a low level on the principle of incapability of attack (NOD: non-offensive defence).[13]

Wherever positive interdependence is found in international relations it is always based on a mutually beneficial economic exchange. Even at the time of détente between East and West there were considerable structural obstacles to such exchange between East and West, in particular the poor performance of the economies of *Realsozialismus*. The transformation of command economies into market economies, striven for everywhere since the global political revolution, continues to call for major efforts by the reform states. The road to substitutive division of labour of the kind that characterises the mutual economic relations of the Western industrial countries will be a long and laborious one. Yet all efforts must be directed towards the development of competitive economies in the eastern half of Europe, i.e. on upgrading. Only such economies will ultimately facilitate mutually beneficial exchange, only such economies will become fully capable of integration in the EC internal market.

The deconstruction of confrontation will have to go hand in hand with the building of contacts and communication if positive interdependence is to be achieved also on the plane of human relations. Such contacts and communication are of course substantially easier since the system turn than ever before. They can increase the reality content of the perception of one another and extend the ability to place oneself in the position of the other (empathy). This gives rise to the counterpart of the former deterrence constellation of typical enemy perception, i.e. to realistic pictures of the world around. Even a decade after the end of confrontation much remains to be done at the level of town pairing and youth travel, of exchange of sportsmen, pupils, students, teachers and scientists, in the field of joint research projects, the organisation of exhibitions, festivals and film weeks, etc. Activities of civil society in such fields can support cooperation at the political and economic level and promote an increase in cooperative interdependence also at the social level.

Confrontational interdependence has thus come to an end in the East–West context, where it had reached exemplary exacerbation. Nevertheless it can, as a historical state of affairs, be now, in retrospect, analysed as a typical ideal type. However, confrontational interdependence can be observed not only in the now historical East–West context: in the 1960s/1970s and in the early 1980s it also existed between the Soviet Union and China.[14] Here, too, a political reorientation and a restructuring of relations has been observed since about 1985. ideological confrontation plays hardly any part now between Russia and China; there is no longer an arms race; economic exchange is marked by a remarkable growth rate; contacts and communications, while not possible to an unlimited extent, are easier than in the preceding decades.

On the other hand, the classic model of acute confrontational interdependence can still be observed in many regional conflicts. Their causes and mechanisms are no different from those described, though the ideological component is usually unimportant, while domination-related power-political rivalries are in the foreground.[15] Such confrontational interdependences can be observed in many places in the Middle East and in the Gulf region, but also in the politically virulent relations between India and Pakistan – these moreover have a nuclear weapons component. Wherever confrontation is aggravated, i.e. confrontational interdependence builds up, in the zones of regionally limited political turbulence, there the same approach will have to be tested for overcoming such interdependences as during the East–West conflict: deconstruction of ideological confrontation (where present) and search for common behaviour principles, trust building, reorientation of security policy in the direction of incapability of attack, abolition of economic boycott and serious efforts for economic exchanges, termination of a policy of occlusion and a search for intensified contacts and communication. However, the end of the East–West conflict has also shown that confrontational interdependence can be overcome only if one conflict party, or both conflict parties, undergo profound internal structural changes in politics, society, economy and culture, i.e. especially if authoritarian rule is deprived of its basis.

4. International Economic Interdependence

Global goods export in 2000 was of the order of magnitude of 6,000 billion dollars. Of this total, 70 per cent was accounted for by the Western industrial countries and about 30 per cent by the developing countries including the former state-trade countries, while it should be pointed out that the least developed countries accounted for only 0.5 per cent of global exports. These data are an indication of the weight distribution in the global economic system. In particular they show that the main weight of the global economy continues to lie unchanged with the OECD countries; in spite of all the changes that have meanwhile taken place in international politics not much will change in this respect. The OECD share of global export in 1988 was already much the same. The structure of worldwide direct investments (FDI) conveys a similar picture: about 75 per cent of the FDI are localised in the industrial countries (the triad), the rest in developing countries. More precisely: two thirds of this are in just ten developing countries. Regardless of these basic conditions – the tenacious centre–periphery structure of global economics – universal worldwide effective economic interdependences are not to be missed. Thus for instance the repeated drastic raising of the oil price by the OPEC cartel in the 1970s and early 1980s had considerable consequences for the net importers of energy, among both the industrial and the developing countries. The petrodollars earned in these countries flowed back, by way of 'recycling', into the global finance system (i.e. the OECD countries) and, for instance as commercial credits at very favourable terms, reached the developing as well as the former East-bloc countries. A far from efficient use of the credits as well as other factors then contributed to the international debt crisis. Inability to service the credits in time or to repay them eventually got even great creditor banks in leading industrial countries into major difficulties. In order to prevent total insolvencies and worldwide domino effects international rescue actions became necessary, then as well as later (e.g. in the 'Asian crisis'). The Western industrial countries were affected by these problems just as much as the OPEC countries, the Comecon economies of the still existing *Realsozialismus* and the newly industrialising countries of the Third World, especially those of Latin America. The growing American budget and trade balance deficit, which under the Reagan administration was financed by credits and led to a high interest level, alone increased the indebtedness of the Third World, which was based on short-term and medium-term credits at variable interest rates, by about one-third and thereby contributed to a substantial increase in the burden of the debtor states.

Various forms of globally effective economic interdependences can also be observed in other sectors of the global economy. Thus for instance the policy of massive grain imports by the former Soviet Union temporarily drove up the price level of grain, with immediate consequences for the many net importers of grain in the Third World. Not infrequently an above-average demand for specific goods causes production expansions everywhere, which in the years following result in overcapacities and sometimes in the collapse of the worldwide price level in the area concerned. Such connections have always been, and still are, part of the everyday processes in a globally interlinked world economy. It should, however, be remembered that the OECD gravitational centres of the global economy possess very different capacities and resources for dealing with this kind of problem from those of the peripheral economies.

Moreover, attention should be paid to interdependences arising on the basis of structural change: the more economical use of raw materials in industrial production and less material-intensive new products are reducing the raw-material intensity of production processes and products. Raw-material importers like Japan are in the forefront of this restructuring, which has worldwide consequences as a result of international competition. Raw-material exporters in industrial and developing countries worldwide could suffer from such an unhitching of industrial production from raw-material demand; for them the 'terms of trade' would continue to develop unfavourably if not counteracted by a tremendously increasing demand for raw materials by countries like China and India. It is also to be expected that automatisation and robotisation of industrial production, especially in the world's high-wage countries, will reduce the proportion of the wages bill of total production costs, with the result that certain industries will again become competitive against the low-wage countries. In the end result this would be a reversal of a process that, in the 1970s, was described as a 'new division of labour'. If it prevailed, the earlier relocation of below-average productive industries from high-wage to low-wage countries would partly be counteracted by a back-relocation of such industries. There exist therefore economic interdependences that intensify, but there are also some, albeit on a smaller scale, that move in the opposite direction.

Global economic interdependence is today mediated mainly by transnational enterprises. At an estimate, there are about 55,000 of these at present; they own some 450,000 affiliate companies abroad. The importance of transnational enterprises consists, first, in that the major part of international capital traffic is handled by transnational banks. Besides, some 80–90 per cent of the international trade of market economies is handled by transnational enterprises, with 30–40 per cent of this goods traffic being accounted for by purely intra-company trade, i.e. not between independent enterprises but between affiliate companies of the same enterprise. Similarly, a large part of international technology transfer takes place through such enterprises, mostly as intra-company transfer. A substantial part of workforce migration at the level of specialised and management employees also takes place within these enterprises. If they are active in the consumer goods field, such enterprises, especially in respect of durable goods, transfer globally effective consumption patterns and lifestyles as a result of 'demonstration effects'.

International intertwining due to transnational enterprises is thus of varied character and is not confined to flow of goods. Traditionally such enterprises used to be active in the raw-materials field; after 1950–60 a diversification took place, chiefly in the processing industry (initially non-durable consumer goods, later durable goods and machines); by now they are far more active than the public realises in the services sector (banks, advertising, market research, airlines, hotel chains, fast-food restaurants, data processing, etc.). A growth industry of a new type is the frontier-transcending data traffic based on transnational computer communication networks, the nerves as it were of transnational enterprises and of a global information economy whose development at present moves in its first dramatic boom phases of a logistical growth curve.[16]

A global interdependence of a special kind and order of magnitude exists on the plane of international financial markets. Whereas trade in goods and services at present amounts to about 7,000 billion dollars per year, transactions between individual currencies are taking place up to an order of magnitude of 2,000 billion dollars per stock-exchange day – this comes to about 500,000 billion dollars in a year or about seventy times the global annual trade in goods and services.

Obviously such capital movements are no longer connected to a goods and services traffic of a corresponding order of magnitude. Supported by the development of new communication technologies and a spreading liberalisation and deregulation of capital traffic a unified global financial market has come into being in the international financial market places, where deals are made round the clock. In view of the speculative deals done in the international money market, deals that are largely removed from real economic processes, this market has been described as a single great gambling hell or as 'casino capitalism'. Even experts regard the processes taking place there as 'rather obscure'. Nevertheless, there is no comparable simultaneous interdependence in any other economic sphere – as proved every day by the more or less synchronised stock exchange movements in Tokyo, Hong Kong, Frankfurt, London and New York.

The international financial market is not only largely independent and globally organised, but it is also essentially autonomous and uncontrolled. Certainly the individual national issuing banks have difficulty, at critical times, in standing up to the self-referential dynamics of this economic sector. Attempts to establish a new international financial regime as a successor to the Bretton Woods system have so far been unsuccessful.

5. International Ecological Interdependence

Over the past thirty years the realisation that there is such a thing as a global ecological interlocking has noticeably grown. Ecological interdependence shows itself in negative aspects: in the consequences of the nuclear accident at Chernobyl, in the suspected worldwide effects of the ozone hole and the greenhouse effect and in other serious matters such as the progressing desertification. In themselves the environmental problems are not new: in the Mediterranean area, for instance, extensive tree felling at the time of the Roman empire led to long-term, in a sense permanent, karstification of entire coastal regions. Alongside the present global problems some regional environmental crises have also become greatly aggravated.

As things stand at the moment, environmental problems will become more acute in the foreseeable future rather than less, which means that ecological interdependence will become a fact that international politics will have to take into account even more than over the past decades.[17] In the Western industrial countries more than limited correctives are not at present in sight, even though system-immanent possibilities of correction are quite considerable: air. water and soil, hitherto regarded as free commodities, are entering into production calculations as overheads, which will probably lead to a more economical and prudent use of them. Resource-saving and energy-saving technologies would become a matter of course in such circumstances. However, a changeover to ecology-friendly production processes and products requires substantial restructuring, which is not likely in the short term but not difficult in the medium and long term. In all probability the Western industrial societies will have to be the pacemakers of such ecological restructuring if it is to be globally achieved at all.

In the former socialist industrial economies over-exploitation of resources was particularly marked. This was due to the fact that these countries were pursuing forced industrialisation programmes with the intention of catching up with, or overtaking, the Western industrial countries. Today the demands of economic restructuring from command to market economies combine with the imperatives of ecology-compatible management. It is unlikely that environmental compatibility will be assigned top priority.

Beyond numerically limited scientific circles any sensible environmental awareness is still largely lacking in the developing countries. At the present state of development, or non-development, consideration for the environment is not considered justifiable. Moreover, the ecological ruthlessness during the industrialisation processes of Western and Eastern industrial societies is, historically correctly, pointed out.

At best, under the prevailing conditions, the detrimental ecological effects will stagnate in the western industrial countries, or decline relatively; in the former socialist industrial countries they will increase and, later perhaps, stagnate; in the developing countries, which include a still environment-insensitive China, they will probably increase considerably. On a worldwide view, there will hardly be an environmental relief on the scale necessary. That is why the trend towards a further ecological disruption and impoverishment of the world will intensify and subsequently provoke appropriate dramatic action constraints.

Since water and, more especially, air have no frontiers and since both are carriers of a frontier-transcending transport of harmful chemicals the old sovereignty armour will be pierced or become obsolete just as in the military sphere. Most states in the world are both producers of harmful chemicals and sufferers from harmful chemicals produced by others. Just as there is no defence against rockets, so there is none against 'ecological attacks' by others, any more than they in turn can defend themselves against such effects. From this situation results an inescapable compulsion to political coordination. However, what scope this will have and what success still remain an open question.

If the prospects of an 'environmental foreign policy', which would help enforce national interests elsewhere, are slight or non-existent, there will be no alternative to reaching an 'ecology partnership' on a 'good neighbour' basis. First steps have been taken in that direction: international and regional organisations have formulated principles of an appropriate environmental policy and adopted directives and conventions (climate, ozone layer, protection of species, desertification). Statements of principle as a rule confirm people's right to an intact environment. States are invited to enforce appropriate measures. Whereas, in the past, there have been limiting clauses – e.g. that environmental measures must be compatible with economic growth and maintenance of living standards – there has been a clear direct upgrading of environmental protection in some countries in the past few years.

Even though the directives and conventions for environmental protection may still fall short of the needs and the magnitude of environmental problems, they are nevertheless often more precise today and no longer just of a declamatory nature. At the level of the United Nations, above all in its environmental programme (UNEP), as well as in the regional context, especially within the European Union, progress can be recorded with respect to a strategically understood and in detail verifiable environmental policy. By way of contrast, however, declamatory policies still prevail on an all-European plane (e.g. within the framework of the UN Economic Commission for Europe, ECE). In other words, essential aspects of international environment-protecting policies are now recognised: protection of climate and ozone layer, protection of species, provisions against desertification, containment of frontier-transcending air pollution, provisions against acid rain and acidification of soils, detoxication of rivers and seas, prevention of marine pollution from the land, prohibition of burning of waste on the high seas, sinking or dumping of industrial waste, etc. Measures in these and other areas demonstrate that the complexity of regional and global ecological connections and the consequences of catastrophic interference in the ecological cycle can no longer be ignored.

Destruction of the environment, however, has a dynamic of its own in the face of which many countermeasures seem feeble. The problem is not unlike the problem in the armament dynamic. Here, too, certain driving forces, e.g. of weapons technology and its continuous innovations, have such a striking effect that attempts to intervene (such as arms control) always seem to fall short of what is required. In both these areas there is a need for considerable political corrections in the individual national-state framework and in the frontier-transcending coordination of regional and international environmental policy if the actual scale of existing ecological interdependence is to be managed. If, as a result of pressure from an articulate and organisation-competent part of the population, it proved possible to accomplish such overdue corrections effectively, there would still be the task of enforcing such a policy in the former socialist countries and in the developing countries.

Ecological interdependence is thus a reality of growing importance, be it in the sense of continuing frontier-transcending processes and socio-economic impoverishment, or in the sense of increasing political coordination in eliminating the most serious developmental mistakes or even in a joint struggle against the causes of an ecology-damaging development. The task really demands the existence of a world ecology organisation on the model of the powerful World Trade Organisation (WTO).

6. Institutional Interdependence on a Global Plane

Whereas the international system has meanwhile a basis of nearly 200 states, a significant increase of institutional networks can be observed between them on the global and regional plane. Such networking takes place both at the level of international governmental organisations (IGOs) and on that of international non-governmental organisations (INGOs). In the narrow sense of the concept there are today some 250 IGOs, many of which were only set up after 1960, while the number of non-state organisations amounted to about 5,500 in the mid-1990s. Besides, the number of agreements concluded by governments with one another has meanwhile risen to over 17,000.

Heading the list of state international organisations is the United Nations and its special organisations, which are found most frequently where relatively dense economic, social and cultural networks already exist.[18] This last observation applies especially to the OECD states and there above all in the context of the European Union and the Nordic Council. It is interesting that in the IGOs set up since 1960 the economic tasks are listed first and social concerns second, whereas more recent security-oriented IGOs are of numerically lesser importance. This trend indicates the stronger economic networking in partial areas of the international system that has taken place over the past few decades. It has, however, also been found that IGO membership correlates sooner with economic performance in the industrialising countries than in highly industrialised societies. In the security sphere, contrary to the postulates of some theories, no link has been found between the growing number of IGO memberships and a decline of warlike involvements. This state of affairs reflects a major weakness of numerous international governmental organisations on a regional plane (thus especially in the case of the Organisation of American States, the former Organisation of African Unity, now the African Union, and above all the Arab League), whereas, in contrast, a zone of stable peace has come about within the European Union, which exhibits a particularly high degree of networking.

The interstate networks at governmental level are thus characterised by diverse effectiveness. While the United Nations is of importance with regard to information, consultation and declamatory politics, policies within its specialist organisations are being thoroughly coordinated in certain areas of politics, which means that political interdependence is brought about. This applies generally to the European Union, whereas the fate and effectiveness of other inter-state organisations, for instance the Gulf Council and the Association of South-East Asian Nations (ASEAN) are still uncertain and open.[19] At the same time, developments on the all-European plane between 1973/75 and 1989/90 have shown that an originally not very promising bloc-transcending enterprise like the CSCE process can, with perseverance and some goodwill make progress even in relations between ideologically divided states. After 1989/90 the CSCE process developed into the OSCE since the original system antagonism no longer existed. By way of contrast, the Third World countries were able after 1973, the year of the first 'oil price shock' (OPEC), initially to achieve a remarkable counterweight to the industrial societies (Movement of the Bloc-Free, Group of 77, etc.), which, however, produced no lasting effect in the long term. Between most states in the international system coordination and political cooperation usually take place silently and the majority of states conform to the rules. As public attention is focused on spectacular and, above all, conflict-type events in international politics, the above elementary state of affairs receives too little attention, even though it represents an essential segment of a routinely growing international interdependence.

Unlike the IGOs, the INGOs, the non-governmental organisations, are associations of individuals or groups with comparable interests or parallel lobbying thrust. They include a diversity of organisations, such as the International Philatelist Association, the Rotary Club, Amnesty International, the Socialist International, the International Chamber of Trade, the International Peace Research Association (IPRA), etc. Such organisations can, but need not, seek to influence governmental agents and IGOs. Non-governmental organisations can contribute to the formation of frontier-transcending awareness, help the emergence of transnational loyalty and mobilise attention to specific social concerns on an inter-societal plane. This too promotes the socialisation of sectors of international relations, and social movements and interests can internationalise themselves as a result. For obvious reasons this process does not take place across the board, since it presupposes orders of dominance and societies in which a free organisation of individuals and groups is possible and legitimate. This is essentially the case in societies of the Western type, so that, logically enough, the greatest institutional network on the societal plane can be observed between just those countries. Just as on the plane of international governmental organisations – apart from publicity-driven performances of the type of Greenpeace and a few others – most processes within international non-governmental organisations, as well as between them and governmental organisations, take place in relative silence and routinely.

All sectors of the international system in which economic and ecological interdependence continues to advance will record continual growth of such international non-governmental organisations.[20] In consequence a policy internationalising itself continues to gain in respect of institutional basis and material substratum.

7. Worldwide Cooperative Functional Interdependence

Quantitative extension of frontier-transcending communication and international traffic inevitably demands appropriate regulations in the areas concerned.[21] Their early history goes back to the nineteenth century: in 1863 the first international postal conference was held in Paris; in 1874 the representatives of twenty-two states signed the international postal convention; the secretariat of the conference, then established, was transformed in 1878 into an international organisation that is now known as the Universal Postal Union (UPU). All sovereign states are members of this organisation.

International regulations were also set up in the field of telegraphy as early as the 1960s. These concerned the structures of charges, the settlement of services and the standardisation of communication equipment, with special attention to agreements on the intersections of national telegraphy systems.

With the growing importance of radio and television these areas, too, came within the responsibility of the International Telecommunications Union (ITU). The extent of frontier-transcending administrative and technical coordination emerges from the fact that from the Federal Republic of Germany alone more than a billion international calls have been made since the mid-1990s, nearly all of them self-dialled ones. Besides, nearly every technological innovation in international communications, such as the use of communication satellites for international telephone traffic and data transmission, requires new regulations and international organisations (such as INTELSAT). The fleet of aircraft of members of the International Civil Airlines Organisation (ICAO) – excluding the USSR and the People's Republic of China – amounted to 9,723 aircraft (above 9 t max. starting weight) as early as 1987. In 1999 Germany alone recorded 2 million aircraft movements, as well as 135 million arriving and departing air passengers, 2 million tonnes of air freight and 270 tonnes of airmail. Such a scale of air traffic requires strict worldwide standardisation, especially in the security sphere. Without continuous cooperation at state and private level there could be no landing and overflying rights, or agreements on air routes, flight plans or flight tariffs – all of these nowadays regarded as routine services by air travellers. Of all frontier-transcending traffic, international air traffic is the most sensitive area because the greatest dangers stem precisely from it, especially if, regardless of temporary downward phases (global economic boom, terrorism) the substantial growth rates of the past three decades were to continue. Even international shipping is no longer thinkable without international regulations. In 1998 the world's merchant fleet comprised just under 40,000 ships totalling some 400 million GRT. Admittedly, international shipping is less regulated than air traffic and, despite the existence of some 300 cartels, is organised more on a market basis. Regulations within the framework of the International Maritime Organisation (IMO) are concerned with the safety of navigation and with the avoidance of environmental risks. Looked at historically, frontier-transcending shipping was regulated first on inland waterways. Thus the Rhine Shipping Commission was set up at the Congress of Vienna in 1815; in 1856 the International Danube Commission was created. Along with agreements on safety and the avoidance of risks in international shipping, a contentious area, internationally, is. above all, a 'fair' share-out of freight handling. These contentious issues are to be resolved by a United Nations Convention on Liner Conferences, formulated by the United Nations and designed to regulate the activities of shipping companies.

Any innovation in frontier-transcending communication and international traffic, especially if originating from private enterprise, will sooner or later require international regulation. This has become evident over the past few years mainly in the field of data transmission, where growth rates are exceedingly high. With increasing internationalisation of the services industry, telecommunication and data transmission generally are becoming a branch of steady growth. Appropriate new attempts of coordination and regulation may therefore be expected both at the state and the private level.

However, the trend towards cooperative functional interdependence in the area of frontier-transcending communication and international traffic should not blind us to two facts: while a quantitative increase in both activities is undeniable, we should not overlook the fact that communication and traffic have also clearly grown quantitatively at the national level, at least in the western industrial countries and the newly industrialising countries. Quantitative investigations show that such frontier-transcending activities, measured by intra-state communication and national traffic, have, over many decades right into the reconstruction phase after the Second World War, relatively declined and that the absolute quantitative growth should not simply be regarded as an indicator of internationalisation. Thus the average American family (of 3.4 persons) of the 1970s made roughly 3,700 domestic telephone calls and only one single overseas call, or, put differently: compared with one million inland telephone calls there were only 272 overseas calls. Tables show that intra-state communication had increased above average. Needless to say, this state of affairs is linked to the order of magnitude, the dense infrastructure and the high mobility of US society; it has only slightly changed in favour of international communication since: in 1998 just short of 650 billion domestic calls were made in the U.S.A., as against only 4.5 million calls abroad – that is about 0.7 per cent of all telephone calls. In societies of the size of the U.S.A. it can be assumed, in any case, that, in view of the information and communications overload, national rather than international information will be exchanged. In industrial countries of medium size, such as Germany, Britain, Italy and Canada, as well as in the small industrial countries of the Scandinavian type, there has, however, been a marked relative increase of the international component since the 1980s, i.e. an internationalisation of communication. But even there the limited orders of magnitude should be considered. In Germany, for instance, the proportion of foreign telephone calls of the total of calls in 1998 amounted to a mere 2.6 per cent.

A second observation concerns the danger of regarding cooperative functional interdependence as a global area-covering phenomenon. In reality this interdependence is clearly graduated. In the highly industrialised societies of the West, i.e. in the OECD area, it is a fact that cannot be missed. In West–East relations (at the time of the East–West conflict) and, even more so, in West–South relations, while there is functional interdependence, this is, just like product exchange, investment streams and technology transfer, marked by considerable asymmetry. One must consider such asymmetry in order to avoid the misunderstanding that cooperative functional interdependence, under present-day international conditions in the areas referred to, is always balanced to the advantage of all. In actual fact, viewed globally, there are clear centre-periphery structures: on the one side cluster formation with dense network structures and on the other one-sided dependence of peripheries – an enduring state of affairs that used to be correctly described as structural dependence in dependence discussion in the past.[22]

What has been observed concerning communication and traffic can also, by way of supplement, be applied to education and science. Despite considerable international communication in the field of education, science and research, the relevant institutions and organisations continue to be largely anchored in their various national systems. Research, for instance, is only beginning to be organised in a frontier-transcending way. Recent community programmes of the European Union's science and research policy are making only a marginal change to this (even for western industrial countries) still basic state of affairs. Even in EU Europe, study abroad is the exception rather than the rule, in spite of a broad spectrum of offers and an increasing recognition of certificates. There can as yet be no question therefore of fully differentiated functional cooperation with area-covering consequences in the fields of education, science and research. What we find are centre–semi-periphery–periphery–sub-periphery structures: in this case with the U.S.A. as the centre, the rest of the OECD world as semi-periphery (*sic*) and the remaining world as periphery or sub-periphery – disregarding a few threshold countries, which, in some areas, are on the way towards developing a semi-periphery structure.

8. Internationalising Normative-moral Interdependence

Studies of international politics frequently refer to the anarchy of international order. If this image is considered correct, one should really speak of international disorder. The formulation reveals the elementary situation that the international system, viewed from the angle of international law, is still essentially based on individual sovereign states without a superior authority. States were, and continue to be, the real subjects of international law, both in classic and in modern international law. For this reason, equality of states, reciprocity and prohibition of intervention are enduring principles of interstate intercourse, realised through diplomatic relations. However, an order based largely on the right of self-judgment and self-help is somehow viable only if there are ways and means of coordinating the actions of its sovereign members. Unregulated anarchy then, at least, gives way to 'regulated anarchy', peaceful coexistence and, at best, international cooperation. Viewed closely, however, peaceful coexistence and cooperation are, regardless of all mainstream theory, far more often the rule than the exception in the international system – otherwise sovereign states would be settling many more conflicts in a warlike manner than is actually the case.

There exists therefore a multitude of restrictions on the freedom of action by states, restrictions that are evidently acceptable even for sovereign individual states. These are of bilateral, regional or global scope and are grounded in treaties, customary behaviour and a multitude of recommendations, decisions, resolutions and declarations. In their formulation a particular role is played by the numerous international and regional organisations, headed by the bodies, organisations and special organisations of the United Nations. Such restrictions are the outcome of cogent law (*ius cogens*), as well as of 'soft law', both of which assume regulatory significance for interstate relations even without the existence of an obligatory international sanctioning power. This offers a chance that a normative-moral interdependence, transcending the individual states, will be established on the international plane; hopefully, this will progressively grow denser and will also be secured by international regimes.

This process finds its most obvious expression in the development of a general prohibition of force in modern international law. This represents a significant break with classic international law, which did not know any legal norms that would have obliged states to preserve peace. From the international law perspective of then, war could not be eliminated from international politics, because international law only accepted the task of containing any wars. International lawyers are therefore entirely right when they point out that classic international law was not an unambiguous force for peace. The transition to the prohibition of force only occurred in the twentieth century and with it classic international law came to an end.

This process proceeded step by step. While there was still some doubt on whether the statutes of the League of Nations contained a partial or general prohibition, an unambiguous general prohibition of war was laid down in the Briand–Kellogg Pact (1928), with the contracting states declaring that they condemned war as a means of resolving international conflicts and that they renounced it in their reciprocal relations as a tool of national policy. Finally, the statute of the United Nations extended the prohibition of war to a general prohibition of force. Thus there no longer exists any juridical basis for the sovereign states' right to wage war. International law has become an international law of peace.

Whereas in classic international law there were two equal juridical states: war and peace, the international law valid today obliges the states to maintain peace. There is a general duty to keep peace as the supreme goal of international politics, a duty founded in the statute of the United Nations and derivable from it. Only self-defence continues to be permitted, though the interpretational difficulties in the definition of aggression, force and self-defence do not touch upon the fundamental option of present-day international law in favour of peace and against war. The so-called law of war (*ius in bello*), designed to check unlawful acts in war with a view to reducing human suffering, is accentuated rather than weakened by the qualitative change from classic to modern international law. That is why the various efforts in past decades to extend and deepen international-law stipulations for the protection of victims of armed conflicts within the framework of 'humanitarian international law' are entirely consistent.

The definitional grey area and the ineffectiveness of such law against arbitrary violent actions by individual states or military alliances are obvious – but they change nothing about the fundamental reorientation of international law in the respect mentioned. With regard to the protection of human rights, a further area of evolving normative-moral interdependence on the international plane, the obligatory nature of the relevant general legal principles is similarly not yet universally accepted. Even so, there can be no doubt that human rights policy and protection of human rights have become major issues of international policy and that relevant actions cannot remain without practical consequences – as proved in the former Soviet Union and in Eastern Europe during the second half of the 1980s. This is all the more significant as individuals had no legal standing in traditional international law.[23]

The Human Rights Declaration of the United Nations of 1948, which heralded a new era of international protection of human rights, was, as its name implies, a declaration of moral-political significance and awareness-creating intent. On the basis of all people's equality, freedom and right to live it formulated specific legal guarantees, concrete personal rights to freedom, active civil rights and social rights. Against this, the two UN covenants or conventions on civil and political rights, as well as on economic, social and cultural rights (1966) have become mandatory law among those states that joined these conventions. Admittedly, even they do not create any directly applicable intra-state right that the individual could invoke: execution of the legal norms continues to be entrusted to the sovereign state.

The International Covenant on Civil and Political Rights emphasises the right to life and rejects torture and slavery, it moreover confirms the right to personal freedom and security, as well as free movement, equality before the law, the right to freedom of thought, conscience and religion and unhampered freedom of opinion. It acknowledges the right of free assembly, as well as the right of association with others and of participation in the shaping of public affairs. It expressly emphasises the right of voting in the sense of genuine, periodical, universal, equal and secret elections in which the free expression of the voter's will is guaranteed. It rejects discrimination on grounds of race, skin colour, gender, language, religion, or political and other opinions, of national or social origin, of fortune, birth or other status; protection of minorities is guaranteed. The International Covenant on Economic, Social and Cultural Rights recognises the right to work and to fair and favourable working conditions, as well as the right to representation of interests in the framework of trade unions and every individual's right to social security and an adequate standard of living for himself and his family. Everyone's right to health and education was also included in the catalogue.

While on the international plane different interpretations of human rights were for a long time widely separated, it proved possible in the western European area, with the European Convention on Human Rights of 1950 (and its supplementary protocols) to codify relatively homogeneous legal ideas and to accomplish a corresponding institutionally secured protective system (until 1999, the European Commission for Human Rights, after 1999, the reformed European Court of Human Rights). On an all-European plane, too, mainly in connection with the Conference on Security and Cooperation in Europe (CSCE) and an expanding European Council human rights policies were ultimately successful, even though it took the revolutionary upheavals in the eastern half of Europe to achieve this. The most comprehensive formulation of the new consensus was reflected in the *Document on the Meeting of the Conference on the Human Dimension of the CSCE* in Copenhagen in June 1990. This document is a kind of Magna Carta for the new Europe and may be regarded as a guiding prospectus of the CSCE successor organisation, the OSCE.[24] Alongside the welcome developments within Europe after 1989/90, the difficulties of achieving global normative common ground between states of diverse orientation, needless to say, continue unchanged. It will take much effort and prolonged processes to achieve common principles of behaviour and agreement in normative orientation in a world that is heterogeneously structured. Even greater efforts will be needed for translating such principles and norms locally into practical politics. More than in any other dimension of international interdependence the yardsticks of judgment should here allow for the scope and the difficulty of the task. Consideration of the astonishing growth of importance of international human rights policy over the past few decades even justifies cautious optimism.[25]

9. Summing Up

By interdependence the *Duden* dictionary understands 'the reciprocal dependence of all prices; also: the dependence of one country's policy on that of other countries'. Reciprocal dependence, but also one-sided dependence, is therefore the keyword that defines the core of the interdependence concept in this definition. Immanuel Kant's more accurate definition was: 'coming into effective relationships with one another'.

Kant's formulation of over 200 years ago has meanwhile acquired an increasing degree of reality. There can be no doubt that the scope and intensity of interdependences, just as the speed with which they arise and maintain themselves, as well as any consequential effects, have increased. The scope of interdependences today is 'more global' than ever before and their intensity has undoubtedly increased quantitatively.[26] Technological innovations nowadays render a historically incomparable speed of global communication possible at favourable prices. As for the consequences of such transformations in the global political, economic, social and cultural scene, it is just those parts of the world that would deliberately like to seal themselves off against them that are unable to do so. As evidenced by North Korea, as an extreme, downright pathological borderline case, the resulting costs are exceedingly high.

Nevertheless, examination of the diverse interdependence relations in the world shows that we are not dealing with a globe-covering equally positioned situation. Instead, realistic analysis reveals a clear space-geographically recognisable structure: the world's gravitational centre is characterised by cluster formation of the leading industrial countries with each other. On the basis of dense and symmetrically located exchange processes and a high degree of networking, the OECD triad structure has evolved. This is based on subject-articulated sub-clusters, which are more or less equally located (congruent): thus we have correspondences between the structures of goods exchange, investment streams and technology transfer, as well as of information flows and communication networks. And the structure patterns of these areas are again, as expected in a solid structure development, comparable to the political, institutional and functional-cooperative networks. In this dominant gravitational centre, the OECD world, dense, complex, congruently located and more or less symmetrical interdependences can be observed. In this the centre of world hierarchy constitutes itself and with it also the centre of the hierarchy of international division of labour, i.e. the hierarchical structure of international value creation at the peak of which, based upon high intensity in research, capital and manpower, the production of high-quality investment goods, consumer durables, technological products and services is localised.

Proceeding from this focused cluster formation, we can usually observe in the rest of the world typically asymmetrically localised centre–semi-periphery–periphery–sub-periphery structures: the further we descend from the centre, the OECD world, towards the peripheries, the less can we observe any reciprocal equally located networking. Proceeding from the Kantian formula we might state: immediately below the central area of the international hierarchy the societies (semi-peripheries) are slowly and laboriously achieving reciprocally effective relationships; among the peripheries of the international system such a process is, as yet, hardly taking place; among sub-peripheries it is not taking place at all. Peripheries, as before, are relatively unilaterally and asymmetrically dependent, aligned towards specific semi-peripheries or centres. This is the reason for the difficulties of establishing, between peripheries, effective organisations of regional cooperation and not just paper tigers like, for instance recently, the African Union (AU). Below the centres, among semi-peripheries, and especially on the level of peripheries, this layered hierarchy emerges as a corresponding stratification of international division of labour: at the lower end of the international value creation hierarchy, i.e. at the peripheries, we find raw material production and a fragile subsistence economy, as well as a research-poor and labour-intensive production of simple goods; in semi-peripheries we find the production that, in terms of value creation, lies between the peak production of the OECD gravitational centre and the simple production at the peripheries. The production and export statistics of the countries concerned accurately testify to this state of affairs.

Against the background of such a realistic stratified overall picture of the world the question posed above, about the interdependence of interdependences becomes tentatively answerable. Such interdependence reveals itself in the subject-conditioned necessary congruence of cluster structures within the gravitational centre. The density of the exchange of goods, capital, technology and services demands a corresponding density of information and communication, as well as of institutional coordination and functional-cooperative collaboration. The requirement of congruence to be understood functionally further deepens the establishment of a differentiating structure as a result of redundant and configurative causation.

Like the clusters at the peak of the international hierarchy, so parallel structural features are also displayed by centre-periphery relations across all subject areas. As we move from the peak of the hierarchy towards the peripheries, the extent of asymmetrical dependence ('dependent reproduction') and marginality increases in all subject areas. The interdependence of interdependences therefore establishes itself in line with the structural models predominant in the world. If one keeps this structural models before one's eyes, such an information-rich picture of the world provides the basis for a reality-conformant, i.e. qualified, concept of 'globalisation' and globality. In that case this concept, which has by now become an almost randomly used concept, would define the range and scope and above all the real stratification of structures and processes through which the various parts of the world 'enter into effective relationships with one another' in the most diverse manner.[27]

Another point to be remembered is this: a survey of the different segments of the international system in respect of their interdependence content shows – as elucidated earlier – that the positive peace-policy expectations implicitly, but occasionally also explicitly, associated with the concept of interdependence are being fulfilled only in one segment – in the area of symmetrical interdependence, i.e. within West–West relations. Perhaps it would be useful to speak, in such a context, of an emphatic interdependence concept: this relationship structure is, as we have shown, relatively homogeneous in system-political terms (rule-of-law states of Western type); it is moreover characterised by comparable highly productive and efficient economic profiles and a resultant dense material interlocking (substitutive division of labour), as well as by dense institutional networking at both government and non-government level. The extent of self-regulation is relatively high; there are explicit mechanisms for settling conflicts; as a consequence of its dense structure this pattern of relations creates a constraint to permanent coordination both at government level and between social groups. The arrangement is widely felt to be reasonably fair, which lends it legitimacy. Nothing comparable can be observed with regard to asymmetrical interdependence, such as North–South relations or any relations between centres and developing regions; nor indeed with regard to confrontational interdependence, which once marked East–West relations and today characterises regional conflicts. In both instances, viewed in retrospect but related to the present, critical argumentation, aimed at overcoming confrontational or asymmetrical interdependence, aims at the components of symmetrical interdependence: at common principles of behaviour and the strengthening of equally located material networks, at coordination of behaviour through an intensification of institutional networks and the search for just distribution in the sense of fairer 'pay-offs' on the basis of increasingly symmetrical reciprocal relations.

On the basis of experience, therefore, symmetrical interdependence becomes a normative guiding perspective in analysis and practice. The development of this type of interdependence increases the probability of civilisation of international politics. At the same time we cannot ignore the fact that this state of affairs depends on a great many premises and that the concept is a very demanding one. Translating this concept outside the OECD world, i.e. (in population terms) to four-fifths of mankind, ensuring that other parts of the world are, as a result of a fundamental structural transformation, eventually, each on a regional basis, positioned in a symmetrical-interdependent manner is certainly a major challenge – more than a single century's task.

Notes

1. Contributions to this include Beate Kohler-Koch, 'Interdependenz', in Volker Rittberger (ed.), *Theorien der Internationalen Beziehungen*, Sonderheft 21/1990 der *Politischen Vierteljahresschrift*, Opladen 1990, pp. 110–130; James N. Rosenau and Hylke Tromp (eds), *Interdependence and Conflict in World Politics*, Aldershot 1989; Jaap de Wilde, *Saved from Oblivion. Interdependence Theory in the First Half of the Century*, Aldershot 1991, A retrospect to the interdependence debate is provided by Manuela Spindler, 'Interdependenz', in Siegfried Schindler and Manuela Spindler (eds), *Theorien der internationalen Beziehugen*, Opladen 2001, pp. 89–116.
2. An analytical bridge between interdependence analysis and globalisation analysis is found in Michael Zürn, 'From Interdependence to Globalization', in Walter Carlsnaes et al. (eds), *Handbook of International Relations*, London 2002, Chapter 12.
3. The data in the subsequent empirical branches are taken from readily accessible data handbooks, such as *Der Fischer Weltalmanach* (annual), *Global Trends* (biannual), as well as the *World Development Report*, published annually by the World Bank.
4. See Ralf Roloff, *Europa, Amerika und Asien zwischen Globalisierung und Regionalisierung*, Paderborn 2001; Reinhard Rode, *Weltregieren durch internationale Wirtschaftsorganisationen*, Halle 2001.
5. See Roloff, *Europa, Amerika und Asien*.
6. For a differentiated conceptualisation of these problems see Robert Gilpin, *War and Change in World Politics*, Princeton 1981, as well as the broadly conceived monograph by Paul Kennedy, *The Rise and Fall of the Great Powers*, New York 1987.
7. See Chapter 6 of the present book.
8. See Dieter Senghaas, *The European Experience*; David S. Landes, *The Wealth and Poverty of Nations*, New York 1998 (on this also my extensive review in *Leviathan*, vol. 28, no. 1, 2000, pp. 142–153).
9. An early seminal analysis of this state of affairs can be found in Ulrich Menzel, *In der Nachfolge Europas. Autozentrierte Entwicklung in den ostasiatischen Schwellenländern Südkorea und Taiwan*, Munich 1985.
10. See Ulrich Menzel and Dieter Senghaas, *Europas Entwicklung und die Dritte Welt. Eine Bestandsaufnahme*, Frankfurt/M. 1986, Chapter 7.
11. This Listian perspective is developed in Dieter Senghaas, *Weltwirtschaftsordnung und Entwicklungspolitik. Plädoyer für Dissoziation*, Frankfurt/M. 1977, as well as in Samir Amin, *La déconnexion*, Paris 1985 (see also my piece on S. Amin in *Entwicklung und Zusammenarbeit*, no. 6, 2001, pp. 196–199) and recently also Ha-Joon Chang, *Kicking Away the Ladder. Development Strategy in Historical Perspective*, London 2002.
12. See Dieter Senghaas, *Konfliktformationen im internationalen System*, Frankfurt/M. 1988, Chapters II and III. A comprehensive retrospect in idem, 'War der Kalte Krieg ein Krieg? Realitäten, Phantasien, Paradoxien', in *Leviathan*, vol. 31, no. 3, 2003, pp. 303–322.

13. See Dieter Senghaas, *Friedensprojekt Europa*, Frankfurt/M. 1992; Ernst-Otto Czempiel, *Neue Sicherheit in Europa. Eine Kritik an Neorealismus und Realpolitik*, Frankfurt/M. 2002.
14. See Senghaas, Konfliktformationen, Chapter VI.
15. For analyses of regional conflicts see Karl Kaiser and Hans-Peter Schwarz, *Weltpolitik im neuen Jahrhundert*, Bonn 2000; Mir A. Ferdowsi (ed.), *Internationale Politik im 21. Jahrhundert*, Munich 2002.
16. On the structural transformation in the global economy see Mathias Albert, Lothar Brock, Stephan Hessler, Ulrich Menzel and Jürgen Neyer, *Die Neue Weltwirtschaft. Entstofflichung und Entgrenzung der Ökonomie*, Frankfurt/M. 1999.
17. See Ernst Ulrich von Weizsäcker, *Erdpolitik. Ökologische Realpolitik als Antwort auf die Globalisierung*, Darmstadt 1997, 5th edn. A well-founded comparative and methodologically complex examination is found in Günther Bächler, *Violence Through Environmental Discrimination*, Dordrecht 1999.
18. On the facts generally see Volker Rittberger and Bernhard Zangl, *Internationale Organisationen. Politik und Geschichte*, Opladen 2003; Eva Senghaas-Knobloch, 'Beiträge internationaler Organisationen zum Frieden in der Welt', in Astrid Sahm et al.(eds), *Die Zukunft des Friedens*, Opladen 2002, pp. 213–230.
19. See the five-volume series published by Björn Hettne, András Inotai and Osvaldo Sunkel, *The New Regionalism*, New York 2000–2.
20. See Thomas Risse, 'Transnational Actors and World Politics', in Carlsnaes et al. (eds), *Handbook of International Relations*, Chapter 13.
21. See Dieter Ruloff, *Weltstaat oder Staatenwelt? Über die Chancen globaler Zusammenarbeit*, Munich 1986.
22. See Dieter Senghaas (ed.), *Imperialismus und strukturelle Gewalt. Analysen über abhängige Reproduktion*, Frankfurt/M. 1972, idem (ed.), *Peripherer Kapitalismus. Analysen über Abhängigkeit und Unterentwicklung*, Frankfurt/M. 1994.
23. See Peter J. Opitz, *Menschenrechte und internationaler Menschenrechtsschutz im 20. Jahrhundert*, Munich 2002.
24. This document is published in Senghaas, *Friedensprojekt Europa*, pp. 191–210.
25. See Thomas Risse et al. (eds), *The Power of Human Rights. International Norms and Domestic Change*, Cambridge 1999.
26. See David Held et al., *Global Transformations. Politics, Economics and Culture*, Oxford 1999.
27. See also Dieter Senghaas, 'Die Konstitution der Welt – eine Analyse in friedenspolitischer Absicht', *Leviathan*, vol. 31, no. 1, 2003, pp. 117–152, as well as Chapter II in the present book.

Chapter 9

MODERN DEVELOPMENT PROBLEMS AND THEIR IMPLICATIONS FOR PEACE POLICY

1. Modern Development Problems

Over the past fifty years, in particular, both national and international organisations, as well as scholarship, have been concerning themselves with the problems of modern development. Prior to that, mention was only rarely made of 'developed' or 'underdeveloped' countries; more often mention was made of 'pays capitalistes avancés' and 'pays retardataires', 'plutocratic' and 'proletarian' nations, 'la société globale' and 'la société locale', and finally 'centres' and 'peripheries' – i.e. structures described by François Perroux in the 1950s as 'économie dominante' and 'économie dominée'.[1] The concept of 'developing countries' also came into use after 1945. This fact is surprising as modern development problems are much older. They can be traced back to the eighteenth century, when historically unprecedented modernisation and, in consequence, productivity leaps were recorded in England, first in agricultural and then in industrial production. Since then there has been the problem of delayed or 'catch-up development' – a fundamental structural problem of the modern world and one with major peace-policy implications.[2]

1.1 Challenge and Responses

The modern development problems arise when a gulf of knowledge and organisational ability exists between societies, especially between their economies, or if such a gulf is opening as a result of unequally spreading technological and organisational innovations. In that case, in the course of time, a less productive economy is confonted by a more productive. Between them a capability and competence gradient develops. If the exchange is maintained, a displacement competition arises between the more highly developed and the more backward economy. The leading society, or peak economy, will then be able, effortlessly to flood the national and international market, at favourable prices, with the goods produced with its more modern technology and its higher productivity. Unless protective measures are in place, the goods produced in the less advanced society with its old technology, low productivity and outdated design will simply be run into the ground by competition. Moreover, if the gradient between the more highly and the less highly developed economy is particularly great, efforts by the less developed society to check the trend are often discouraged from the outset. Their performance and innovation readiness are then at risk of petering out altogether, since the more competent peak economy can exert its superiority in every respect: in respect of production methods, the products themselves, as well as its ability to pursue innovations in every direction. In a sense an economy that has accomplished a breakthrough in important fields of technology and products is always more capable and knows more in all respects.[3]

Displacement competition is therefore a comprehensive phenomenon; it reveals itself not only in the competition pressure of more cheaply priced goods. Societies exposed to a competence gradient are, in an open global economy, forced to the margin over a broad front. They are, as the present-day development discussion puts it, peripheralised or marginalised. If they succumb to a broad peripheralisation pressure, their traditional lifestyles decline: they suffer social regression. They are simply overcome from outside. Or else they are functionally transformed into attachments or outposts of the more highly developed societies. As the history of such peripheries shows, this was not infrequently helped along by military pressure or by superior military might.

In the second case, the functional transformation of dependent societies into pendants or outposts of the more highly developed societies, there arise, viewed from the angle of the peak economies, exclaves of the type of monocultures or plantation economies. In these, a few commodities, such as sugar, coffee, tea, and also mineral products, are produced for the market of the more advanced economy. Such exclave economies are internally disrupted structures, in which no balanced or broadly effective potential arises. What does arise is structural heterogeneity.[4] Admittedly, in the event of high demand by the rapidly industrialising and advanced societies for agricultural products or unprocessed raw materials, considerable growth may be triggered in the exclaves of the less advanced economies. However, the result is often no more than a short-lived pseudo-boom. As a rule such exclave economies remain divided between an outward-directed growth pole and a more or less stagnating remaining economy.[5] If, as a result of economic-cycle and/or structural changes in the peak economies and in the global economy, the demand for agricultural products and raw materials declines – this has happened during economic crises and during global-economy structural change – then the externally stimulated growth in the relevant sector collapses and the scant resulting effects (linkages) of such growth in the remaining economy evaporate. The society thus affected is then, as a rule, thrown back to a meagre subsistence economy. Much the same reproduction dynamics apply if, as a result of outsourcing industrialisation, the industrial countries utilise certain developing countries for the production of labour-intensive and/or harmful-chemicals-intensive products of a low degree of finishing. In this case the exclave character emerges in the existence of so-called 'free production zones'.[6]

Modern development history shows that the processes described were observed not only between industrialising Europe and the rest of the world, but also within Europe itself, where regions with comprehensive development breakthroughs existed in the nineteenth and twentieth century, though alongside extensive regions, such as southern and eastern Europe, where displacement competition, chiefly from the industrial centres of north-western Europe, had led to actual peripheralsation. The problems described are therefore really worldwide; they did not leave Europe, the starting point of these problems, untouched – a fact that is often forgotten today.[7]

However, a totally different reaction to a developing competence gradient is also thinkable and can actually be observed in reality: the replacement competition described and the peripheralisation pressure can be seen as a challenge; by strenuous efforts it can be opposed. The gulf between the leaders of development and those lagging behind is regarded by the latter as an opportunity: by means of imitation, suitable protective measures and focused development projects the developmental lead is to be reduced or entirely eliminated. The development-policy slogan is then: catch up and even overtake! In this case we would observe an active and innovative response to replacement competition and peripheralisation pressure, totally different from being passively overpowered from outside, or even from a monoculture alignment of the weaker economy to the requirements of a lead economy in respect of agricultural produce, raw materials and finished goods of a low degree of processing. A precondition for a constructive reaction, admittedly, is that the gulf between leaders and catchers-up is not too great and that certain necessary intra-societal conditions for a successful catching-up process are given.

The history of Scandinavia, North America, Australia and New Zealand, and more recently also East Asia, shows that such active responses to replacement competition are possible and that attempts at catch-up development are not always doomed to failure from the outset, in spite of the competence gradient.[8] Lagging can therefore be also seen as an opportunity. An attempt is then made to defeat the more highly developed economy with its own weapons by copying its technology, thus saving development costs, and by conquering foreign markets with high-quality goods that are more favourably priced than would be possible if manufactured by old industrial societies with higher wages and infrastructure costs. Such opportunities were successfully taken up by Japan after 1945 and, following Japan, by the newly industrialising countries of Taiwan and Korea.[9]

1.2 Reasons for Different Roads of Development

If the international competence gradient between more and less advanced economies leads, in one case, to the overpowering of the less advanced societies, while, at other times, it is utilised as an opportunity for an innovative response, the question naturally arises about the reasons for such different reactions. In this context it is useful to remember an earlier, particularly clear-sighted, development theoretician and practician: Friedrich List (1789–1846).[10] List, who was the first to recognise the overall problem of catch-up development, argued from the viewpoint of his time, but his arguments are still important. He had England of the industrial revolution before his eyes; British industry's replacement competition was observed in many parts of the European continent. Theoretical and practical discussion culminated in the question of whether the European continent, or the U.S.A., would be able successfully to resist this English replacement competition or whether these economic zones would simply be steamrollered by British goods and British know-how. List in his day discussed the problem of catch-up development with regard to the continental European states, which were still in a transitional phase from a feudal-aristocratic system to an industrial society. His reflections made it clear that, in the first half of the nineteenth century, the development opportunities depended on the scale and the range of the defeudalisation process taking place in those societies. What List in his day, after extensive experience in the U.S.A. as a non-feudal lagging economy, regarded as the basis of successful development, namely, appropriate social and economic conditions, still applies as an essential prerequisite of developmental processes today.

According to his ideas, which have, since the middle of the past century, been buttressed by extensive economic-history research into early and less early cases,[11] feudal autocracy had to be replaced by far-sighted and efficient administration, including a bureaucracy that would have to look after the cohesion of a nation in course of development. An aristocracy grown limp with privilege had to be replaced by a business world oriented along profit and material prosperity; serfdom was to be replaced by a free peasantry; well-nourished and well-paid workers were regarded by List as one of the bases of increasing productivity of labour; the beneficial effects of freely creative scholarship and the arts were contrasted by him with the results of traditional fanaticism as revealed in religious wars and the Inquisition; an intellectually and socially mobile society was seen by List as the opposite of rigidified traditional societies. Development therefore had something to do with the mobilisation of forces that had been lying fallow in traditional society. If that process was impeded, or only half-started, or interrupted, then development blockages would result. Freedom and free movement figure as important prerequisites of a development process. A stable national framework is just as important as reliable rule of law and the widening of self-administration; a free entrepreneurial spirit in all strata of the population, as also a circumspect and long-term planning and a non-corrupt public administration (today called 'good governance'); a widely ramified transport network of roads, railways and canals, and a multiply branched education system. If there was one aspect to which this early theoretician of development problems assigned a certain priority, then it was his respect for immaterial spiritual forces, i.e. 'invisible capital', as against material values: stimulation and promotion of intellectual work and a spirit of invention, of knowledge and abilities, in short, of intellectual competences – these were to List a source of energy and strength scarcely replaceable by natural resources.

Another reflection of List is likewise still worth remembering and can be regarded as well founded in economic history: he found that a prerequisite of development processes from the very start is an efficient agriculture. The tasks of agriculture are many: for one thing, a growing urban population has to be fed by an ever smaller number of persons employed in agriculture. Next, industry has to be supplied with agricultural raw materials. Nor can agriculture avoid, in the early phase of industrialisation, having to support industrialisation and the creation of an infrastructure by means of an overt or covert transfer of resources. Moreover, the agricultural sector is an important market for industrial products of everyday use and for agricultural equipment. In spite of major demands and burdens an affluent demand has to remain in the rural area if the overall economic development dynamics are to be maintained. This consideration makes it clear that it is a mistake to attempt a successful industrialisation without a productive agriculture: agriculture plays an important, though often disregarded, strategic role in development processes. Yet this matter-of-course realisation had been more or less forgotten in the development programmes of the late nineteenth and the twentieth century. Eyes were focused on the developmental success of the industrialising lead economies, forgetting that their industrial development had specific antecedent agricultural and industrial prerequisites.[12] It took the many developmental failures of the past few decades to lend new life to this elementary realisation: countries without institutional agrarian reform and without agrotechnical modernisation remain incapable of liberating their development potential; as a rule they get into bottlenecks and allow disastrous structural defects to arise.

1.3 Lessons from Development History

What other lessons are there to be learned from successful or unsuccessful development processes? The problem of mobilising intellectual resources, the so-called human capital, has already been touched upon: countries that in the literacy drive of their populations and in the development of higher educational establishments (specialised colleges, people's universities, technical and general-education universities) lag behind have not only been less inventive than societies with a differentiated range of educational facilities but have also impeded the social mobility of their societies. As a result intellectual resources are left to lie fallow. One need only compare the development in Scandinavia, where, embarked on by church and state, a widespread literacy drive was pursued at an early date, with the situation in large parts of southern and south-eastern Europe, where neither the church nor the state showed much interest in the intellectual emancipation of their people. In this context it is also interesting to note the difference between the educationally eager East Asian societies (Japan, China, Korea, Taiwan and Singapore) and other parts of the Third World (especially the Islamic–Arab region), where no such efforts can be observed. It is also a fact that a disproportionate mobilisation of intellectual capital can offset a lack of natural resources. In this way even small countries with small natural resources can achieve a high-quality specialisation in the niches of the global economy (an example is the meanwhile much admired Finland as a European newly industrialised country in the twentieth century and, more recently, East Asia).[13] Of major importance for the development process is the evolution of a widely branching infrastructure: with increasing division of labour and the resulting need for networking of individual economic branches and sectors an efficient infrastructure becomes an indispensable requirement for the mediation of economic activities. Since infrastructure is a public asset, individual enterprises cannot be expected to make the public investments needed for the development of a national economy. Infrastructure therefore becomes a public task and the countries that have correctly realised this situation have thereby served their national developmental process well.

Nowhere in modern history has there been a successful development as the result of the free interplay of free forces. More or less state intervention has always been of major importance. Even in conditions of liberated forces, development is not an automatic process. This emerges particularly from the foreign-trade framework conditions under which the development processes must evolve. This aspect, too, had been clear-sightedly analysed by Friedrich List: today he is remembered chiefly as a champion of so-called protective tariffs for infant industries. If the problematic impacts of lead economies upon catch-up societies are to be prevented, or if these impacts are to be filtered and canalised, appropriate protective foreign-trade measures, such as protective tariffs, are necessary. These were to enhance the survival prospects of infant industries in developing societies. However, List's argument, confirmed by subsequent economic history, was more differentiated. He wanted protection chiefly for such industries as produced mass consumer goods, because these are of crucial importance for broadly opening their own domestic market. Protection of the production of precious and high-value luxury consumer goods was not considered sensible. Foreign machines and know-how were to be deliberately fed into the production process, though with the proviso that they do not simply overpower technological knowledge already existing. Here a major role is played by the ability to focus foreign technology on one's own needs. Besides, it had to be pointed out then, as it has to today, that protective measures are no panacea: according to the state of development they can be useful or harmful, and they can be abolished prematurely, or too late. In the critical early phase of a catch-up development it is important to find the correct branch-specific and sector-specific dose of openness outward and protective measures (selective dissociation or association). What is needed is a qualified mixed strategy of partial detachment from lead economies and partial alignment to them. Finding the appropriate mixture ratio and the correct road is a task for superior state policy.[14] The trick is neither to overtax nor to undertax a developing economy – an experiment based on trial and error, with no advance guarantee of success, with a need to weigh up long-term economic perspectives and short-term enterprise-economic profitability calculations against each other.

In this context attention should be drawn to an unambiguous lesson from recent development history: selective protective measures are helpful only in conjunction with appropriate domestic development efforts. If a country isolates itself without making simultaneous internal development efforts, such protectionism leads to failure. Recent development history of the nineteenth and twentieth century provides ample evidence of this. Thus, protectionist measures were frequently used not for the deconstruction of traditional development blockades, such as old-fashioned agrarian structures and continuing privileges for oligarchic groups, but for their reinforcement. In consequence, in the latter case it was not an orientation towards competition and hence towards innovation that prevailed, but protection of a mentality focused on unearned income.[15]

Getting development processes on the right road is therefore not an easy task: for one thing, a damaging displacement competition originating from higher developed societies has to be fended off, while, on the other hand, know-how existing elsewhere has to be deliberately utilised in one's own context, thereby saving development costs. Within the country itself successful development depends on a broad-spectrum network between agriculture, industry and commerce, on the mobilisation of an appropriate *linkage* potential.[16] In reality, however, we all too often observe industrialisation leading to withdrawal effects to the detriment of agriculture and to the one-sided advantage of urban conglomeration centres (urban bias). The resulting exacerbation of political, socio-economic and cultural divisions then becomes a breeding ground for many aggravating social catastrophes: the collapse of agricultural self-sufficiency, drift from the country, mass impoverishment in the countryside, excessive urbanisation, structural unemployment and underemployment, and finally an uncontrollable population growth, which with an unrelenting dynamic of its own, wrecks or diminishes partial development successes. These manifold negative experiences show that only a broad-spectrum mobilisation of unused resources in all parts of society, and especially in agriculture, can lead to success. As a rule this calls for prior or accompanying reforms, without which industrialisation efforts remain stuck in their beginnings and usually end in failure. Added to the skill of correctly creating the foreign-trade framework conditions of development programmes, there is therefore the practical trick of demolishing detrimental internal structures and creating space for new development opportunities.[17]

1.4 The Political Content of Development Options

Such reflections may appear abstract or technocratic, but they are of course intended quite concretely and describe entirely political states of affairs. Protective foreign-trade measures favour or disadvantage specific interests. Progress of literacy as the basis of intellectual emancipation contributes to social transformation and undermines traditional positions of power. Infrastructural measures favour the regions in which they are effected. In all development processes there is a permanent conflict between rural areas and urban conglomeration centres. This means that development processes cannot simply be 'unreeled'; they are the result of political conflict constellations. Development processes are channelled, each into a specific direction by specific relations of forces: if, for instance, the power of the landed oligarchy and of commercial capital remains unbroken, the emergence of an exclave economy is more or less inevitable. If, on the other hand, in the political clash between these forces and an emerging bourgeoisie, the entrepreneurial forces together with a unionised urban working class, supported by a nascent middle class in the services sector, come out victorious, then a national-capitalist development road is probable. Other fundamental constellations could be mentioned.[18] Such contexts also make it clear that development, wrong development or even underdevelopment cannot be simply attributed to the presence or absence of natural resources or climatic conditions. They also explain why technocratic development programmes, attempting to stage development by bypassing political power situations, are usually bound to fail. Understanding modern development problems therefore requires a theoretical understanding of political economy.

1.5 The Lesson of the Failure of Real Socialism

The political content of development processes was always visible with the classics of the old development discussion. It was only displaced after 1945 in a more and more one-sided economic-theoretical orientation. On closer inspection, it emerged after 1945 chiefly in the area of the really-existing socialism, with which the development discussion was not normally concerned.[19] The lessons of this, eventually unsuccessful, experience should also receive appropriate attention in the development discussion.

If, as happened in the Stalinist development model, society's free spaces are eliminated, one of the most important development resources, the free unfolding of individuals and groups, is destroyed. If, as happened in this model, agriculture is permanently bled white, negative effects on the economy as a whole are unavoidable. Overemphasis on heavy industry bypasses the daily needs of consumers. As a result, performance motivation dries up and social apathy takes over. If the services sector is neglected or, on ideological grounds, mistakenly regarded as 'unproductive', division of labour and networking of productive forces are bound to be impaired. Total isolation from the world outside, i.e. a policy of autarky, deprives a society of the stimuli for innovation. This produced a doubly negative effect in real-socialism: in addition to the elimination of any competition from outside, internal competition as a potential source of innovation was eliminated as well in the state-trade countries. In consequence, innovation had to be planned technocratically; this was more or less successful only in the armaments area. Real-socialism also proves that growth is a necessary, albeit not a sufficient, condition for development. What matters is what grows, and how vigorously, and under what distribution conditions.

What was lacking in real-socialism – more and more – is immediately obvious from a development-history point of view: the emancipation of society vis-à-vis the state and party monopoly, especially the transition from a kind of despotism to enlighted absolutism and eventually democracy; the creation of spaces for political freedom as a starting point of self-activating social forces; political participation and self-administration; an agrarian reform informed by worldwide experience, i.e. the high productivity of self-managing medium-sized enterprises networked the basis of cooperation; an increase of labour productivity in all parts of the economy by a shift of growth priorities from raw-material and heavy industry to consumer industry with support for a technologically advanced engineering industry; development of the infrastructure, as well as appreciation and promotion of the services sector; an increasing opening to the more distant outside world by an intensification of the exchange of people, goods, technology and capital. A reconstruction of these societies was long overdue after an initial phase of extensive growth. As we know, it came too late: the internal contradictions could no longer be managed within the framework of the real-socialist *ancien régime*. In an environment characterised by considerable dynamism they were bound to escalate with the result that more or less revolutionary transformation situations – predictable and long predicted – became inevitable. As with any real revolution it was just the precise date (1989–92) that was not predictable.[20]

Attempts to steer an entire development process from a centre is bound to result in failure. Simply leaving development processes to the free interplay of forces can succeed only in exceptional cases – and these have scarcely ever occurred in history. What has to be done, therefore, is set social forces free and let them unfold under framework conditions that do not overtax them, but do not undertax them either. This has always been a difficult task and it is no easier today when the gulf between lead economies and stragglers has, over the past few decades, become bigger rather than smaller. This fundamental structural state of affairs is one of the reasons why development problems, manifesting themselves as of *longue durée*, have become one of the core problems of international politics.

2. Implications for Peace Policy

What are the peace-policy implications of the modern development problems set out above? We should differentiate between two problem areas: on the one hand, the problems resulting from the internal revolution of individual societies as a consequence of development processes and, on the other hand, the problems affecting the international system.

2.1 The Conflict Liability of Development Processes

1. Development, as well as faulty development or underdevelopment, implies social change, i.e. descent of old social groups (classes and strata) and the rise of new ones. This downward and upward mobility is, as a rule, highly

charged with conflict and, according to old historical experience, pervaded by violence. Not only are interests affected on which fair compromises might be found, but also identities endangered by social change or newly established. If a conflict of interests is overlaid by a conflict of identities, the resulting political disputes are especially violent. Decades might pass before a new institutional framework and its political rules are considered more or less legitimate: during this period long-term conflicts are mostly inevitable.

The practical question arises concerning the scale of violence, or the prospects of non-violence in such social confrontations. Experience teaches that political participation combined with a focused policy of fairness of distribution can help diminish the scale of violence. This experience is confronted by another, according to which, during a prolonged initial phase of development processes, socio-economic inequality tends to increase rather than decrease. A policy of distribution fairness or social equity therefore requires a long breath because it only becomes fully effective in a later developmental phase, especially when, as a result of lobbying conflicts, a widespread democratisation of political participation opportunities has been achieved. What can today be observed in the Third World as the result of modernisation conflicts – political instability all the way to civil-war-type clashes – has a century-old history also in the early development of Europe, except that political, social, economic and cultural revolutions nowadays occur in a much shorter time span than in the lead societies of Europe. In consequence the problems are aggravated; practical management of the conflicts becomes exceedingly difficult, all the more so as the employment of modern media dramatises political conflicts to an incomparable degree. Development processes therefore inevitably jeopardise any traditional 'social peace': the social transformation makes agreement on the new political premises of social order necessary. This means that, for a long time, we have to expect, in development processes, more or less violent conflicts rather than enduring social peace.[21]

2. Development also implies conflicts about the upward mobility and against the downward mobility of individual states, societies and nations in the hierarchy typical of the world. a hierarchy based essentially on the stratified structure of the international division of labour. Two sets of problems are of particular importance here: the hegemony position of a lead economy and the problem of catch-up development aiming at upward mobility and the prevention of peripheralisation.

For the past 250 years a hegemony position in the global economy and in international politics has only been attainable on the basis of technological and organisational innovation through globally leading economic sectors. Such a performance profile is, essentially, not the result of the exploitation of other societies, even though this might help, but the result of unparalleled productivity breakthroughs in one's own economy as the sum total of competences achieved. Hegemonic peak economies are of course tempted to exert their superiority in world eco-nomics by advocating free trade and attempting to enforce it worldwide. Free trade implies that the *économie dominante* can fully employ its own economic potential as the prospects of a successful replacement competition are favourable for it from the outset. And although the general assumption of classic liberal theory – that a free-trade global economic system implied cosmopolitan welfare gains for the global economy as a whole – is correct in principle, the real unit, however, is not the global economy around which economic action revolves, but the individual variously developed national economies.[22] Cosmopolitan welfare gains can mean very different things for those concerned: for the peak economy, as a rule, further growth opportunities, for a few states with a skilful strategy for catch-up development the possibility, or acceleration, of upward mobility by attaching themselves to the growth engine at the peak of the global economy and by embarking on a broadly effective catch-up development. For many others, however, management under free-trade conditions means the danger of peripheralisation and eventually a real peripheral development, either in the sense of a monoculture alignment to the requirements of the peak economy (as often in the case of global boom phases) or in the sense of socio-economic and sociocultural regression (especially in the case of global recession phases).

A policy concerned with a country's own development opportunities can be observed mainly under conditions of a dependent upward mobility that eventually leads to a widespread catch-up development and thus to success. What matters in these circumstances is fending off, or channelling, the displacement competition from outside and initiating a state-supported development policy for the deployment of one's own productive forces. Such measures, as a rule, are not short-term ones as they are aimed at the opening up of human capital and a publicly promoted industrial policy. Since catch-up development is not an automatic process, but requires measures within the national framework, such 'development nationalism' has to be seen as an important means for the release of a country's own development potential, its national economy. From a development-policy viewpoint it does not therefore make sense to reject any emphatically national policy, one that steers the economic process, from the outset. In judging such 'nationalism' we should ask whether it serves an across-the-board development of the society concerned or if it is no more than a demagogical or militant means for preserving the status quo. Any nationalism of the latter kind needs to be fundamentally criticised, especially from a peace-policy viewpoint, because it usually serves the concealment of an offensive-expansionist policy. And quite often such a policy is pursued towards the outside only in order to consolidate and cement the existing status quo against social forces pushing forward as a result of development processes.[23]

The idea, championed at present also among the peak economies of the global economy (the club of OECD countries), that free trade is welfare-promoting under all circumstances is no less problematical today than it was in the eighteenth, nineteenth and twentieth centuries. Today's most highly industrialised countries did not, in their own development history, adhere to this motto at all. On the contrary, they pursued a nationalist development policy aligned to their own development interests, a policy of deliberate protection and subsidies and of public support for developmental measures ('industrial policy').[24] This obvious orientation, a kind of survival strategy, reflects the ever-present virulence of the competence gradient in the global economy. Free trade was always the exception rather than the rule in economic history.

2.2 Five Peace-policy Problem Areas of International Politics

What then are today's experiences and their peace-policy implications from the viewpoint of modern development problems? At least five areas of experience should be distinguished.

2.2.1 The Potential Reappearance of Modern Hegemony Crisis Problems

One of the most important peace-policy questions for the future concerns the so-called 'hegemony crisis problems', when the virulence of catch-up development undergoes political exacerbation. This set of problems, which used to recur cyclically in the past, resulted in the context of the rise and fall of 'great powers' from the clash between hegemony candidates and existing hegemony powers. This state of affairs is well documented over the past 500 years and transparent also from theoretical viewpoints.[25] It is the consequence of different innovation capability and divergent growth rates of ' ageing powers' in contrast to 'young, dynamically upward-mobile powers that are coming into being' and which succeed in acquiring a new economic-technological base of resources resulting in new lead sectors for an international division of labour.[26] This gives rise to a world-political constellation in which conflicts develop about the future of the world order; in an extreme case the result is major wars for hegemony, i.e. global or world wars.[27]

Today the U.S.A. is a hegemonic power, unquestioned in military respects and in other dimensions perhaps perceived exaggeratedly. If the official document *The National Strategy of the United States of America* in the autumn of 2002 pointed out that the U.S.A., by means of a forced mobilisation of its own resources, would have to strive to prevent the geopolitical rise of a comparably powerful state, then this document acurately anticipated a potential global hegemony crisis problem.[28] China in particular is being identified as a potential candidate for geopolitical upward mobility; the rest of possible powers (such as the European Union, Japan, India, Russia, Brazil) are regarded as improbable contestants. In actual fact, China's future road of development is not unambiguously mapped out either economically or politically: is China (like Japan and West Germany after 1950) going to follow the *'trading state'* model and, moreover, qualify and optimise its economic basis in order, eventually, to achieve an *'upgrading'* of its position in the hierarchy of the international division of labour (as South Korea and Taiwan succeeded in doing after 1960) or will China, faced with enormous problems within the country pursue a cultural-chauvinist economically nationalist course? Even close China watchers dare not answer these questions definitively one way or the other, which means that a future hegemony crisis problem cannot be unambiguously forecast.[29] One thing is certain: this set of problems, which time and again have characterised the modern world of states at the peak of its hierarchy, has simply not come to an end with the present unquestionable military and the by no means equally unquestionable economic-technological and cultural supremacy of the U.S.A.[30]

Alongside this set of peace problems at the top of the international hierarchy four other problem areas need mapping out.

2.2.2 The OECD World

After some 100 to 150 years of successful catch-up development, today's highly industrialised societies of the West (OECD) have achieved internal profiles that permit them to act amongst each other in a free-trade manner.[31] This situation is reflected by substitutive division of labour, i.e. in competition in all essential branches of the economy, all of which are marked by high productivity. Thus in this core segment of the global economy we find a tendency towards symmetrical interdependence of a substantial order of magnitude. These are societies with a high degree of political stability, with broad opportunities for democratic participation, based on political systems characterised by the rule of law. Economically speaking, these are high-wage countries with powerful domestic markets. A substantial measure of symmetrical economic intertwining and overarching institutional networking results, among the members of this club, in a more or less fair distribution of profit opportunities. On the basis of a trilateral coordination of economic policies between the U.S.A., Japan and the European Community a mutual economic-policy adaptation takes place, which has so far prevented global-economic disputes of a no longer controllable order of magnitude. Generally, however, even the club of

OECD economies shows that even under peak economies the modern development problems, i.e. the structural dangers of a displacement competition, continue to be virulent:[32] by means of appropriate state measures these peak economies, too, promote and protect potentially new lead sectors whose successful development would ensure an appropriate lead in the global economy (innovation protectionism). But they also protect, albeit in the individual case with retro-effect, ageing industrial branches and sub-branches, through preservation protectionism, against competition from young upwardly mobile industrial societies (newly industrialised countries). The free-trade arrangement between the OECD economies is therefore always threatened from two sides – a problem clearly reflected in the continual, mostly crisis-triggered, discussion on neo-mercantilism or neo-protectionism.

Despite such cushioned virulence we must not overlook the fact that the 'OECD world' represents a zone of stable peace. Neither is there any threat of military force in connection with conflicts of interest, nor is it thinkable that military force could be applied in the mutual relations of the OECD states. The 'OECD peace' is a considerable achievement, especially if one considers that 120 years ago leading industrial countries found themselves in imperialistic conflicts and that two world wars were subsequently fought between them. The probability of this type of conflict is slight today. In view of the unprecedented interweaving of interests conflict settlement by institutionalised ways of negotiation and relevant regulation systems ('international regime') are far more likely. Interwoven interests lead to concerted behaviour.

2.2.3. North–South Relations

By way of contrast, no comparable symmetries exist in relations between the Western industrial societies and the world's developing regions, either in political or in an economic respect. On the contrary, these relations are characterised by profound asymmetries. Here the modern development problems emerge in full: the peak economies of the OECD club are confronted by economies that have passed through a peripheral development and are attempting, with more or less success, to embark on a catch-up development. Only in East Asia have there been real development breakthroughs implying an upward mobility. Elsewhere we find rather problematical, and quite often disastrous, results. These relations reveal their asymmetry in the unequal relevance to one another: to the industrial countries, which in their economic activities essentially orbit around themselves, the Third World – with the exception of about ten threshold countries and the energy-producing states – is of limited importance, whereas the developing countries in their external economic activities remain basically oriented towards the industrial countries. Above all, the structural consequences of these relations tend to be asymmetrical: for the industrial countries their external economic activities in the Third World are only supplementary fields of activity for already diversified and high-quality economies; for the developing countries these relations may imply income opportunities, which, however, are directed to widely different uses – whether used for productive investments or used for consumption, or indeed simply wasted. Yet even productive investments are not invariably development-enhancing: indeed, as a result of wrong priorities, they can trigger drastically wrong developments. If, however, one could assume more or less correct priorities – and this is a rather unrealistic assumption – a supplementary international social policy would be necessary at least for the least developed countries, a policy to be understood as support for national developmental efforts. Viewed realistically, however, long experience teaches that even a resource transfer from the centres of the global economy to the peripheries is by no means always development-promoting: unless subject to conditions it can result in a consolidation of old structures or in wrong allocations. In this respect, too, correctly set focuses of development policy – correct in respect of List's above described criteria – are important.

As for the degree of conflict intensity in North–South relations, we cannot proceed from a broadly established across-the-board North–South conflict in the sense of antagonistic organised conflict parties. For that the developing countries are too heterogeneous a structure. Besides, they do not possess any effective collective organisations; their interests are therefore difficult to articulate, coordinate and assert. In all probability there will no longer be a great uniform conflict front line between the industrial and the developing countries; instead there will be multiple small conflict front lines resulting from specific problems, for instance from assumed dangers (in consequence of nuclear, biological and chemical rearming in the Third World) or as a consequence of profound political and socio-economic upheavals, which already, albeit so far only on a limited scale, are producing streams of economic refugees. Yet even these minor conflict front lines are not numerous; at present only the Middle East and the Gulf zone are to be assessed as globally dangerous – not Latin America, black Africa, the ASEAN area or East Asia. In southern Asia, admittedly, there is a threat between India and Pakistan, which, given certain impacts from outside, might be limited to a regional conflict.[33]

2.2.4 The New West–East Relations

Relations between the Western industrial societies and the societies of real-socialism that collapsed after 1989–92 were in danger of an opening gulf that might easily translate into a chronic peripheral development. However, such a development is not inevitable: it can be counteracted by appropriate local reform measures and substantial rehabilitation help from outside. Nor should it be overlooked that the egalitarianism forcibly imposed by real-socialism might become a positive aspect in the transformation process: long experience teaches that initially egalitarian societies are more capable of development than those marked initially by gross inequality. Moreover, the formerly real-socialist societies, which have been in transition to democratic rule-of-law states with a market economy, have a considerable well-trained human capital at their disposal, which could, without difficulty, be further enhanced and qualified. It is obvious, however, that these societies have, owing to a liberalisation of their external economic relations on the basis of dogmatic free-trade premises, been exposed to an equally comprehensive displacement competition, to which, because of the weakness of their own transformation economies, they are unable to stand up. On the other hand, there is a need for a selective opening up to the world market in order to get out of the defensive circle of their past planned economies and to link up with new technological developments in products and production methods. The trick, in these cases too, will be to fend off a ruinous displacement economy, or to channel it towards their own needs, while urgently seeking an attachment to the global economy. As always in such situations, there is a danger of wrong decisions one way or another, either in favour of a defence against displacement competition that lasts too long and is too comprehensive, or one that is too short and not comprehensive enough, and that, in either case, internal development efforts remain inadequate, resulting in a repetition of age-old development-policy experience.

However, it is entirely thinkable that, unlike in North–South relations, reconstruction and transformation assistance will, in this system of relations, produce visible successes within the relatively short period of two decades – not only because, in the case of eastern central Europe, the Baltic and (albeit still with considerable limitations) south-eastern Europe it encounters receptive structures, but because it is integrated into a comprehensive concept of a European peace system, the EU's opening to the East. A structure of durable peace in Europe will only be attainable if an economic levelling out is achieved between Western and Eastern Europe, or, in other words, if Europe splits economically, viable all-European institutions will not be achieved.[34]

2.2.5 South–South Relations

Apart from a few exceptions, economic relations among the developing countries are of slight importance in terms of magnitude. That is why, at present, it seems rather hopeless to try effectively to counteract conflicts in this area through the creation of economic interdependence. Power-political disputes – as a glance at the Third World reveals – erupt here quite undisguised, while sober economic interests frequently play a much slighter role than political aims of gaining power, or especially of maintaining or extending power. These so-called 'new wars', which are based on the rule of warlords and markets of violence ('warlordism') reflect a downright chronic socio-pathological state of affairs.[35] Yet, given appropriate political coordination, the developing countries could easily solve the most important problems of their own development among themselves: despite a low, but nevertheless differentiated, development level they could be reciprocally exceedingly useful to one another. The danger of being overpowered and steamrollered by a partner of a comparable level of development is not nearly as great as the one resulting from the gradient between the peak economies of the industrial world and themselves. But such an outlook of 'collective self-reliance' has not so far fallen on fertile ground in the developing countries, which is the reason why, except for newly industrialising countries, their foreign-trade relations remain tied into old bilateral structures of the colonial type.

3. Summary

The modern development problems, starting with England's agrarian and industrial revolution, if not before, have increased in virulence over the past decades. Power-cyclical disputes arose about the leading positions in the global economy, i.e. modern hegemony conflicts. Moreover, the problem of catch-up development became increasingly politicised as the development issue was becoming an important point of reference of regional and worldwide political dispute. Added to this is the fact that, with easier international information and communication, demonstration effects between advanced and lagging societies become more marked, so that development gradients are tolerated less and less. Without an equilibrium of possessions, 'when everyone is tolerably well situated', as Fichte once put it, peaceful relations within societies and between societies can hardly be expected.[36] A policy of active distribution fairness is therefore a minimum condition for social peace within and between societies. As for the peace-policy implications, an answer referring to the classic position of 'peace through trade', or even 'peace through free trade', is far from satisfactory. In development history, this slogan was directed against the power-extension policy and the conquest policy of the European dynasties in the seventeenth, eighteenth and nineteenth centuries, while simultaneously, in the long term, the cosmopolitan interests of the rising bourgeoisie were to be promoted. The modern development problems, which are concerned with facilitating catch-up development, were not, or not adequately, considered. Today, especially in view of the gross asymmetries in the world, these problems are undeniably of fundamental importance in determining the constitution of the world. Hence the variable aspects of the security dilemmas can no longer be understood without an understanding of the preceding development dilemma. This basic state of affairs alone catapults the development problems straight into the centre of the discussion about the conditions of possible peace in the single-state, regional and global context.[37]

Notes

1. An early seminal development-policy discussion with theoretical implications was held in the second half of the nineteenth century in Romania; this is documented in the journal *Review*, then published by Immanuel Wallerstein, vol. 2, no. 1, 1978 (*Romania. Early Theories of Development*). The debates that took place there were significantly inspired by Friedrich List (see below); François Perroux, 'Note sur la notion de pôle de croissance', *Économie appliquée*, vol. 8, 1955, pp. 307–323.
2. The classic author on this state of affairs is Friedrich List, *Das nationale System der Politischen Ökonomie* (1841), Tübingen 1959.
3. See Dieter Senghaas, *The European Experience. A Historical Critique of Development Theory*, Leamington Spa/Dover, NH 1985; Ulrich Menzel and Dieter Senghaas, *Europas Entwicklung und die Dritte Welt. Eine Bestandsaufnahme*, Frankfurt/M. 1986.
4. See Dieter Senghaas, *Weltwirtschaftsordnung und Entwicklungspolitik. Plädoyer für Dissoziation*, Frankfrt/M. 1977.
5. In simply structured cases we can speak of a dual economy; as a rule, however, we are dealing with stratified structures with internal symbiotic relationships: hence the more appropriate concept 'structural heterogeneity'.
6. On the latter case see Folker Fröbel et al., *Die neue internationale Arbeitsteilung*, Reinbek 1977.
7. This state of affairs is the central subject of Senghaas, *The European Experience*.
8. Senghaas, *The European Experience*, as well as in particular Ulrich Menzel, *Auswege aus der Abhängigkeit. Die entwicklungspolitische Aktualität Europas*, Frankfurt/M. 1988.
9. See Ulrich Menzel, *In der Nachfolge Europas. Autozentrierte Entwicklung in den ostasiatischen Schwellenländern Südkorea und Taiwan*, Munich 1985.
10. From the wealth of List's writings see especially his principal work, *Das nationale System*. A general tribute is in Dieter Senghaas, 'Friedrich List und die moderne Entwicklungsproblematik', *Leviathan*, vol. 17, no. 4, 1989, pp.561–573, as well as idem, 'Friedrich List (1789–1846)', *Entwicklung und Zusammenarbeit*, vol. 40, no. 6, 1999, pp. 164–168.
11. See mainly Paul Bairoch, *Révolution industrielle et sous-développement*, Paris 1974; idem, *Die Dritte Welt in der Sackgasse*, Vienna 1973; Alan S. Milward and S.B. Saul, *The Economic Development of Continental Europe 1850–1914*, London 1977; Iván Berend and György Ránki, *Economic Development in East-Central Europe in the nineteenth and twentieth Century*, New York 1974; Sidney Pollard, *Peaceful Conquest. The Industrialization of Europe, 1760–1970*, Oxford 1981; Cynthia Taft Morris and Irma Adelmann, *Comparative Patterns of Economic Development, 1850–1914*, London 1988; David Landes, *The Wealth and Poverty of Nations*, New York 1998; Harmut Elsenhans, 'Geschichte und Ökonomie europäischer Eroberung, Leipzig (unpubl. manuscript).

12. See Samir Amin, *Die ungleiche Entwicklung*, Hamburg 1974; Bairoch, *Die Dritte Welt*; W.A. Lewis, *The Evolution of the International Economic Order*, Princeton 1978; Hartmut Elsenhans (ed.), *Agrarreform in der Dritten Welt*, Frankfurt/M. 1979.
13. On Finland see Senghaas, *The European Experience*, Chapter 2.
14. See Senghaas, *Weltwirtschaftsordnung*, as well as Samir Amin, *La déconnexion. Pour sortir du système mondial*, Paris 1986.
15. Fundamentally Hartmut Elsenhans, *Das internationale System zwischen Zivilgesellschaft und Rente*, Münster 2001.
16. See W. Leontief, 'The Structure of Development', *Scientific American*, vol. 209, no. 3, 1963, pp. 148–166; Albert Hirschmann, 'A Generalized Linkage Approach to Development with Special Reference to Staples', *Economic Development and Cultural Change*, vol. 25, suppl. 1977, pp. 67–98; Jane Jacobs, *Cities and the Wealth of Nations. Principles of Economic Life*, New York 1984.
17. All the doctrines of development history listed in this secton – of both successful and failed cases – demonstrate how extremely one-sided, i.e. economistic, a large part of the development discussion over the past few decades has been and how, gradually, ancient and often obvious insights into development processes have had to be 'rediscovered'. This state of affairs can be documented in particular by the World Bank programmes as evidenced in the annually published World Development Reports. For the past two decades new features are being propagated year after year that can only be described as such if one assumes an extreme oblivion of history. In reality these are development-historical truths. See my brief and pointed contribution, Dieter Senghaas, *Wider den entwicklungstheoretischen Gedächtnisschwund. Die Auswege aus der Armut sind bekannt*, in Reinhold Thiel (ed.), *Neue Ansätze zur Entwicklungstheorie*, Bonn 1999, pp. 350–354; see also the instructive volume by Louis Emmerij (ed.), *Economic and Social Development into the XXI Century*, Washington 1997.
18. See Senghaas, *The European Experience*.
19. See Roman Szporluk, *Communism and Nationalism. Karl Marx versus Friedrich List*, New York 1988.
20. On early predictions see Senghaas, *The European Experience*, mainly the East European authors quoted in Chapter 6, also my own prediction in 1982. Useful to an understanding of the revolutionary transformations in the real-socialist countries is, interestingly enough, the classic author on the diagnosis of such a situation, namely, Alexis de Tocqueville, *Der alte Staat und die Revolution* (1856), Bremen n.d. (Collection Dieterich, vol. 232).
21. See chiefly Chapter 2 of the present book.
22. See Paul Bairoch, *Economic and World History. Myths and Paradoxes*, New York 1993, esp. Chapters 2 and 3.
23. On this set of problems and different types of development nationalism see Dieter Senghaas, *Wohin driftet die Welt? Über die Zukunft friedlicher Koexistenz*, Frankfrt/M. 1994, Chapters 2 and 3.
24. See now, fundamentally, Ha-Joon Chang, *Kicking Away the Ladder. Development Strategy in Historical Perspective*, London 2002.
25. See Paul Kennedy, *The Rise and Fall of the Great Powers*, New York 1987.
26. See Robert Gilpin, *War and Change in World Politics*, Cambridge 1981.
27. See Jack S. Levy, *War in the Modern Great Power System, 1495–1975*, Lexington 1983; William R. Thompson, *On Global War*, Columbia 1988; George Modelski, *Long Cycles in World Politics*, London 1987; idem (ed.), *Exploring Long Cycles*, London 1987.
28. The President of the United States, *The National Security Strategy of the United States of America*, Washington 2002. There it is said unmistakably:

> The President has no intention of allowing any nation to catch up with the huge lead the United States has opened since the fall of the Soviet Union more than a

decade ago ... Our forces will be strong enough to dissuade potential adversaries from pursuing a military buildup in hopes of surpassing or equaling the power of the United States.

On the hegemony crisis problems, especially in the 1980s see Dieter Senghaas, *Die Zukunft Europas. Probleme der Friedensgestaltung*, Frankfurt/M. 1986, Chapters 1 and 2.

29. In this context see Günter Schubert, *Chinas Kampf um die Nation. Dimensionen nationalistischen Denkens in der VR China, Taiwan und Hongkong an der Jahrtausendwende*, Hamburg 2002.

30. See G. John Ikenberry (ed.), *America Unrivalled. The Future of the Balance of Power*, Ithaca, NY 2002; John J. Mearsheimer, *The Tragedy of Great Power Politics*, New York 2001; Joseph S. Nye, *Das Paradox der amerikanischen Macht. Warum die einzige Supermacht der Welt Verbündete braucht*, Hamburg 2003; Michael Mann, *Die ohnmächtige Supermacht. Warum die U.S.A. die Welt nicht regieren können*, Frankfurt/M. 2003; see also Tony Judt, *America and the World*, in: New York Review of Books, vol. 50, no. 6, 10 April 2003, pp. 28–31; Werner Link, *Imperialer oder pluralistischer Frieden? Plädoyer für eine Politk der kooperativen Balance*, in: *Internationale Politik*, vol. 58, no. 5, 2003, pp 48–56.

31. See Chapter 6 of the present book.

32. The background of these problems emerges from Michael E. Porter, *The Competitive Advantage of Nations*, London 1990.

33. See the detailed studies in Karl Kaiser and Hans-Peter Schwarz (eds), *Weltpolitik im neuen Jahrhundert*, Bonn 2000; Mir A. Ferdowsi (ed.), *Internationale Politik im 21. Jahrhundert*, Munich 2002.

34. See Dieter Senghaas, *Friedensprojekt Europa*, Frankfurt/M. 1992.

35. See Mary Kaldor, *Neue und alte Kriege*, Frankfurt/M. 2000; Erhard Eppler, *Vom Gewaltmonopol zum Gewaltmarkt?* Frankfurt/M. 2002; Herfried Münkler, *Die neuen Kriege*, Reinbek 2002.

36. Johann Gottlieb Fichte, 'Zum ewigen Frieden – Ein philosophischer Entwurf von Immanuel Kant', in Zwi Batscha and Richard Saage (eds), *Friedensutopien. Kant, Fichte, Schlegel, Görres*, Frankfurt/M. 1979, p. 91.

37. See Dieter Senghaas, 'Die Konstitution der Welt. eine Analyse in friedenspolitischer Absicht', *Leviathan*, vol. 31, no. 1, 2003, pp. 117–152.

Chapter 10

INTER-CULTURAL DIALOGUE IN THE LIGHT OF CULTURAL GLOBALISATION

Since the middle of the 1990s the concept of 'globalisation' has massively moved to the centre of political and economic discourse. We know from the history of publicly effective concepts that such a process invariably mirrors real states of affairs. Yet the by now current concept becomes problematical if – as frequently happens in industrially highly developed countries – it assumes worldwide parallelisms; these then create a questionable or even a false picture of the world. The truth is that this world is still characterised by exceedingly different partial structures or part-worlds, which, however, relate to one another in hierarchical stratification, i.e. they do not exist each by itself.[1]

This statement applies not only with regard to the political economy of the world, i.e. the observable existence of symmetrically interactive centres and of asymmetrically interdependent centres, sub-centres, semi-peripheries, peripheries and sub-peripheries, but also with regard to politically relevant context-specific cultural profiles. The latter fundamental fact – the embedding of cultural profiles in specific, nowadays largely economically determined societal formations of the above-listed kind – has to be understood if one wishes to arrive at a fruitful inter-cultural dialogue.

1. On the Culturally Relevant Contexts of the Global Economy

At the top of the global society we can, between the advanced industrial societies (OECD world), observe boundary-abolishing processes that lead to the development of complex cultural interdependences in all dimensions (politics, economy, society, culture). This process has advanced furthest in the economic area. An example is the forced development of the European internal market, which is today characterised by a free-trade-motivated mobility of the decisive economic factors. The interdependences that have meanwhile arisen are marked by symmetry and substitutive division of labour – i.e. all participating economies, whether small or large, tend to produce capital-intensively, know-how-intensively and technology-intensively; they are in all sectors comparably competitive and they export one and the same type of high-value goods across the frontiers. This results in considerable competition, though simultaneously in frontier-transcending integrated markets. As competition takes place on the same level of competence, the result might be described as globalisation de luxe: a symmetrical penetration of the markets with comparable, i.e. substitutable, goods. Apart from nature, all the participants, including the consumers, profit from this type of division of labour.[2]

Outside the OECD economies, however, such a state of affairs can be observed globally only in incipient stages and at a few individual locations, Globally, as in past decades or even past centuries, there exists a substantial productivity and competence gradient between the high-productivity economies and the less productive ones. The less productive economies are exposed to a dramatic displacement competition; they are under peripheralisation pressure, i.e. in danger of being forced to the margin of the global economy, of being peripheralised or even marginalised.[3]

Needless to say, the productivity and competence gradients and the resulting asymmetrical displacement competition are not equally pronounced everywhere. And, naturally, there are different reactions by the less productive economy (*économie dominée*) to the overwhelmingly more productive *économie dominante*. Demolition and ruin, i.e. regression, is one of the possible reactions and it is by no means the rarest (see black Africa today). Another possible and empirically observed reaction is a partial sealing itself off, along with an attempt to survive under self-chosen conditions ('import substitution industrialisation'), an example, until recently, would be Latin America. The third, more unusual type of reaction might be described as an innovative response to the challenge: here all forces are mobilised in order to stand up to the displacement competition and, if possible, counteract it. In that case a displacement competition is initiated against the more productive economy: the challenger is beaten with high-quality simple, and later more complex, products manufactured at first at low wage costs; this leads to a 'dependency reversal', a displacement competition in the opposite direction, from the latecomers in development against the old industrial countries (e.g. East Asia over the past few decades).

Unlike this exceptional case, however, globalisation most often results, in the less productive societies and economies, in the phenomenon that development researchers have for some decades correctly described as 'structural heterogeneity'. This concept is used for a social and economic structure in which different productivity levels and production methods, hierarchically stratified, interlink with each other – rather in the spectrum of the high-productivity affiliate firms of multinational corporations on the one hand and a scanty self-supply economy on the other. In between there is a fragile industry and an inflated service sector. The familiar consequence of this structure, in which a gradient of capital and technology equipment, of organising ability and competences, is integrated is usually a widening of the gulf between rich and poor, between privilege and marginality in one and the same society. Economic growth then results not in a diminution but in an increase in structural heterogeneity. The homogenisation of the economy, necessary for a successful development, does not take place. In consequence the familiar social disasters of developing countries – the topics of development-political discussion since the 1960s – are accentuated.[4]

A few decades ago a fulminant Latin American development discussion took place about 'transnational capitalist integration with simultaneous national disintegration' – this problem was the core of the so-called *dependencia* discussion – but meanwhile the problems for this type of countries in the world have become more pressing. The productivity and competence gradients, and hence the peripheralisation and marginalisation pressure, have not become any less in the meantime, but have increased. Some authors (e.g. A. Cordova, F.H. Cardoso, R.M. Marini, A. Quijano and O. Sunkel) have reflected on the case of Latin America, others (especially Samir Amin) on Africa and the rest of the world, and others yet have made observations on the starting situation of a 'world system analysis' (I. Wallerstein).[5] The globalisation problems ('transnational capitalist integration'), as they today affect the major part of the world, are not therefore an unfamiliar phenomenon, nor is their frequently inexorable consequence: 'national disintegration' as the result of an asymmetrical displacement competition from the centres of the global economy down to its sub-peripheries. For the developing societies of the world it has existed long before the concept of globalisation became current. It should therefore be useful once more to examine the facts of a globalisation *avant la lettre* in order to avoid the logical trap of assuming the experience from the area of OECD globalisation de luxe to be representative of the world as a whole.[6]

2. Structure-analogous Cultural Profiles

Viewed from the economic area, we find a remarkable structural analogy with regard to cultural globalisation. Here, too, a stratified picture is necessary. Frontier abolition is taking place, but this has very different forms according to whether we move in the OECD world or in the rest of the world.

Within the OECD world increasing cultural exchange is perceived as qualitative enrichment, no matter whether it originates in other comparably developed societies or in the rest of the world. It intensifies the variety of cultural impulses, whether in art, in film, in music ('world music') or in literature. This variety increases an anyway ample culture on offer; this further accentuates an extensive postmodern flair of these societies. Mixtures of styles come about, in the form of either hybridisation, cross-overs or similar mixes.[7] In broad-strata popular art such processes are interesting, often culturally exciting, but politically they are largely unimportant. Evidently these varied impulses can be absorbed without the societies concerned even beginning to find themselves in identity crises. Above all, such a pluralising and more colourful cultural scene does not, or at least not yet, threaten the core stock of political culture, i.e. the meantime routine acceptance of plurality and the tested ability to cushion and constructively manage it by means of well-tested institutionalised measures. Disregarding the spatially containable problem of the integration of migrants, we are dealing here with a cultural globalisation de luxe.

In contrast, the situation in the developing societies of the world is, as a rule, totally different. There the cultural influence from abroad, coming mostly from the economically, technologically and media-effectively superior OECD world, is perceived as an attack on one's own (mostly already crumbling) identity. The foreign culture imposing itself from the centres is then viewed in terms of an aggressive, again asymmetrical, cultural displacement competition. Once more, as in the economic field, there are three fundamental ways of reaction: regression as a consequence of overtaxing; an upsurge of resistance as an expression of defence (this is, admittedly, found also locally in highly developed societies, e.g. in the past in France against an overwhelming cultural influence of the U.S.A.); and occasionally an innovative reaction: something new emerging as the result of an initially overpowering challenge.

As a rule, however, displacement competition, as in the economy, leads to the emergence of structural heterogeneity, this time in a cultural respect.[8] In that case societies, as a result of cultural globalisation, divide into strata of different mental and cultural orientation. There are 'Westerners', who have no problem with Western culture (plurality of interests and identities, individualism, equality of the sexes, self-determination, etc.). On the contrary, they want to see their own societies taking on a comparable cultural model as soon as possible, which is perceived as civilisatory progress and is expected to lead out of structural dependence. Then there are those striving for a kind of mixed programme, i.e. a synthesis of the modern and of traditional cultural models. Then there is a considerable number of those who wish to save their own culture but do not wish to do without the blessings of foreign technology. These have been described as 'half-modernists' because they only want to modernise science and technology, but do not wish to see culture put under pressure to change. Then there are traditionalists who often see in the past only what they themselves project into it and who thus become representatives of the process that has been called the 'invention of tradition'. Finally there is the fundamentalist reaction, which, both locally and internationally, responds aggressively to the challenge of Western culture ('the devil', 'Satan'), in the extreme case with locally or internationally staged terrorism. Admittedly, the cultural content of this last-named reaction is minimal to non-existent. Terroristically motivated violence wishes to spread terror and thereby mobilise additional sympathies from those thinking alike. Above all, terror is understood as a means of seizing power. Culture, more especially religion, is as a rule functionalised quite openly in a power-opportunist manner, resulting in non-culture or, in extreme cases, culturally or religiously dressed-up macro-criminality.[9]

The observed mix of any politically-culturally motivated reaction largely depends on the success or failure of socio-economic and political transformation processes. If, as in East Asia, the transformation processes (viewed long-term) are more or less successful – in which case one observes an 'upgrading' – cultural changes may be painful, but are, willy-nilly, characterised by adaptability and willingness to learn.[10] If, on the other hand, societies find themselves in a deep and moreover increasingly chronic development crisis, i.e. a crisis without hope of its end, then, in parallel with the aggravating structural heterogeneity in the economy and social stratification, the cultural fault lines are accentuated and a breeding ground is created for a broad spectrum of mostly simultaneously observed types of reaction. In conditions of a chronic development crisis, of a 'downgrading', the local cultural conflict inevitably develops into a permanent, usually militant, conflict about the direction of public order, i.e. into an entirely public and highly political event. The result is a cultural struggle in the serious meaning of the concept: to a clash on differing options in the shaping of public affairs. Cultural conflicts then resemble power struggles, which are constitutional struggles because they concern fundamental issues of the future societal order. The best example are Islamically characterised societies with the issue of theocratic or secular models, or indeed mixed models ('God's state as a republic'), as observable, for instance, in Iran for the past few years and to this day.[11]

Cultural struggles of this kind reveal existential identity crises in the form of power conflicts. Cultural and awareness heterogeneity can then be observed not only on the all-societal plane, or in individual social strata, but also in the individuals. This state of affairs has nothing to do with the consequences of a cultural globalisation de luxe, of a steadily self-enriching cultural scene, of a playful postmodern freedom of choice. In extreme cases, conflicts of this kind (Algeria, Iran, etc.) are life-and-death clashes.

It is advisable, therefore, just as in the economic (and general) globalisation discussion, to distinguish between different contexts and their characteristics also in the cultural dimension of globalisation, while at the same time viewing the economic and cultural profiles, especially those of political culture, in their usually conflict-charged contexts and in their realistically existing interlocking.

3. Conclusions for a Fruitful Inter-cultural Dialogue

What conclusions follow from the above considerations for the cultural dialogue that is often described as inevitable today?

That which can today be observed in the developing societies of the world under conditions of economic and cultural globalisation and in the face of profound social change, is reminiscent, if not in every detail then certainly in its main features, of European experiences nowadays largely repressed in public consciousness. After all, Europe – or, more precisely, northern and western Europe – is the continent that, since the early modern age and more especially since about 1750, for the first time in world history, as a result of social mobilisation, became the cradle of dramatic modernisation thrusts and corresponding mental experiences of upheaval. Their concomitants were profound system-political, or socio-political, conflicts, as well as cultural struggles of the above-mentioned kind in the various societies.

The present-day political, socio-economic and sociocultural changes in the world's developing societies are thus not unfamiliar to the history-conscious observer of European development history. As once in Europe, so we can now observe worldwide a dramatic social mobilisation, i.e. a deruralisation or urbanisation of societies, a widespread literacy progress, as well as the politicisation of traditionally rather apolitical but now organisable populations. As a result we find, from a secular point of view, a pluralisation of increasingly politicised class-specific and stratum-specific interests and identities. Moreover, there arises the modern coexistence question that becomes the fundamental constitutional question: what obligatory institutional measures are found in a pluralising society for the peaceful management of inevitable fully politicised conflicts and are accepted as legitimate? These were the problems that haunted the modern history of Europe and these same problems today characterise the political conflicts in large parts of the extra-European world.[12]

The politically virulent cultural identity crisis of many present-day societies right across the world (including the former region of real-socialism) cannot be mastered by exclusive recourse to a society's own tradition or by a pure takeover of foreign offers, even though both can occasionally be observed. The solution, as once in Europe, can only be the outcome of compromises resulting from political conflicts. Such power-position-conditioned compromises must be wrested from the traditional status-quo powers, because most of the time these are orientations against their will. This was no different in Europe. None of the civilisatory accomplishments that are today regarded in Europe and in the Western world as fundamental for the structure and the establishment of public order (protection of individual basic rights, equality before the law, separation of powers, etc.) were key principles in the pre-modern political order of the old Europe. They all are, just as the regulatory idea of toleration, a very late product of civilisatory development in our Western longitudes.[13]

With regard to Europe it should not be forgotten that the civilisation of the modern social conflict, as it may now be observed in the core countries of Europe, was at no time embedded, as it were, in the cultural genes of the old Europe. It is the outcome of decades or centuries of a history of conflicts. And in the south of Europe the civilisatory accomplishments of the development of a modern political culture became the basis of political order only recently, after the end of the fascist regimes in Portugal and Spain, as well as of the military dictatorship in Greece; in eastern central Europe and in the Baltic they only emerged after the collapse of real-socialism. In eastern and south-eastern Europe and in the Balkans the organisational principles of modern political systems and their cultural contents still only exist as a façade or on the surface and are therefore continuously in danger of relapse.

No one who understands his own European culture, in particular the meanwhile widely esteemed plurality-oriented political culture as the historical result of a conflict-rich and often convulsive learning process, will, faced with tense socio-political conflicts elsewhere, assume, in a holistically culture-essential manner, the existence there of unshakeable homogeneous cultural profiles ('Asian/Islamic values'). On the contrary: it has long been obvious that extra-European cultures, as a reflection of aggravating socio-economic change and the resulting political conflicts, get into conflict with themselves, i.e. they differentiate themselves by strata and mentally and thus become self-reflexive. Sensibly staged, this 'clash within civilisations', this state of affairs that cannot be missed in developing societies, facilitates the inter-cultural dialogue, especially if on the European (Western) side the real European history of conflict is remembered, so that the starting point is a realistic image of themselves.[14] As for this last premise, it would be useful for Europeans (Westerners) to remember:[15]

- That in their pre-modern, i.e. old-European societies, which in many places lasted well into the nineteenth and, in their final aspects, into the twentieth century, those corporative-collectivist values, stratified by social classes and estates, were a matter of course, the values that today are elsewhere and in an anti-Western manner propagated, for instance as 'Asian values', values that were simply representative of traditional societies and might therefore be labelled also Andalusian, Swabian, Anatolian, Nipponese, Punjabi, etc.

- That the (nowadays fortunately spelled-out) assumption in declarations of fundamental human rights that all men are born free and equal in dignity and rights was considered in the old Europe – as clearly and unmistakably documented in the then legal system – a strangely deviant and absurd idea.
- That the abstract individual (i.e. the individual regardless of class, sex, skin colour, age, intelligence, etc., an individual as such not really existing) was, in the major part of European history, not even known and therefore, as a counter-fact presumed legal entity, did not exist as a person in law, though eventually, after many political, and especially constitutional-political, disputes, it became the quintessence of modern law.
- That the equality of the sexes before the law, let alone in fact, was not even thought of.
- That religious freedom as a basic right was for a long time unknown, later controversial and fiercely rejected (even by the reformatory faiths) and, by the Catholic Church was accepted only in the 1960s (Second Vatican Council).[16]
- That toleration was rejected in the old Europe because it was regarded as an attitude that would allow the world to become anti-Christian (toleration as the root of the anti-Christian world, 'the first-born of all abominations')[17]
- That with the confessionalisation of the Christian religion (disregarding a few bridge-builders, the Irenics) intolerance, regarded in the Christian Middle Ages as unproblematic and more or less routine. became militant not only on the side of the Counter-Reformation, but especially on the Reformation side, all the way to the establishment of self-assured and explicitly propagated intolerant theocratic communities of Zwingli and Calvinist origin, reminiscent of Taliban rule – moreover, for a time, also in Britain's North American colonies, founded there by people who actually had escaped religious persecution in the old Europe, persecution based on militant intolerance.
- That in any event there was no tolerance or mercy for minorities – heretics, pagans and Jews (let alone for Muslims), that censorship and fettering of the intellect were an everyday event and that freedom for science, as we understand it today, did not exist.
- That, in the understanding of the age, men did not really possess rights, but were tied into communities with duties only; buttressed and protected by a broad range of 'police powers' (occupational, moral,

domestic and economic police), confirmed in a rich, affirmative 'police science', the precursor of modern political science.

- That morality and virtue, duties and customs, anchored in communities steered the class-bound individual along a road of substantially prescribed, socially defined heternomous morality, since individual autonomous ethics were unknown or, where demanded, opposed and rejected.
- That the modern idea of the individual as an autonomous subject, i.e. the modern image of the person as against the old-European community-based image of the individual that, as a primarily socio-moral being, had to be tied into a guardian-type public system, amounted, especially in Europe, to a caesura, a downright cultural revolution – a caesura that became inevitable as a consequence of modernisation processes and social change.

While the old Europe was characterised by a mandatory power-backed and guarded social idea in the various aspects of feudalism and of a cameralistically mercantilist *ancien régime*, it was only the rise of the bourgeois market society and its gradually emerging proletarian foundations that placed the individual upon himself or threw him back upon himself.[18] This transformation and transition resulting from anti-feudal bourgeois, and later anti-bourgeois proletarian, movements triggered emancipatory impulses, but simultaneously provoked reactionary opposition all the way to intellectual and political movements of theocratic counter-revolution. Their former topoi, meanwhile faded in Europe, are, however, found today worldwide in many developing societies: the rejection and critique of individualism, liberalism and secularism, the decline of manners and culture presumed in such critique, the critique of pluralism generally and of tolerance of a plurality of values, especially as the roots of social lawlessness, moral disorientation and corruption.[19]

We are dealing here with topoi that can be observed, not in the margin but at the centre, especially also in Germany's intellectual and cultural history, especially in its relevant political groupings and movements well into the twentieth century. In the light of the – meanwhile fortunately overcome – debate on 'German values', which were set up against the values of western enlightenment and Anglosaxon pragmatism ('culture vs. civilisation'), even more so in the light of cultural-political pleas for a 'German authoritarian state' in contrast to the corroding pluralism of Western political order (still strong in the 1920s and prominently championed), it should not be too difficult, especially in Germany, to understand the context of the public discussion of values at present observable in extra-European countries or to appreciate the political significance of such debates: in different variants of development nationalism they reflect, as they did once in recent European history, development-conditioned, more especially misdevelopment-conditioned problems.[20] Thus the old, and lately revitalised, debate on 'Slav values' in Russia, the cultural struggle there between 'Westerners' and Slavophiles, should be understood as a reflex of chronically unresolved all-societal problems. These defensive reactions, apart from a certain local colour, were and are everywhere founded in comparable anti-Western projections – 'occidentalism'. They are the counterpart of so-called 'orientalism', the current generalising projections of the West with regard to extra-European societies.[21]

Europeans (and Westerners) should therefore participate in an inter-cultural dialogue in the knowledge of their own real history. They should have previously understood that many politically motivated cultural debates at present taking place in the wide world had their analogous precursors in Europe and that the cultural struggles observed today are not unfamiliar, let alone new, so long as one recalls one's own past. Such an entry into the dialogue has been found to work discursive 'wonders' in that it protects against a mostly unconscious essentialisation of a late phase in European (Western) culture (this would equate European culture as such with modern value opinions and organisational principles of public order); such an approach also counteracts any temptation of essentialising other cultures (still in comparable upheaval), i.e. of perceiving them in Herder's fashion as of quasi-monadic spherical shape. The point is that any essentialist self-image and any essentialising image of another leads any cultural debate into a cul de sac, the more so if, as happens not infrequently, it takes place under politicising conditions. A fruitful cultural dialogue therefore presupposes knowledge of the paradigmatic argument that characterises the real history of every cultural sphere, especially all global regions.[22]

As for the extra-European partners of such a dialogue, it would be important that these do not allow themselves to be elevated into representatives of cultures or religions, nor to be forced into such a position, since in view of profound acute cultural conflicts within cultures such 'representative representatives' do not in fact exist. What we do find are representative champions of the most varied trends, who have long been present, though quantitatively diverging, in all cultures marked by structural heterogeneity. There they are in conflict with one another: traditionalists and modernists, theocrats and secularists, value-preservers and post-modernists, enlighteners and contra-enlighteners, progressives and reactionaries, universalists and communitarians, unbelievers and fundamentalists, status-quo followers and dissidents. Their differences are often to be found not so much in specific cultural contents that are regarded as not exchangeable or not negotiable; instead these controversial and often antagonistic positions reflect modernisation-conditioned analogous socio-economic and socio-political problems that transcend the individual cultural orbits, or also analogous action perspectives for their management and mastering – all this today outside Europe, but no different from what it used to be in Europe itself.

Positions of the above type are therefore primarily development-context-conditioned and by no means exclusively culture-specific; otherwise the parallel conflict constellations across historical periods and individual cultural spheres, along with their culture-struggle positions would be hardly explicable. Thus today's arguments of militant Islamism of the theocratic type are – without prior acquaintance with them – accurately repeating the arguments of the theocratic counter-revolution put forward after 1789 as a reaction to the laic state of the French type.[23] In scripturalist orientation all orthodoxies of whatever provenance are in agreement worldwide. And just as once in Europe, so today, in conditions of a politicised culture conflict, above all in the Islamic countries, the attempt to deconstruct 'sacred texts' is followed by withdrawal of teaching licence, or indeed an attempt against life and limb, and often enough flight into exile as the only way of saving one's life. Arguments against the vote for women and against the electability of women are today as unimaginative and cranky as in the past.[24]

These and other examples prove that history repeats itself more often than we, in our fast-living and history-forgetting age, realise. Anyone attempting to stage inter-cultural dialogues today should proceed from really existing cultural worlds and not from a fiction of homogeneous cultures. And, conscious of history, he should be aware of the recurrence of analogous conflict constellations and make this fact itself the subject of the dialogue. This requires, first of all, the removal of self-created cliché-type mental blockages: mainly the widening of one's intellectual horizon with regard to history and a globally oriented comparative analysis.[25] This would counteract an increasingly counterproductive routine, the observable freewheeling of many well-meaning dialogues, which are mostly only abstract meta-dialogues. Thus, newly oriented, inter-cultural dialogues would become important contributions to a gradually emerging globality, a globality marked by multiple cross-references. Their basic problems can be summed up as follows: pluralisation and plurality of individual societies and of the world as a whole are the central challenge: the constructive response to be aimed at is tolerance and coexistence, the result of collective learning experiences that always remain at risk of relapse. Inter-cultural dialogues, meaningfully directed, could be of considerable benefit in the search and staging of necessarily multiple context-specific answers, but also of general answers slowly crystallising.[26]

Summing up, there are a few clear peace-policy-significant points to remember for the inter-cultural dialogue:

- It is necessary to observe the contexts of politically relevant self-articulations of culture, i.e. their embedding in specific action contexts to be explored by an analysis of the individual societal formations along with their reference to a worldwide milieu.
- Attention should be paid to the ambivalences, the ambiguities, the internal fissures, as well as the internal conflicts that are already to be observed in most testimonies of traditional culture in individual cultural spheres. Thus the Old Testament does not only make a plea for beating swords into ploughshares and spears into pruning hooks (Isaiah 2; 4), but also for the opposite: 'Beat your plouwshares into swords and your pruninghooks into spears!' (Joel 3; 10) Traditional Chinese philosophy, which mainly reflected on the facilitating of public order in a practical manner, was marked not only by controversies but by downright antagonistic positions. Facts of this kind, which can be observed also elsewhere, mostly remain underexposed in inter-cultural dialogues. A realistic cultural image would therefore have to start much earlier, i.e. at the shaping of the individual traditional culture. That, too, would counteract any essentialisation of culture.[27]
- It should further be noted that culture and especially religion become politically relevant in so far as their demands enter into the political opinion process, will process and decision-making process, i.e. into the current processes of the political system and thereby acquire political weight.[28] The inter-cultural dialogue has to do with such politicised culture and religion, rather than with their presumed 'original' self-articulations, which are mostly misinterpreted anyway.
- A meaningful inter-cultural dialogue therefore always moves in the field of tension of those controversies and conflicts that the various cultural trends in the individual cultural spheres are conducting within themselves and against each other. Thus the change in the self-understanding of individual cultures and the sequence of corresponding paradigms, which find themselves in conflict with each other, also become a subject of the dialogue.
- A historical and present-oriented comparative observation (comparativistics) is an indispensable method for inter-cultural dialogue. Without historical or comparative orientation, dialogues are in danger of sliding into the routine of a well-intentioned but unproductive exchange or into the cul de sac of self-created incomprehension.

Notes

1. See Dieter Senghaas, 'Die Konstitution der Welt – eine Analyse in friedenspolitischer Absicht', *Leviathan*, vol. 31, no. 1, 2003, pp. 117–152.
2. See Chapter 6 of the present book.
3. See Chapter 9 of the present book.

4. A detailed analysis of the problems of structural heterogeneity is found in Dieter Senghaas, *Weltwirtschaftsordnung und Entwicklungspolitik. Plädoyer für Dissoziation*, Frankfurt/M. 1977.

5. Significant contributions of the quoted and other authors are published in Dieter Senghaas (ed.), *Imperialismus und strukturelle Gewalt. Analyse über abhängige Reproduktion*, Frankfurt/M. 1972; idem (ed.), *Peripherer Kapitalismus. Analysen über Abhängigkeit und Unterentwicklung*, Frankfurt/M. 1974; idem (ed.), *Kapitalistische Weltökonomie. Kontroversen über ihren Ursprung und ihre Entwicklungsdynamik*, Frankfurt/M. 1979.

6. Globalisation *avant la lettre* and its present form is particularly illuminatingly analysed in Osvaldo Sunkel and Michael Mortimore, 'Transnational Integration and National Disintegration Revisited', in Björn Hettne, András Inotai and Osvaldo Sunkel (eds), *Comparing Regionalisms. Implications for Global Development*, London 2001, pp. 54–92.

7. From a wealth of literature see Bernd Wagner (ed.), *Kulturelle Globalisierung. Zwischen Weltkultur und kultureller Fragmentierung*, Essen 2001.

8. An early analysis in Hans Bosse, 'Sozio-kulturelle Faktoren von Unterentwicklung. Überwindung von Unterentwicklung als Lernprozeß', in *DGFK-Informationen* (Deutsche Gesellschaft für Friedens- und Konfliktforschung), Sonderheft Schwerpunkt II, Bonn 1974, pp. 33–44.

9. See Mark Jürgensmeyer, *Terror in the Mind of God. The Global Rise of Religious Violence*, Berkeley 2000; Martin Riesebrodt, *Die Rückkehr der Religionen. Fundamentalismus und der Kampf der Kulturen*, Munich 2000; Henner Fürtig (ed.), *Islamische Welt und Globalisierung. Aneignung – Abgrenzung – Gegenentwürfe*, Würzburg 2001; Thomas Scheffler (ed.), *Religiom between Violence and Reconciliation*, Beirut 2002; Harald Barrios and Andreas Boeckh (eds), *Resistance to Globalisation. A Comparison of Three World Cultures*, New York 2003.

10. See Klaus-Georg Riegel,' "Asiatische Werte" – Die Asiatisierungsdebatte im Kontext der Globalisierung', *Zeitschrift für Politik*, vol. 48, no. 4, 2001, pp.397–425; Manfred Mols, 'Bemerkungen zur Globalisierung in Ost- und Südostasien', ibid., pp. 427–447. See also Peter Birle, Jörg Faust, Günther Maihold and Jürgen Rüland, *Globalisierung und Regionalismus. Bewährungsproben für Staat und Demokratie in Asien und Lateinamerika*, Opladen 2002.

11. See Gudrun Krämer, *Gottes Staat als Republik. Reflexionen zeitgenössischer Muslime zu Islam, Menschenrechten und Demokratie*, Baden-Baden 1999.

12. See Chapter 2 of the present book.

13. See Dieter Senghaas, *The Clash within Civilizations. Coming to Terms with Cultural Conflicts*, London/New York 2002.

14. On the significance of such a realistic self-portrait, not only for the inter-cultural dialogue, but also for the further development of Europe, see now Emanuel Richter, *Das republikanische Europa. Aspekte einer nachholenden Zivilisierung*, Opladen 1999.

15. On the facts listed below the following is especially illuminating: Ernst-Wolfgang Böckenförde, *Vom Wandel des Menschenbildes im Recht* (Gerda Henkel lecture), Münster 2001.

16. Particularly informative on this subject: Hans Maier, *Wie universal sind die Menschenrechte?* Freiburg 1997.

17. On this and the next two points especially Henry Kamen, *The Rise of Toleration*, London 1967.

18. See Böckenförde, *Vom Wandel*.

19. See the excellent article by Christoph Marx, 'Fundamentalismus und Nationalstaat', in *Geschichte und Gesellschaft*, vol. 27, 2001, pp. 87–117; also Wolfgang Reinhard (ed.), *Die fundamentalistische Revolution*, Freiburg 1995; Martin Riesebrodt, 'Die fundamentalistische Erneuerung der Religionen', *WeltTrends*, no. 30, Spring 2001, pp. 9–27.

20. On the German debate see Paul Nolte, *Die Ordnung der deutschen Gesellschaft. Selbstentwurf und Selbstbeschreibung im 20. Jahrhundert*, Munich 2000; Stefan Breuer, *Ordnungen der Ungleichheit. Die deutsche Rechte im Widerstreit ihrer Ideen 1871–1945*, Darmstadt 2001. Particularly illuminating for the debate on 'German values', or an orientation by

'culture' in contrast to an orientation by 'civilisation' see the controversy between the brothers Heinrich and Thomas Mann: Thomas Mann, *Betrachtungen eines Unpolitischen* (1918), Frankfurt/M. 2001.

21. On this now Ian Buruma and Avishai Margalit, *Occidentalism. The West in the Eyes of its Enemies*, New York 2004. A fundamental examination of orientalism, in this case relating to east Asia, can now be found in Eun-Jeung Lee, *'Anti-Europa'. Die Geschichte der Rezeption des Konfuzianismus und der konfuzianischen Gesellschaft seit der Aufklärung*. Münster 2003. See also Heiner Bielefeldt, *Philosophie der Menschenrechte*, Darmstadt 1938.

22. The change of paradigms in the development of world religions is set out in an exemplary fashion by Hans Küng, *Das Christentum. Wesen und Geschichte*, Munich 1994; idem, *Das Judentum. Die religiöse Situation der Zeit*, Munich 1991; idem, *Der Islam*, Munich 2004.

23. See the presentation of post-revolutionary France in Johann Baptist Müller, *Religion und Politik*, Berlin 1997, Chapter IV, as well as, by way of comparison, Sadik J. Al-Azm, *Unbehagen in der Moderne. Aufklärung im Islam*, Frankfurt/M. 1993.

24. Insightful on the background of these problems: Ronald Inglehart and Pippa Norris, 'The True Clash of Civilizations', *Foreign Policy*, March/April 2003, pp. 63–70.

25. See Martin Marty and R. Scott Appleby, *Herausforderung Fundamentalismus. Radikale Christen, Moslems und Juden im Kampf gegen die Moderne*, Frankfurt/M. 1996.

26. See, from a philosophical angle, Heinz Kimmerle, *Interkulturelle Philosophie zur Einführung*, Hamburg 2002; Franz Martin Wimmer, *Interkulturelle Philosophie*, Vienna 2004; from a politological angle Harald Müller, *Das Zusammenleben der Kulturen. Ein Gegenentwurf zu Huntington*, Frankfurt/M. 1998.

27. See, in detail and in comparative analysis, Senghaas, *The Clash within Civilisations*.

28. The conditions in which a political issue or a controversy become relevant to politics are elucidated in Ernst-Otto Czempiel, *Internationale Politik*, Paderborn 1981.

Chapter 11

FUTURE OUTLOOK

'Get into effective relationships with each other' – that was Immanuel Kant's conceptual definition of what today is commonly described as broadening and deepening worldwide interdependences. Kant already had a cautious surmise in his writings of what is now quite patent, but nevertheless is noted rarely or casually in the discourse on peace: the fact that 'getting into effective relationships' leads to extremely divers situations in the world and, as a result, calls for a correspondingly differentiated situation assessment with differentiated consequences for peace in practice. The One World, to which a multitude of political comment refers, is in reality a world split into partial worlds, which, admittedly, do not exist in isolation from one another, but, as set out in this book, are related to each other within a single complex structure.[1] The really existing world is characterised not by homogeneity, but by structural heterogeneity in the sense sketched out in the Introduction and explained in this book.

One of the partial worlds – let us call it, as was done in this book, the OECD world or simply World I – embodies the materially, communicatively and institutionally densely networked gravitational centre of the world. The prehistory of World I is the history of rival, war-inclined modern power-states along with their characteristic competitive interests. This prehistory ended in the Western part of Europe after the Second World War. This was followed by that new World I configuration that, in some partial areas, especially in the EU context, can be labelled postmodern because essential characteristics of the classic modern world of states, associated with national statehood, have lost some of their importance or were downright overcome. In this partial world a continuous coordination of political strategies, in one of the partial areas even integration (see Chapter 6), is taking place on a relatively symmetrical basis the prerequisites of which were set out in detail earlier on. These welcome conditions are not irreversible since a change in their prerequisites can also change them, i.e. regression cannot be ruled out. It is precisely at this point that the renewed debate on the transatlantic drifting apart – a consequence of a presumed unipolar hegemony position of the U.S.A., or indeed of imperially behaving American power politics – should be focused.[2]

In another partial world, let us call it World II, the experience of the prehistory of World I basically repeats itself, except that here, in the East Asian sphere, the process proceeds in speeded-up form without having as yet reached the developmental stage when a regional integration arrangement comparable to the EU might be possible. Such a stage cannot be ruled out, but presupposes that Japan will keep to its trading state orientation, that China chooses the option of a trading state and not a power state and that the U.S.A. will pursue, in that sphere, a circumspect policy of an essentially trading state orientation. These, too, are prerequisites for which there is no guarantee that they will actually come about. The danger of a classic power conflict about regional hegemony positions in this sphere cannot at present be dismissed; it will essentially depend on the direction in which China will develop, on how Chinese–American relations will evolve and on how Japan will fit into a regional arrangement.

A further partial world, World III, is characterised by the fact that it faces a transnationally capitalist integrated and institutionally networked gravitational centre (World I), into which its members, the individual states, are selectively (i.e. not all together as a collective agent or a cooperating collective) integrated. In this world (we have become used to calling it the 'Third World') we find some aspects of modernity, especially an often still reasonably functioning state apparatus, in some cases a more or less differentiated economy and a tendency towards a corresponding social stratification. However, all these aspects are thwarted by a serious structural heterogeneity. As this heterogeneity is scarcely being deconstructed, and indeed is often aggravated, this world should more properly be called pseudo-modern. Transition from World III to World II (the latter is, in a sense, the new modern world) is not ruled out in principle, but, as explained in a preceding chapter, depends on whether appropriate reforms and development strategies are embarked upon.

Yet another partial world, World IV, was characterised in the first post-colonial phase by seemingly modern, though in reality fragile pseudo-modern aspects: 'fragile pseudo-modern' because they were superimposed on a narrow base without economic dynamics of its own. This world is in a process of decay and is meanwhile characterised by many pre-modern features: the rule of warlords (warlordism) and endemic civil wars, by locally mounted, but often internationally interconnected, markets of violence and the collapse of what infrastructure had survived as the colonial legacy, by a spread of societal lawlessness and social hardships hand in hand with a self-enrichment of the warlords and their clients, and the upper stratum generally.[3]

These four partial worlds are characterised by more or less pronounced dynamics of their own; but they are in turn embedded in a worldwide hierarchy of stratified-structural dependence. In this world there is a geographically localised cluster formation determined by World I as the starting point of a centre–semi-periphery–periphery–sub-periphery structure. Moreover, as the past few decades have shown, limited upward and downward mobilities, as well as split experiences, can be observed in that hierarchy. The different developmental stages of these partial worlds, and the world constituted by them, define the world's fundamental problems for a foreseeable time. To maintain oneself in a hierarchically structured construct in which interdependences of all kinds are increasing (see Chapter 8), and in which the competence gradient is at the same time accentuated, defines – from the top, the OECD gravitational centre (World I) down to the world of eroding statehood (World IV) – the world's fundamental problem: the development dilemma. And although the security dilemma can be observed right across the world, it only becomes comprehensible in its specific aspects if one understands these as a reflection of the strikingly different constituent partial worlds. At the top of the world hierarchy it is, according to its specific contextualisation, self-contained and cushioned, and in part overcome (see Chapter 6); in World IV it is virulent in a Hobbesian manner; in the in-between positions the present dilemma situaton is reminiscent of the war-prone power history of modern Europe until the Second World War and its intra-societal precondition: the non-existence or the not-yet-existence of a hexagonal society (see Chapter 2).

In the real world, peace policy therefore has entirely diverse tasks, which have been extensively discussed in this book and only need a brief summary here: in World I the task is reliable management of symmetrical interdependence, which today includes also the skilful fending off of a unipolar world-order policy of the U.S.A. because the consequences of such a policy are today elsewhere accepted less than ever before, or no longer accepted at all, and because it provokes the formation of an opposing power.[4] In World II the task is the containment of a potentially developing regional hegemony conflict through the creation of a counteracting arrangement of regional cooperation; here the EU could be a model. Only thus can we prevent the security dilemma in this sphere from becoming of an independent history-affecting magnitude of a virulent nature. An important prerequisite of preventing this from happening is a further maturing process of the economies affected, and also in the further development of emerging societies into genuine hexagonal societies (see Chapter 2). In World III the task is the long-known one of initiating broad-spectrum effective development processes and simultaneously (extremely difficult!) regional exchange arrangements. Only development processes with across-the-board effect lead to the construction of hexagonally structured societies and political systems – and thereby the civilisation of the modern social conflict (see Chapter 9). By way of contrast, peace policy in World IV faces a task of the most elementary nature: the overcoming of the absence of social rules, resulting from the disintegration of state institutions, as well as the establishment of a solid monopoly of power. This, however, will only acquire legitimacy if it is seen to be moderated by rule-of-law controls and enjoys legitimising reinsurance by widening democratic participation. Such participation requires a solid material base, i.e. a developing and progressively differentiated economy (see Chapter 9). As the actual and the possible peace-policy-disturbing potential, that is embedded in the separate partial worlds and in their interactions, is of major importance to the further course of world history, a world order policy deliberately counteracting these disturbing potentials acquires increasing importance. As yet, world order policy is not a widely effective history-making force; what can be observed are first developments in that direction. However, put quite soberly and without emphasis, mankind has a long-term survival chance only if the rifts, inequalities and dramatic injustices of the real world are at least successfully reduced or levelled out, if not totally overcome. This is a peace-policy task for the century: its successful management will inevitably fail unless long-term objectives are already successfully aimed at in strategic day-to-day policies here and now.[5]

Notes

1. See Dieter Senghaas, 'Die Konstitution der Welt – eine Analyse in friedenspolitischer Absicht', *Leviathan*, vol. 31, no. 1, 2003, pp. 117–152.
2. See the special issue *Die Neue Weltordnung* of *Internationale Politik*, vol. 58, no. 5, 2003, with contributions by Karl Kaiser, Ivo Daalder/James Lindsay, Hans-Peter Schwarz, Robert Cooper, Christian Tomuschat and Werner Link. For a splendid analysis from a journalist author see Ulrich Speck, 'Macht und Widerstand. Amerikas Rolle in der unipolaren Weltordnung', *Merkur*, vol. 57, no. 5, 2003, pp. 395–404.
3. The state of affairs has triggered an interesting debate on so-called 'new wars'. See Mary Kaldor, *Neue und alte Kriege*, Frankfurt/M. 2000; Erhard Eppler, *Vom Gewaltmonopol zum Gewaltmarkt?*, Frankfurt/M. 2002; Herfried Münkler, *Die neuen Kriege*, Reinbek b. Hamburg 2002.
4. According to the 'realistic' theory of international relations, based on the globally relevant distribution of power potentials, supported by the present champions of a unipolar world power status of the U.S.A., the emergence of counter-power formation is downright inevitable in such a constellation. This is a theory-immanent prognosis which, however, is being significantly disregarded by the practitioners concerned. This state of affairs impressively confirms Karl W. Deutsch's definition of power, when, in *The Nerves of Government. Models of Political Communication and Control*, New York 1966, 2nd edn., he formulated 'power as the ability to afford not to learn' (p. 111). The powerful

believe they can afford not to learn: however, just this is the basis of the learning pathology of power, as Karl W. Deutsch explained in detail in Chapter 13 of his book.

5. See also the thematically wide-ranging contributions in Dieter Senghaas (ed.), *Den Frieden machen*, Frankfurt/M. 1997.

INDEX

* 9 7 8 1 8 4 5 4 5 3 2 5 1 *